INTRODUCTION TO HEALTH CARE
FOR THE ALLIED HEALTH STUDENT

INTRODUCTION TO HEALTH CARE

FOR THE ALLIED HEALTH STUDENT

Updated Edition

John W. Ridley, Ph.D., RN, MT(ASCP)

Australia · Canada · Mexico · Singapore · Spain · United Kingdom · United States

THOMSON
™

Introduction to Health Care
For the Allied Health Student, Updated Edition
John W. Ridley

Custom Editor:
Brett Westerman

Marketing Coordinators:
Lindsay Annett and Sara Mercurio

Production/Manufacturing Supervisor:
Donna M. Brown

Project Coordinator:
Heather Madsen

Pre-Media Services Supervisor:
Dan Plofchan

Sr. Pre-press Specialist
Kim Fry

Rights and Permissions Specialist:
Kalina Hintz and Bahman Naraghi

Cover Image
Getty Images*

Cover Designer:
Phoenix Creative, LLC

Compositor:
Integra Software Services Pvt. Ltd.

Printer:
Global Printing & Packaging

The Adaptable Courseware Program consists of products and additions to existing Thomson products that are produced from camera-ready copy. Peer review, class testing, and accuracy are primarily the responsibility of the author(s).

Introduction to Health Care for the Allied Health Care
John W. Ridley – Second Edition
ISBN 0-759-35210-0

Library of Congress Control Number:
2005934938

International Divisions List

Asia (Including India):
Thomson Learning
60 Albert Street, #15-01
Albert Complex
Singapore 189969
Tel 65 336-6411
Fax 65 336-7411

Latin America:
Thomson Learning
Seneca 53
Colonia Polano
11560 Mexico, D.F., Mexico
Tel (525) 281-2906
Fax (525) 281-2656

UK/Europe/Middle East/Africa:
Thomson Learning
High Holborn House
50-51 Bedford Row
London, WC1R 4L$
United Kingdom
Tel 44 (020) 7067-2500
Fax 44 (020) 7067-2600

Australia/New Zealand:
Thomson Learning Australia
102 Dodds Street
Southbank, Victoria 3006
Australia

Canada:
Thomson Nelson
1120 Birchmount Road
Toronto, Ontario
Canada M1K 5G4
Tel (416) 752-9100
Fax (416) 752-8102

Spain (Includes Portugal):
Thomson Paraninfo
Calle Magallanes 25
28015 Madrid
España
Tel 34 (0)91 446-3350
Fax 34 (0)91 445-6218

Table of Contents

FOREWORD

Allied health and professional health care workers serve an important role in giving care to others. Acting in a professional manner and utilizing a body of medical knowledge and training in procedures to provide optimum care for each patient should be their main focus.

The purpose of this book is to provide those entering various fields of health care with an overview of common subjects needed to understand the foundations of health care. Topics in this book span a body of knowledge common to a number of professions, including emergency medical services (EMS), respiratory therapy, radiography, medical assisting, practical nursing, as well as others requiring licensure, registry, and certification. Basic life support (BLS) is treated on a community response basis. It is necessary for certification that students receive their BLS training as outlined by American Heart Association or the American Red Cross.

People entering the caring professions must prove themselves competent in a number of procedures and must possess information related to self-protection, ethics, and professional documentation of their worthiness to enter the health care sector. It is an awesome responsibility for people placed in the care of those needing spiritual, psychological, and physical assistance. Therefore, a broad-based understanding of the forces driving effective health care must not be ignored or minimized.

INTRODUCTION TO THE CARING PROFESSIONS

OBJECTIVES

Upon completion of this unit of instruction, the student will be able to:

a. Describe the major elements and standards of a typical medical training program

b. Understand the provisions necessary to provide safe and effective treatment for the patient

c. List the major topics required for providing privacy, ethical and moral treatment of the patient

d. Relate the similarities and differences in certification, licensure, and registration of professionals

e. Discuss the benefits of accreditation of health care facilities

f. Identify the hierarchy of administration in a typical health care setting

g. Demonstrate an understanding of legal implications in the provision of health care services

h. List at least ten health care professionals other than the physician, and the major duties of each

SECTION OUTLINE

Introduction to Health Care

Requirements for Maintaining Accreditation

Medical Law and Ethics

HIPAA Legislation In Direct Care

Health Plans and Providers

Opportunities in the Allied Health Professions

Descriptions of Representative Professions

Fairview Park Hospital, Dublin, GA (used by permission of CEO, 1993)

INTRODUCTION TO HEALTH CARE

Health care is important to all of us. The provision of health care is the biggest single industry in the United States. It surpasses the budget of the Department of Defense and all other various governmental entities in the consumption of our gross national budget. Governmental agencies exist solely for the dispensing of funds for providing medical care, for research into disease processes and cures, and for the protection of the consumer of products and health care. More public and private money is spent on health care than any other segment of our national economy.

Health care for everyone, both individual and collective, is the goal of most people. Health care is important to our happiness and peace of mind. It enables us to enjoy life and to pursue the things that are important to us. Protecting the public and ensuring that health care is ethical and available to everyone are among the most important functions of our government. We are protected from unethical practitioners, contaminated food and air, and disposal of wastes in order to maintain a healthy living environment.

Educational Considerations

Education of the health care worker takes into consideration a number of issues:

1. Economy (affordable and effective care)

2. Practices that adhere to currently accepted practices and standards

3. Personnel standards that incorporate a body of knowledge into each profession

Medical Educational Standards

Standards are developed in order to protect you, the consumer, and you, the worker, in order to provide adequate care and to protect you in the workplace. This book is intended to address these aspects that tend to protect both you and your patient. This is paramount in the practice of any sort of profession, particularly the medical professions. You should get your money's worth for the best and most available care. A number of competencies are common to all of the medical professions, and they will be discussed in this book. All health care workers are usually required to know certain things in order to protect themselves and their patients. These areas of study are:

Components of Training Related to All Medical Programs

1. **Bloodborne and Airborne Pathogens**
   The health care worker must have a thorough knowledge of the transmission of pathogens when working with patients. The most common of these are bloodborne and airborne. The bloodborne pathogens encountered most often in the health care arena are viruses called human immunodeficiency virus (HIV) and Hepatitis B virus (HBV). While these by no means comprise all of the organisms with which we will come in contact, they are the most prevalent. The most common airborne pathogen that we have the possibility of exposure to is the tuberculosis (TB) organism. This is a bacteria-like organism that is again growing in prevalence after several decades of decline.

2. **Infection Control (sometimes called Exposure Control)**
   A set of practices has been developed into a plan to decrease the likelihood of exposure to and contracting of diseases. This plan also aids in protecting the patients from unwarranted exposure to disease. This area also includes issues other than infectious diseases, so it is gradually evolving into a more comprehensive program to include effective use of medications and types of chemicals that may be found in the workplace.

3. **Vital Signs**
   Vital signs are indicators of disease states and warnings indicating the potential for serious illness to develop. All medical workers are expected to be observant and to be able to assess patient changes as well as to monitor the prognosis of patients. The correct procedures to follow for the four vital signs – temperature, pulse, respiration, and blood pressure – are the most important set of indicators providing significant medical information to the physician.

4. **First Aid**
   We all have an ethical responsibility to be able to respond to human need according to our ability. This ability to respond to a medical emergency may be the difference in saving the life of a family member or a stranger. Everyone has a stake in being able to respond properly in an emergency in order to stabilize a patient before advanced medical assistance arrives or transport to a medical facility has occurred.

5. **Basic Life Support, or Cardiopulmonary Resuscitation (CPR)**
   Heart disease is one of the most significant health challenges of today. While CPR may be used in other instances of injury or disease, heart disease is the reason the practice is employed in most cases. With the use of these techniques, coupled with better availability of Automated Electronic Defibrillation devices, many lives could be saved annually.

Ethics and Organization of the Health care Delivery System

In the following sections, there is information related to ethics, organization of the health care delivery system, and terms widely used in indicating documentation of the meeting of medical standards established for health care facilities. Both governmental and professional groups have taken measures to ensure that health care institutions and practitioners of various medical professions are effectively trained and monitored. In the following sections, specific training areas will be addressed in order to acquaint the student with the proper information and expertise to provide quality care for those in his or her care.

Delivery of Medical Care

All people deserve appropriate health care and to enjoy a sense of well-being, regardless of their station in life or their status related to having a disease, whether chronic or acute. Those who are stricken by illness, permanent or temporary, should expect to be treated by health care providers who possess not only professional competence, but also the appropriate compassion and caring needed to ensure comfort during illness or recovery.

Organizations have been founded over the years to ensure that health care providers have met the credentials necessary for performing certain duties in a medical facility. These organizations may be on a state or national level, or the profession in which they practice may govern them. All of these organizations exist in order to protect the public from unscrupulous and unprofessional practices. Almost all health care professions require a certain level of credentialing, often with a licensing or registry examination necessary to achieve professional status.

Professional Ethics and Regulatory Agencies

In general, professional groups require certification or registry, while government organizations require licensure. Certification and registry may be viewed as somewhat of a quasi-legal requirement, since most health care organizations will not hire unqualified personnel. Both certification/registry and licensure usually require an examination developed by the professional organizations or a professional testing agency in order to determine competency of the individual prior to the person performing professional duties in a health care facility.

Medical organizations, which exist in order to document that standards of care have been achieved to their satisfaction, have codes of ethics by which they operate. Personal and institutional practices and standards of behavior exist, often in formal documents, to which each member of the professions represented within a medical care facility are to adhere. Definitions of terms related to the mission statements of these professional organizations include the following:

Definition of "Ethics"

Stedman's Medical Dictionary for the Health Professions and Nursing, Illustrated, Fifth Edition (p. 505) defines ethics as:

1. The branch of philosophy that deals with the distinction between right and wrong, with the moral consequences of human actions.

2. The science of morality; the principles of proper professional conduct concerning the rights and duties of health care professionals, their patients, and their colleagues.

Ethics/professionalism

There is a blending or blurring of distinction for these two words. These words may be used in adjective or adverb forms, and they may mean different things to different people.

Code of ethics

Compiling an organized set of ethical issues is often a legal matter and might include, but is not limited to:

1. Bill of Rights for the patient

2. Rights to privacy

3. Rights to self-dignity

Ethics more than set of rules

Michael Bissell and Teri Cosman state, "Ethics consists of far more than abiding by rules, procedures, and guidelines ... [ethics] represents an expression of conscience".[1] But the practice of ethical behavior includes much more than the surface activities a health care practitioner may perform. In the health care arena, there is a responsibility for all medical workers to treat people as they should be treated as well as handling sensitive information that should not be disseminated to the general public. Laws related to the treatment of patients and protection of patients and their privacy are established and often modified as society and procedures change.

Appearance and grooming

Patients regard the health care practitioner or other medical worker as more "professional" and place more trust if the person is dressed and groomed in a professional manner. A clean and properly dressed health care worker does a great deal to engender confidence in the patient as to the medical worker's abilities. Some safety issues are also involved, and as an example, consideration is given to dangling jewelry and artificial fingernails that may interfere in the performance of medical procedures or get tangled in equipment. Long hair may pose a risk for transmitting infections to patients, as hair is often covered with organisms and other materials.

Oath of Hippocrates, Nursing Creed, Mission Statements

Essentially, these documents include the following requirements:

1. Do not harm anyone intentionally.

2. Perform according to sound ability and good judgment.

3. Do that for which training has occurred, not more.

4. Do not become involved in anyone's care out of curiosity, but only deal with those to whom assigned. Only information that is needed to provide the appropriate level of care should be obtained or solicited.

5. Facts about patients are not to be part of personal conversations but kept confidential.

Professional Societies

Most professional groups have a statement or statements governing the ethical practice of their respective associations. These groups generally reflect in their codes or creeds the major themes of reliability, accuracy of procedures, assessments, and confidentiality.

---

[1] Teri Cosman and Michael Bissell, "How Ethical Dilemmas Induce Stress – Ethics and the Clinical Laboratory," Medical Laboratory Observer 36, no. 8 (1990): 1404–1407.

Hospital Code of Ethics

Most hospitals and medical clinics have a code of ethics, which often includes a Bill of Rights for patients. Basic tenets of the Patient's Bill of Rights will include the following:

Professionals Should Not:

1. Be impolite to a patient or his or her family; always treat the patient with respect and in a professional manner

2. Discuss a patient's ailment with him or her. This is the role of the physician or his or her assistant or other designated person.

3. Discuss various types of therapy chosen for treatment

4. Prescribe or suggest changes in medication or means of treatment

5. Discuss a patient's physician or his or her designated assistant with the patient or his family or yield information of a confidential nature to anyone except those who need to know

Professional Organizations Provide:

In matters of registries and certification, those who present themselves to the public as practicing professionals must meet the standards for entry into the profession. Most often there are continuing requirements for remaining in good standing with the respective accrediting bodies.

State Licensure Laws

Most states require licensing for a variety of health care professions, while others accept certification or registry as an official means of ensuring competency of a number of practitioners. There are basically two types of state licenses.

1. Personal Licensure

2. Facility Licensure

PROFESSIONAL ETHICS AND REGULATORY AGENCIES

State and Other Government Licensure Laws

1. The term "licensure" refers to the **legal** requirement to meet certain conditions in order to enter into a profession

2. Reasons for licensure – protection of the public

    A. State Licensure

    Licensure is generally a function of state government, although some federal agencies require licenses as well. Licensure is necessary in most instances to protect the public from unscrupulous would-be practitioners of a profession. Harm could arise when someone holds him or herself out to be competent and in actuality has not met the training, educational and other intangible requirements for licensure.

    B. Certification

    Certification may be required by, or accepted as a form of licensing by, governmental agencies. It is a quasi-official means for determining that certain steps have been fulfilled for achieving a body of knowledge. Certification generally refers to training more than formal educational requirements, but it can contain both formal educational and didactic material as well as manual task-related functions that adhere to certain mandated standards.

C. Accreditation
Facilities voluntarily ask for accreditation in order to present themselves as abiding by a certain set of standards associated with given professions or institutional standards, such as a hospital that encompasses a number of occupations that are addressed. This meeting of the requirements for accreditation assures the public that the institution is seeking to provide a high standard of care and is a form of self-policing.

Hospital Organization

The hierarchy of a hospital organization is well entrenched, although some of the names for certain offices within the facility have changed over the years. Where one falls within the framework of the organization usually depends on level of education and responsibility given to the individual in the health care facility. The administrator, or the highest-ranking official of the hospital, is now known generally as the chief executive officer (CEO), which is the same terminology used in most business enterprises. This would reflect the greater demand on health care institutions to be more cost conscious and to employ good business practices, which was not thought to be necessary in past years. Many of the officers of the various departments are currently called assistant administrators and are often categorized by the area over which they exercise authority and responsibility. For example, the larger hospitals may have an administrator for finance, computer services, clinical services, and so on.

Lines of Authority in a Typical Hospital Setting:

1. Board of director includes chief of staff, administrator or CEO, attorney, business leaders
2. Chief of professional services
3. Department supervisors for all ancillary departments, such as laboratory, pharmacy
4. Section supervisors of areas within a major department
5. Shift supervisors who report to section supervisors
6. Staff (considerable ranking among staff, with the professional staff of people who are licensed, registered, or certified at the top of the group in their scope of duties and responsibility)

REQUIREMENTS FOR MAINTAINING ACCREDITATION

Continuing education

1. Often provided or financed by institution and required for facility accreditation
2. May be sponsored by accrediting and licensure bodies as a part of the protection of the profession and insurance of continuing competence of its members
3. In licensure, registry, and certification of personnel, continuing education is often a legal requirement in order to have a license renewed on a routine basis

Committee Functions

Committee members, chosen because of a particular expertise each individual possesses, handle most accreditation requirements and related issues of health care delivery. Some committees are multidisciplinary and have members from several departments within the hospital. Some committees also retain members from outside the facility in order to get input from the community. Examples of typical committees are:

1. Infection/Exposure Control Committee
   This committee will include, but is not limited to: physicians, nurses, laboratory personnel from the various departments within pathological services, custodial/housekeeping, food service, and pharmacy

2. Tissue committee
   Will include surgeons, pathologists, and other professionals and paraprofessionals

Legal, Moral, and Ethical Concerns

1. Legal

   A. Hospital documents are legal documents.

   B. Legal requirements entail that the categories of who, how, and when work is done, and by whom it was ordered, is documented. Often, insurance reimbursement is denied in the absence of this information.

   C. Dispensing of results to the patient is normally only done by the physician or his designated practitioner.

2. Ethical

   A. Maintain confidentiality of patient's condition and results of procedures and medical tests

   B. Do no tests unless ordered through proper channels (usually by physician)

   C. Give no results given directly to patient without guidance of the physician

MEDICAL LAW AND ETHICS

Introduction

Medical law and ethics are inseparable in their relation to the rights of patients. Patients have an entitlement to certain expectations in their medical care; their rights as citizens do not end at the doors of medical facilities. As listed in the introductory portion of this book, the patient's Bill of Rights is a written document to inform patients about their rights when they are receiving medical care. Legal issues may arise if these rights are violated, and medical workers may be held culpable if the patient's rights are violated. The intent of this section is to inform the medical worker/student as to how to treat patients humanely, legally, and ethically and avoid any legal entanglements. A well-informed practitioner would avoid many of the pitfalls that may lead to litigation against the medical worker, such as negligence and malpractice.

Confidentiality for Medical Information and Records

Any information you obtain from a patient or any privileged information about the patient is considered confidential. This information includes the patient's history, diagnosis, current condition, and/or plan of treatment. The medical worker is not allowed to reveal that a patient is even being treated in many cases. The only time this information may be shared with others is when a signed release statement has been prepared or when imparting information to another medical care provider who has the need to know the information. Information for insurance purposes and information transmitted to another medical care professional for continuity of care is allowed within established guidelines (HIPAA will be discussed later). Again, the medical care worker should never discuss anyone's condition, treatment, or any personal information to those who does not have the right to know, even family members.

Basic Rules to Observe for Confidentiality

1. Never discuss the patient or his condition with family and friends. On a practical basis, a medical care worker should not be involved in matters that are not directly related to the performance of their specifically assigned and reasonable duties for the position.

2. Never discuss the patient's illness in his or her presence with another worker or family member. There is evidence that patients may hear everything you say, even if in a comatose state. In any condition, a patient may misinterpret what you have to say.

3. Refer questions by the patient regarding disease and treatment to the physician in charge of the patient's care. The patient and his physician are the only people legally and ethically able to divulge information of any type to another party.

Standards for Legal and Ethical Issues

Legal and ethical standards are developed in order to provide safe medical care for the patient and to protect the caregiver. Ethical or moral activities and laws that have been developed to govern the legal aspects of care are often the same and are inextricable. The medical worker may be faced almost daily with decisions to make about what is the morally or legally correct thing to do. Often, there is an attorney on the hospital board, or an attorney on retainers, to provide insight into questions of legality when policies and procedures are being developed and implemented.

1. **Legal standards**

   These standards are developed within the legislative and judicial departments of our country. If a worker fails to follow the legal standards and does not work within the scope of practice established for the particular profession, he may be liable for legal action.

2. **Ethical standards**

   Ethical standards are based on moral standards and are in some cases based on religion or customs. Many laws have been traditionally developed based on the religious practices of various groups of peoples.

Sample Legal and Ethical Questions

Often, legal and ethical dilemmas result in arguments by people who have an interest in an issue. An example of this difference of opinion is in the right to life. Questions regarding this issue involve more than the rights of one person. Some of these legal and ethical questions are:

1. Do all of our citizens have the right to life and the pursuit of happiness?

2. Does this include the unborn, and, if so, at what period of gestation does the fetus become a person, or a separate entity?

3. Should the tissue of an aborted fetus be used to provide medical treatment for people suffering illnesses that might be aided by transplanting tissue from the fetus?

4. Is euthanasia ever legally justified, such as in assisted suicides like those performed by Dr. Jack Kevorkian, the Michigan pathologist?

5. Should a person have the right to refuse water and food in order to die if the disease or condition is terminal, or should medical intervention force the person to be nourished?

6. Does a person on public assistance including Medicare deserve to have continuous treatment for an incurable condition, but not a person whose insurance limits the amount of treatment that may be received? Does a person of a lower socioeconomic group deserve the same treatment as someone of a higher status?

Standards of Confidentiality

Most medical workers will be faced with at least some of these questions as well as others of their own in the course of their duties. Many medical facilities have ethics committees including clergy, legal personnel, and citizens interested in the development of standards to use in the workplace. Some of these committees may even be statewide or national in scope. Most assuredly, we will hear more of these issues in the next few decades as technology evolves and more and more personal information becomes available through technological means. Health care workers should be aware that a record of accessing a patient's or an employee's records by computer leaves a trail that may be followed. Disciplinary action for unwarranted intrusion may follow an attempt to gain access to private records. In many cases, workers have been surprised by a visit from computer services personnel, asking why some individuals have accessed certain files.

Health Insurance Portability and Accountability Act (HIPAA)

The Health Insurance Portability and Accountability Act (HIPAA) of 1996, an act of Congress, took effect on April 14, 2002. The purpose of this legislation is to protect the privacy of the patient's health information and records. Many agencies, such as health care insurers, routinely purchased and otherwise obtained individual patient records in the past in order to determine premium charges or even to deny insurance coverage for certain patients and their families. Also, commercial efforts for companies that wished to establish a base of customers and private information for sale to certain businesses were becoming more prevalent. These regulations protect medical records and other individually identifiable health information, whether on paper, in computers, or communicated orally for recording. There are also offshoots of this legislation affecting institutions other than the health care industry. One example of this is Family Education Rights and Privacy Act (FERFA), which affords students certain rights with respect to their educational records. FERFA is designed to protect the records of students enrolled in any educational institution, and is intended to protect the privacy of individual students.

HIPAA and FERFA were the first attempts, but others will surely follow, to establish federal privacy standards to protect patients' medical records and other health information provided to health plans, doctors, hospitals, and other health care providers. The plan was developed by the Department of Health and Human Services (HHS), and in addition to protecting patient records, these new standards provide patients with access to their medical records and more control over how their personal health information is used and disclosed. A consistent format is provided for privacy protections for consumers of medical care nationwide. In instances where current state laws already provide protection or are more stringent than the federal law, the state laws are not affected.

Congress asked HHS to provide a plan for patient privacy protections as part of HIPAA. As a means to transfer health information from provider to provider, and for insurance reimbursement, HIPAA encourages electronic transactions and provides requirements to safeguard security when sharing health care information between medical facilities and any agency with the need for acquiring individual patient records. Verification should be done electronically in the cases of health insurance, HMO, and preferred-provider plans, health care clearinghouses that maintain records for large institutions, and medical care providers who provide financial and administrative transactions, such as enrollment information, billing of patients and plans, as well as insuring eligibility for family members.

Almost all health insurers, pharmacies, physicians, and other health care providers were required to begin compliance with these regulations on April 14, 2003. A number of agencies requested exemption from the timeline, and Congress allowed some small health plans to have an additional year to comply. HSS provides assistance to health care providers to assist them in transitioning to a more structured manner of obtaining, using, and transmitting information. A website is provided from medical care providers to ask questions about the rules and obtain explanations and descriptions about specific components of the rule. These materials are available at at http://www.hhs.gov/ocr/hipaa.

Important Facts About HIPAA Legislation

1. Access to Personal Medical Records

Patients may see and obtain copies of their medical records, request corrections where errors and mistakes are found, and receive assurance that these errors have been corrected. Copies of records should be available within thirty days of receiving a written request. Patients may be charged for the cost of copying and sending the documents.

2. Notice of Privacy Practices

Patients must be advised in writing of their rights after the first visit on or following April 14, 2003, the date when compliance will be required. Patients must acknowledge receipt of this notice of their rights under HIPAA, as usually they will be apprised of their rights when they make an initial visit to a health care practitioner for assessment or treatment. Patients are typically asked to sign a form indicating their understanding of the HIPAA regulations and how they are used to limit the amount of information imparted to a third party.

3. Limited and Specified Use of Personal Medical Information

There are limits as to how information may be used. These limits specify what information will be shared, and they do not include personal information or the patient's entire medical file. In the past, many facilities actually sold information to companies performing research or those interested in marketing a product and desired a population using a particular product. Personal information not related to health care issues may be provided to outside entities, but the patient must authorize release of medical and/or personal information to other health care facilities, providers, insurance companies, or financial institutions. Facilities must reveal dissemination of even demographic information to other agencies that may be studying a region of the country or a particular population group.

4. Prohibition on Marketing

Any information released to pharmacies, pharmaceutical firms, health plans, and so on must be authorized as stated previously by the patient before the information may be transmitted. As an example, many pharmaceutical firms use patient data for research purposes as pertaining to use of medications developed for treatment of specific diseases. Patients usually are asked to sign a release allowing specific information to be passed to an insurance carrier or other agency needing such information.

5. Stronger State Laws

These federal privacy standards give states that have laws requiring privacy protections for patients a minimum standard to insure that effective protections are in effect. One area where this requirement would affect state laws is in the reporting of infectious diseases to state health departments. Certain protections of this information would be in effect for the states in their reporting, tracking, and using information for surveillance purposes. Most states have laws requiring the reporting of certain contagious and communicable diseases. This type of surveillance is necessary to provide more protection for the entire population. Sexually transmitted and foodborne diseases comprise the majority of reportable diseases as required by law.

6. Confidential communications

Patients may request that physicians, their health plans, and other involved offices enact practices that ensure that communication with the patient is kept confidential. A patient may ask that any medical consultation is done at his or her home, or in a private office where access is limited to those performing the consultation or procedure. Most medical treatment facilities and professionals take the responsibility of safeguarding private information from their patients very seriously, as they could be successfully sued if they are careless with information. There have been cases of suits against a medical office or facility when records were carelessly discarded in waste containers in an easily readable form, and where others could retrieve the records.

7. **Consumer Complaints**

Patients may file complaints when they suspect that violation of privacy may have occurred. These concerns may be made in writing directly to the covered provider or health plan or to the Department of Health and Human Service's Office for Civil Rights. Even large corporations, such as pharmaceutical manufacturers and governmental agencies, are subject to sanctions for violations of personal privacy issues. Only information that is necessary for processing medical claims for insurance purposes and in some cases research for determining the usefulness of certain medications and procedures may be solicited from medical professionals. In most cases, patients give their permission for dissemination and use of their personal information, with or without the patients' identification. However, patients are under no obligation to release any of their information if they choose not to do so.

HEALTH PLANS AND PROVIDERS

Health plans and providers include insurance companies that administer health plans, pharmacies, physicians, and other covered entities that formulate policies and procedures for protection of the confidentiality of health information about their patients. Chief components of this protection are:

1. **Written Privacy Procedures**

Written privacy procedures that specify which personnel will have access to protected information and how it will be used is required. Patients must be made aware of how their information will be used. Standards of conduct for professionals most often specify that medical workers should only have access to information necessary for the treatment of patients.

2. **Employee Training and Privacy Officer**

Employers must train their employees in their privacy procedures and designate an individual responsible for insuring that all staff must follow the established privacy procedures. Documentation of this training and the employee's understanding of the requirements is necessary. If an employee fails to follow these procedures, appropriate disciplinary action is mandatory.

3. **Public Responsibilities**

Certain information is required by law to be released and is not covered under the normal requirements for routine treatment, record keeping, and release of these documents. Examples of these exempted categories would be:

A. Emergency circumstances, possibly of an unknown or unidentified victim

B. Identification of a deceased person, or the cause of death

C. Public health needs, as in infectious diseases that require surveillance by public health officials

D. Research that involves limited data or has been independently approved by an institutional review board or privacy board developed for the protection of the public's mental and physical health. Educational research activities also require that a review board adjudge the safety of the process being conducted.

E. Limited law enforcement activities

F. Activities related to national defense and security
In part because of the needs for homeland defense, new safeguards and limits have been established for these types of disclosures. If no other law requires disclosures in these

situations, responsible health care personnel and public officials may continue to use their professional judgment to decide whether to make such disclosures based on their own policies and ethical principles.

4. Equivalent Requirements for Governmental Agencies
This final rule applies to public facilities, such as federally funded health care facilities and insurance provided through the federal or state governments. Penalties against individual workers are provided upon conviction for violation of these laws.

Personal Treatment For Patients Must Include

Respect for Life

It is generally accepted and mandated by law that everyone in the United States has a Constitutional right to life and the pursuit of happiness. When patients are approaching death, it is the objective of the medical community to keep the person comfortable and to continue to treat the patient with dignity and respect. The main goal of medicine is to maintain and assure that everyone is afforded the best quality of life possible. Often, ethical principles are related to the individuality of the person and must be considered. These individual differences are based on age, ethnic background, religion, culture, life experiences, attitudes, family background, and the person's response to illnesses, including the accommodations for the illness that the person must make in his life. All medical care workers must subscribe to the value and sanctity of life, a person's most prized possession. Patient safety and comfort are at the top of a health care provider's list of considerations when dealing with a patient and his or her family.

Legal Considerations

Laws are created to protect society. Failure to obey the law and to report violations of laws may result in fines or imprisonment. Some common elements of law are:

1. Do no harm to the patient. A good rule is "Safety First" for the patient.

2. Do only those things you were taught and stay within the scope of practice for your profession. Involve yourself only with the duties to which you are assigned.

3. Maintain skills by study and participation in continuing education and inservice education in order to maintain up-to-date skills and knowledge.

4. Request guidance from a supervisor when in doubt about any issue.

5. Respect the patient's belongings. Theft is taking anything not belonging to you. Patients are extremely vulnerable to having their possessions stolen, as there is often little opportunity for them to secure their belongings. You also must not ask for nor accept tips from the patient for services rendered to the patient or his family.

6. Defamation relates to statements about someone. A verbal statement is called **slander**, and a written statement is called **libel**. While these charges are difficult to prove, as the harm done to the plaintiff must be established, the proceedings will be at least an inconvenience, requiring the expenditure of money and time for defense. It is a good idea not to speak about others, even if your remarks are true. A jury might disagree with you and place you in the position to defend yourself. Do not make negative remarks about medical practitioners to a patient, his family, or to anyone at all!

False Imprisonment

Patients have the right to leave the hospital with or without the physician's permission. You may not physically restrain the patient from leaving. If you try to prevent the patient from leaving, you may be found guilty of false imprisonment. If it becomes necessary to restrain small children, a parent or guardian must be present. Restraints may be in the form of physical restraints or chemical restraints. Support and restraints may be used with a physician's order, which will limit the amount of restraint or support that may be used. Medicating a patient to keep them immobile is a form of chemical restraint. Physical restraints include anything that

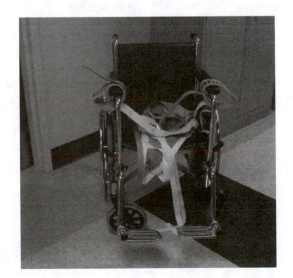

cannot be easily removed by the patient, restricts a patient's movement, or does not permit a person to have normal access to his body or portions of his body. These physical restraints include hand mitts, vests and jackets, wheelchair, safety belts, bars, or any physical barrier against movement. Even bed rails may be considered physical restraints. Only certified police officers and certain state and federal officers have the authority to restrain a patient against his will.

Assault and Battery

Assault and battery are legal issues and have potentially severe legal penalties. To assault a person is an intentional attempt to touch or to threaten to touch a person's body. To commit battery is actually to touch a person without the person's permission. The act does not have to be violent in nature to be construed in a court of law as battery against the person. When we touch a patient in order to provide care, we have implied consent to do so if it falls within the scope of our duties and responsibilities. If you threaten to get another person to help you force the person to do your will, you are committing assault. When providing care, the patient must be informed as to what you intend to do. If the patient is incapable of understanding, a family member should be notified. Not to do so could make you liable for assault, so the following statements address this situation:

1. Always inform the patient of what you are planning to do.

2. Ensure that the patient understands what you have told them.

3. Never carry out a procedure if the patient refuses.

4. Give the patient an opportunity to refuse prior to performing a procedure, and document the refusal for your supervisor's knowledge.

Abuse

Abusing a patient involves doing actual harm to the patient. This violates legal and ethical standards. Legal standards outline penalties for abuse. Abuse is intentional in that it is not accidental and causes harm to the patient. Categories of abuse include sexual, verbal, physical, mental, and even seclusion of the unruly patient. Many subtle issues are at stake here. Abuse will include such behaviors as:

1. Using profanity or harsh and loud words

2. Calling the patient names or reflecting on the person's race, gender, or handicap

3. Embarrassing the patient by bringing up prior unpleasant situations involving him or her

4. Making obscene or threatening gestures of any type

5. Teasing a patient with sexual innuendos or gestures, as sexual abuse may include suggestive language or touching a patient in a sexual way

6. Leaving the patient secluded from other patients, particularly as a means of punishment or behavior modification

7. Removing the patient's means for summoning aid

8. Making verbal threats against the patient or his family

Documentation

Documentation, other than properly performing the prescribed medical treatment, is the next most important task in the medical profession. There is an old adage, "If it isn't written down, it

wasn't done." Most accrediting agencies subscribe to this line of reasoning. Also, to avoid conflict and possible legal action, care must be exercised when describing a patient's behavior while charting a medical procedure or assessment. Do not use subjective words such as "belligerent," "uncooperative," "mean," or "hostile"! Instead, use terms to describe the exact behavior of the patient, using specific activities that are inappropriate. The key word is subjective. Incorporating personal feelings into the description of a patient is not appropriate. Also, the physical and emotional conditions of the patient must be taken into consideration in charting a person's personal affect. Another critical component in assessing a person's behavior is considering the possibility of abuse that the patient may have previously experienced. If you suspect that abuse may have occurred, you are required to report the situation to the authorities so that it may be investigated. In some states, failure to report suspected abuse makes the medical worker or layperson as guilty as the perpetrator of the abuse. All confidential records, including those related to incidents involving patients and staff, must be documented and placed in a secure location. After medical procedures and treatments are performed, records are generally stored in a secure area, such as a storage vault, with access limited to those assigned the task of filing and retrieving records.

Documentation of health care records, in particular the use of certain medications and treatment protocols, must be maintained for specific periods of time. The amount of time they are to be retained may vary by state and local government requirements. Physicians' offices, clinics, and hospitals that cease operations must provide for storage of records in order to access them even years later. Many of these facilities offer the records to the patient upon closing of the offices with the remainder not dispensed to patients placed in permanent storage.

OPPORTUNITIES IN THE ALLIED HEALTH PROFESSIONS

Careers in the Medical Fields

A number of career opportunities exist in the health care provider fields other than those of dentists, physicians, and other professions requiring graduate education and training. The increasing importance of preventive and restorative medicine, as well as advanced diagnostic and maintenance procedures and applications, has fueled phenomenal growth in high schools, community and technical colleges, and senior universities. An increasingly technological role of planning, organization, research, and administration of health care has led to the emergence of a number of professions that may not have even existed a few decades previously. It is indisputable that in the future, many health care personnel will become even more important in the diagnosing and treatment of patients. Technology dealing with both diagnosing and treatment is advancing and becoming more complex daily.

Entry into Allied Health Training and Educational Programs

All personnel employed in the health care environment are required to have a basic level of competency prior to being certified, licensed, or registered as qualified professionals. A number of states require that certain standards be completed before being deemed qualified, and most often when licensure is not required, a voluntary professional organization for each of the allied health fields has emerged to establish minimum standards before a person may present himself or herself as being qualified to practice in the given field of work. A wealth of information regarding information about and entry requirements for selected health care professions is available from the Commission on Accreditation of Allied Health Education Programs (CAAHEP). Not all health care programs are under the auspices of CAAHEP, but information on the eighteen programs CAAHEP administers is available on the Internet (www.caahep.org).

Opportunities in the Allied Medical Professions

There are many rewarding career opportunities in patient care and public health in addition to those of a physician or a dentist. The increased appreciation of preventive medicine and the growing problems of an expanding population in a technological society have placed new emphasis on the important roles of planning, organization, and administration of health care. While most states maintain schools of dentistry and medicine, as well as graduate programs in public health administration and hospital administration, many universities and colleges offer a variety of allied health care programs, usually depending on local need.

Selected Allied Health Professions

No attempt is made here to list all of the numerous allied health care programs that exist in educational settings. A representative listing is presented, including discussions of the duties, educational requirements, and sites from which the student may gain more detailed information regarding the requirements for the specific programs. In addition to identified professions such as medicine, dentistry, and clinical psychology, one may be able to pursue a graduate degree (MS, Ph.D.) in any one of the basic medical sciences, such as anatomy, biochemistry, immunology, neurology, pathology, or psychology. In order to gain entrance to these graduate level programs, one must complete a categorical level examination required by graduate and professional schools.

Employment Outlook

Today's complex national health care system requires professionals in many disciplines. While physicians, dentists, and nurses are at the forefront and are most visible, a growing number of allied health professionals who provide important professional support to the previously listed personnel exists, with a broad array of technical knowledge and skills to enhance and make more efficient the health care industry.

According to demands seen around the United States, health care employment will increase by several million and will account for 17 out of every 100 new jobs through the year 2005 (U.S. Department of Labor Bureau of Labor Statistics). A growing population of people in the retired ranks fuels this, requiring that health care employment projections will grow roughly twice as fast as all other industries. In some states, health care providers of all ranks make up as much as one-tenth of the total workforce and exert a tremendous influence on the individual states' economies.

Categorically Selected Programs

A. Nursing and Related

- Nursing (includes practical/vocational, associate, and bachelor degree RN programs)
- Medical Assistant, regardless of length of program
- Certified Nurse Assistant (state regulations for training may vary)

B. Therapists

- Occupational Therapy – a two-year assistant program in many types of facilities
- Physical Therapy Assistant – typically two-year college program or diploma
- Physical Therapy – typically requires a four-year degree

C. Radiology

- Radiography (includes radiographs and some special procedures under a radiologist)
- Nuclear Medicine Technology (often a degree program)
- Sonography (may require radiography certification prior to entering training)
- Nuclear Medicine (usually a graduate degree program)
- Radiation Therapy (most often a two-year program following radiography certification)
- Radiation Physicist (requires graduate courses or degree)

D. Dental

- Dental Hygiene (works independently with patients under the guidance of a licensed dentist)
- Dental Assisting (assists dentist with many dental procedures)

E. Laboratory Technology

- Medical Laboratory Technician (AD) (performs routine, repetitive procedures)
- Medical Technology (BS) (works independently; supervises technicians and assistants)
- Cytotechnologist, cytotechnician (works with cellular preparations under pathologist)
- Histotechnologist, histotechnician (processes tissue samples for pathologist to study)
- Phlebotomist (collects, stores, and processes blood samples for processing)
- Categorical Specialists, (Microbiology, Virology, Toxicology, Biochemistry, Immunohematology, Clinical Chemistry, Hematology) (requiring graduate level preparation in areas requiring high level of expertise in several departments of laboratory)

F. Pharmaceutical

- Pharmacist (manages, performs skilled work in dispensing medicines, counseling patients)
- Pharmacy Technologist (formulates and measures medications under pharmacist)
- Pharmacy Technician (performs routine, repetitive measuring and packaging of medications)
- Pharmacy Assistant

G. Patient Counseling

- Medical Nutrition (highly trained specialists who provide diet plans for patients)
- Dietetics and Nutrition (ensure proper nutrition is provided for various groups)
- Medical Social Work (provide first-line counseling in areas such as family needs)
- Drug or Substances of Abuse Counselor (work in group settings for addictive people)

H. Direct Patient Treatment

- Physician's Assistant (may be bachelor's or master's degree level)
- Optometry Technician or Assistant (performs acuity measurements chiefly)

I. Respiratory Therapy

- Respiratory Therapist (may be associate's or bachelor's degree level)

J. Other

- Biomedical Engineering (repairs and calibrates sensitive medical equipment)
- Environmental Health (provides for safe and sanitary facilities to avoid epidemics)
- Hospital Administration (administers and manages operations of health care facility)
- Veterinary Technician or Assistant (works to provide assistance to a veterinarian)
- Medical Illustrator (creates artistic drawings of medical procedures and conditions)

Entry into Professional and Allied Health Programs

It is not assured that everyone will be accepted into the program of their choice, as the competition for training programs in many of these professions is intense. But in most cases, competition is not as great as it is for dentistry and medicine, where there are at least several applicants for every position in a class. Advance preparation will greatly increase one's chances of being selected; no one can expect to gain admission to such a program as a last minute applicant who has been rejected by another program. It is also important to be aware that, while adhering to Americans with Disabilities Act of 1990, all medical programs have essential tasks requiring the physical and mental ability to perform many of the tasks and procedures necessary to practice skills associated with the fields. This means that some people will be unable either to enter or to complete certain programs if the person has certain handicapping conditions that would prevent them from performing required tasks. When a graduate-level degree is required, most graduate and professional programs have their own specific undergraduate course requirements, along with a nationally administered entrance examination or regional acceptance preferences. Most programs also require a standardized examination to include aptitude and achievement before accepting the applicant to a program. Acceptance into most programs depends on the grade point average of undergraduate core courses, an aptitude and achievement score, and often an interview.

Sites of National Offices for Allied Health Professions

Following are some general sites that may be researched for information leading to acceptance and completion of general allied health programs. Much information may be gleaned if the career field is researched on the World Wide Web using a search engine and entering the title of the profession. In addition, the professions listed in this section often have sites and addresses that may be accessed for more information.

REFERENCE BOOKS HELPFUL IN CHOOSING A HEALTH CARE PROFESSION

1. *Allied Health Education Directory*. Chicago: American Medical Association, 1978–1996.

2. Wischnitzer, Saul. *Barron's Guide to Medical, Dental and Allied Health Science Careers*, 3rd ed. Woodbury, NY: Barrons Educational Series, 1977.

3. *Peterson's Annual Guides to Graduate Study*.

4. *Health Careers Guidebook by U.S. Department of Labor, Manpower Administration and U.S. Department of Health, Education, and Welfare, National Institutes of Health*, 3rd ed. Washington: U.S. Department of Labor, 1972.

5. *Twenty-Six Allied Careers*, American Medical Assn., Division of Allied Health Education, 535 N. Dearborn St., Chicago, IL 60466.

6. American Society of Allied Health Professions, Suite 700, 11 01 Connecticut Avenue, N.W., Washington, DC 20036.

DESCRIPTIONS OF SOME REPRESENTATIVE PROFESSIONS

Cardiovascular Technologist

Duties

The cardiovascular technologist performs both therapeutic and diagnostic studies under the direction of a physician. The studies may be classed as invasive, noninvasive, or noninvasive peripheral studies of the vascular system. Through cardiological studies, the technologist provides an anatomical and physiological presentation enabling the physician to develop a treatment protocol based on the diagnosis. The technologist may record patient history and compile medical data from various medical diagnoses. The technician performs procedures necessary for creating a record of anatomical and related medical information for the physician.

Requirements for Obtaining Training

A high school diploma is the basic entry level of education required. Many cardiovascular technology students are health professionals, such as nurses or radiographers, before entering the training program. Programs range from one to four years, depending on previously obtained education and training. Some programs certify the student in more than one category of treatment, therefore affecting time required to finish the program.

Accreditation Groups

More specific information may be obtained from one of the following societies:

Cardiovascular Technology

Society of Vascular Technology
4601 Presidents Drive/Suite 260
Lanham, MD 20706-4365
Phone (301) 459-7550 / FAX (301) 459-5651

American Society of Echocardiography
4101 Lake Boone Trail/Suite 201
Raleigh, NC 27607
Phone (919) 787-5181 / FAX (919) 787-4916

Alliance of Cardiovascular Professionals
910 Charles Street
Fredericksburg, VA 22401
Phone (540) 370-0102 / FAX (540) 370-0015

Certification/Registration

Cardiovascular Credentialing International
4456 Corporation Lane/Suite 120
Virginia Beach, VA 23462
Phone (800) 326-0268 / FAX (804) 628-3259

Amer. Registry of Diag. Sonographers
600 Jefferson Paza/Suite 360
Rockville, MD 20852-1150
Phone (301) 738-8401 / FAX (301)738-0312

Cytotechnologist

Duties

Cytology is the study of the structure and the function of cells, and people employed as cytotechnologists generally work in a medical or reference laboratory, always under the direction of a pathologist (physician trained in diseases of the human body and abnormalities of cells and tissue). Cytotechnologists are specially trained technologists who perform procedures designed to detect changes in body cells that may be important in the early diagnosis and treatment of cancer and other diseases. Microscopes are the primary tool of the cytotechnologist, who prepares, treats, and stains slide preparations of body cells, evaluating them for abnormalities in structure and indicating either benign (normal) or malignant (cancerous) stages. A pathologist verifies a representative sample of the cytotechnologist's work.

Requirements for Obtaining Training

Becoming a cytotechnologist requires an extensive educational background in the biologic sciences as well as chemistry and mathematics. People who have exceptional experience in medical technology or advanced microscopy may be able to shorten the length of the training program somewhat. Cytotechnology programs vary in length, but most require at least one year of structured professional instruction following completion of related science coursework as preparation for the program. Clinical training in the form of practical work done under the supervision of a certified cytotechnologist is required. Successful completion of the program and subsequent attainment of professional registry enables the cytotechnologist chiefly to work independently, with a representative portion of the work reviewed by a board-certified pathologist. A good prerequisite degree to possess before entering into a cyto- or histopathology specialty would be that of a medical technologist.

Accreditation Groups

There are several accrediting bodies for laboratory practitioners. The most prominent and most widely held credentials are from the agencies listed. Also, more specific information for career opportunities and certification may be obtained from one of the following societies at the following addresses and sites.

American Society of Cytopathology
Cytopathology Programs Review Committee
400 West 9th Street, Suite 201
Wilmington, DE (302) 429-8802
(312) 738-1336

American Society of Clinical Pathology
Board of Registry
PO Box 12270
Chicago, IL 60612
(312) 738-1336

Diagnostic Medical Sonographer

Duties

The diagnostic medical sonographer typically works in a department of radiology under the direction of a radiologist (physician trained in the interpretations of X-rays and other imaging processes) and provides patient services using medical ultrasound. This is done under the supervision of a physician responsible for the use and interpretation of ultrasound procedures. The sonographer assists the attending physician in gathering technical data required to diagnose and treat certain diseases. A sonographer delivers their service in health care facilities that have a physician who is trained in the use and interpretation of ultrasound procedures. The medical sonographer is responsible for obtaining, reviewing, and integrating pertinent medical history and clinical data from other sources to provide accurate and timely results. He or she will be proficient in the performance of appropriately ordered procedures and the recording of anatomical and physiological data for interpretation by the physician. The sonographer is also responsible for recording and processing sonographic data and observations made during the procedure for presentation to the physician responsible for interpretation of the data. This position requires close contact with the patient, and it is often necessary to teach the patient somewhat to achieve optimal results.

Requirements for Obtaining Training

Medical sonography programs may last for one to four years, depending on the degree of training sought – some areas are highly specialized – and previous training and certification achieved. A high school diploma or General Equivalency Diploma is often required in addition to holding specific qualifications in a clinically related health profession, such as radiography.

Accreditation Groups

More specific information for career opportunities and certification may be obtained from one of the following societies at the following addresses and sites.

Society of Diagnostic Medical
Sonographers
2745 North Dallas Parkway #350
Plano, TX 75093-8729
Phone (972) 239-7367

American Registry of Diagnostic Medical
Sonographers
600 Jefferson Plaza/Suite 360
Rockville, MD 20852-1 150
Phone (301) 738-8401

Emergency Medical Technician – Paramedics

Duties

Although these fields are treated together in this section, the two programs differ in their degree of critical training in assessment and treatment of ill and injured patients. A paramedic is first an emergency medical technician (EMT) in most geographic locations, and then with additional training and education gains the title of paramedic. Both of these professionals work under the supervision of a physician who most often is an emergency physician and who is employed thorough the emergency room (ER) at a hospital that provides trauma treatment. Direction from the physician to the emergency personnel is typically by radio communication or telephone, ensuring the patient is receiving all possible definitive care, as well as enabling the ER to be ready to accept the patient as soon as he or she arrives at the trauma center. The EMT/paramedic is trained to assess the extent of illness or injury and to provide lifesaving and sustaining treatment, stabilizing the patient until transport to an emergency room is completed. All communities and regions have access to ambulance services with trained emergency personnel, which allow them to gain precious minutes of performing lifesaving procedures prior to and during transport by emergency vehicle.

Requirements for Obtaining Training

Most often, the state government provides educational standards for an EMT-transport program. Certification as an EMT trained in transport of patients is required for entry into a paramedic program. Some states require EMTs to be available for fire and rescue departments, and sometimes these programs do not require that the EMT/paramedic be trained for transport of the patient. These EMTs may treat the victims on the location to which the fire/rescue department is dispatched, as well as to provide treatment for the firefighters with problems such as heat exhaustion and smoke inhalation. The sequence of training for the EMT requires six months to one year of training depending on state requirements, and the paramedic programs generally require one to two years in length following the achievement of EMT certification.

Accreditation Groups

More specific information for career opportunities and certification may be obtained from one of the societies at the following addresses and sites. As is the case in this profession, there is an office providing information for the program and another for certification. Some states also have licensing requirements, with stringent prerequisites for entry into programs within the state.

Certification/Registration

National Association of EMT
408 Monroe
Clinton, MS 39056
Phone: (601) 924-7744 / (800) 346-2368

National Registry of EMTs
Rocco V Morando Building
Box 29233, 6610 Busch Boulevard
Columbus, OH 43229-0233
Phone: (614) 888-4484

Medical Assistant

Duties

Medical assisting is an allied health profession in which the practitioners function as members of the health care delivery team and perform either or both administrative and clinical procedures. Administrative duties usually include scheduling, receiving patients, preparing and maintaining medical records, and assembling necessary documents for a proper medical history. Insurance and medical coding procedures, medical transcription, handling communication between health care professionals, and serving as a liaison between the physician and other individuals are important functions of this profession. There is a division of labor among medical assistants, as some choose to perform only business aspects of the practice while others work in direct patient care. Some medical assistants administratively manage the business functions of a medical practice, such as filing insurance claims, billing, purchase of equipment and supplies, and office expenses. Clinical duties require knowledge of and practice of maintaining a clean and safe work area, instructing patients in self-care, taking extensive patient histories and vital signs, and performing first aid treatment and resuscitation. Medical assistants also contribute to the efficiency of the medical office by preparing patients for procedures, assisting with examinations and treatments, collecting and processing specimens, performing selected diagnostic tests allowed under the Clinical Lab Improvement Act of 1988, and preparing and administering medications prescribed and as allowed by state practice acts.

Requirements for Obtaining Training

There are two types of medical assistant programs: two-year programs, which result in an associate's degree, and a one-year program, which results in either a certificate or diploma.

Accreditation Groups

Specific information about the profession and certification may be obtained at the following:

American Association of Medical Assistants'
Endowment
Department of Accreditation
20 North Wacker Dr/Suite 1575
Chicago, IL 60606-2903
Phone (800) 228-2262 / Fax (312) 899-1259

America Association of Medical Assistants
Director of Certification
20 North Wacker Dr/Suite 1575
Chicago, IL 60606-2903
Phone (312) 424-3100

Medical Illustrator

Duties

Medical illustrators manually produce renderings of body parts and procedures that are difficult to recreate by photography or that are best presented in a medium difficult to replicate through the taking of photos. In addition to producing visual art, the medical illustrator may function in an administrative capacity or as an administrative resource. The medical illustrator must have extensive knowledge of biological sciences and body systems related to human anatomy and physiology. The artist must have proficiency in use of microscopes and other imaging devices required to manipulate medical scenes in order to depict the desired rendering. It is also preferable that the illustrator has some knowledge of pathology and human diseases, coupled with a sense of ethics and psychology, as he or she may be dealing with patients and the general population. Extreme accuracy and realism, or an interpretation based on verbal instructions, are necessary to translate a complex idea into a simple explanatory diagram or schematic product. A high degree of skill and experience in the use of various artistic media is required. Most programs only accept a few students per year, as they must interact in all of the various areas of the hospital, and require a diverse practice employing many different medical specialties.

Requirements for Program Entry

All medical illustrator programs are at an advanced level and are based on a two-year master's degree model, following a bachelor's degree in the physical sciences preferably and usually some experience in a medical profession. Most often, the illustrator is required to have a portfolio of his productions to be used in assessing the individual qualifications for entering into a medical illustrator program.

Accreditation Groups

American Medical Illustrator (AMI) Headquarters
2965 Flowers Road S.
Suite 105
Atlanta, GA 30341
Telephone: (770) 454-7933
http://wwwmedical-illustrators.org

Ophthalmic Medical Technician/Technologist

Duties

Ophthalmic medical technicians and technologists assist ophthalmologists (physicians specializing in the care of and treatment of diseases of the eye) by performing procedures assigned to and approved by an ophthalmologist. Ophthalmic medical technicians and technologists often collect data and medical history. Certain repetitive tasks, such as routine procedures required in the examination of the eye, as well as some well-defined medical treatments are performed by these technical personnel under the direction of the physician in charge of the patient's treatment. Diagnostic tests, to include anatomical and functional ocular measurements by use of sophisticated equipment; testing of ocular functions, such as visual acuity, visual fields, and pupillary responses to light stimulation; and intraocular pressure determinations are commonly performed by the technician or technologist. Teaching and instructing the patient in performing self-care and in the use of optical devices are within the realm of the technician and technologist working under a physician specializing in treatment of eyes.

Ophthalmic medical technicians and technologists maintain ophthalmic and surgical instruments by arranging, sterilizing, and storing them for use. The technologist is expected to perform duties at a higher level of expertise than the technician and to operate with considerable technical and clinical judgment. Technologists may also provide instruction and supervise other ophthalmic personnel, such as clerical and technician-level workers.

Requirements for Entry into Training

To enter an ophthalmic medical technician program, an individual must have a high school diploma or equivalent. Technician programs are approximately one year in length. To enter an ophthalmic medical technologist program, an individual must have two years of undergraduate study. The technologist program is approximately two years in length and is comprised of both academic and practical components of training.

Accreditation Groups

Those desiring to become ophthalmic technicians or technicians may learn about career opportunities through:

ATPO
2025 Woodlane Drive
St. Paul MN 55125
Phone: 651/731-7239
Website: http.//www.atpo.org
E-mail: atpomembership@jcahpo.org

Information regarding credentialing of ophthalmic personnel may be received through:

Committee on Accreditation for Ophthalmic Medical Personnel
2025 Woodlane Dr
St. Paul, MN 551 25-2995
Phone (651) 731-2944 / (800) 284-3937

Respiratory Therapist

Duties

A respiratory therapist with advanced credentials and training is qualified to assume primary responsibility for all respiratory care modalities, including the supervision of respiratory therapy technicians. When providing respiratory care for patients, the advanced respiratory therapist is allowed to exercise considerable independent clinical judgment while under the supervision of a physician. The respiratory therapist, usually a technician (entry level), administers general respiratory care. Technicians may assume clinical responsibility for specified respiratory modalities involving the application of well-established therapeutic techniques but must operate under the supervision of an advanced respiratory therapist **and** a physician.

Requirements for Entry into Educational Program

To enter a respiratory therapy program, an individual must hold a high school diploma or equivalent. Programs for the entry-level technician require essentially two years of study, leading to an associate degree. To enter a respiratory therapist technician (entry level) program, an individual must hold a high school diploma or equivalent. Programs range from twelve to eighteen months in length, leading to a certificate of completion and in some cases an associate's degree.

To enter the advanced respiratory therapy (practitioner is called a Therapist) program, a four-year bachelor's degree may be required by some institutions. The advanced-level practitioner administers general care with clinical responsibility and is allowed considerable independent judgment in the treatment of respiratory patients. However, the therapist is required to operate under the supervision of a physician.

Accreditation Groups

Please contact the following agencies for career and credentialing information.

Certification/Registration

American Association for Respiratory Care
11030 Ables Lane
Dallas, TX 75229
Phone (972) 243-2272

National Board for Respiratory Care
8310 Nieman Rd.
Lenexa, KS 66214
Phone (913) 599-4200

Surgical Technology

Duties

Surgical technologists are integral members of the surgical team who work closely with surgeons, anesthesiologists, registered nurses, and other surgical personnel in delivering patient care and assuming appropriate responsibilities before, during, and after surgery. Scrub, circulating, first assisting, and second assisting surgical technologists have primary responsibilities for maintaining the sterile field, being constantly vigilant that all members of the team adhere to aseptic technique.

1. The Surgical Technologist in the Scrub Role (STSR)
   The scrub surgical technologist handles the instruments, supplies, and equipment necessary during the surgical procedure. The STSR has an understanding of the procedure being performed and anticipates the needs of the surgeon. The STSR has the necessary knowledge and ability to ensure quality patient care during the operative procedure and is constantly on vigil for maintenance of the sterile field.

2. The Surgical Technologist in the Circulating Role (STCR)
   The circulating surgical technologist obtains additional instruments, supplies, and equipment while the surgical procedure is in progress. The STRC monitors conditions in the operating room and constantly assesses the needs of the patient and surgical team.

3. The Surgical Technologist in the Second Assisting Role (STSA)
   The second assisting surgical technologist assists the surgeon and/or first assistant during the operative procedure by carrying out technical tasks other than cutting, clamping, and suturing of tissue. This role is distinct from that of the first assistant and may in some circumstances be performed in addition to the scrub role.

4. The Surgical Technologist in the First Assisting Role (CST/CFA)
   The Certified Surgical Technologist/Certified First Assistant is an advanced practitioner who assists the surgeon with exposure, closure of surgical wounds, and maintenance of hemostasis.

As the trend toward less invasive but more technical surgical procedures continues, surgical technologist training has responded by now requiring courses in physics and computer science in addition to other standard robotics courses. The future surgical technologist will operate and troubleshoot the robotics that will carry out many of the steps of a typical surgical procedure.

Accreditation Groups

Please contact the following agencies for career and credentialing information.

Association of Surgical Technologists

Certification/Registration

7108C South Alton Way
Centennial, CO 80112-2106
Phone (303) 694-9130 or
(800) 637-7433

Liaison Council on Certification for the Surgical Technologist
1080 South Alton Way
Centennial, CO 80112-2106
Phone (303) 694-9264, (800) 707-0057

Health Information Administrator

Duties

Entry-level health information administrators may be employed in a number of types of health care settings. Job titles may vary depending on educational achievement, work experience, and titles employed in local places of employment. Common job titles include director, assistant director, manager, reimbursement claims analyst, and clinical information manager, among others. Generally, tasks related to the management of health information and the systems follow specific policies and procedures for proper retrieval and communication of that information only through the proper channels. This includes manipulating the collection of, processing, electronic, and hard-copy storage of, retrieval, and effective communication of that information to include only pertinent information to other health care practitioners. Health information administrators also monitor the uses of information and determine the most efficient use of and management of the databases.

Requirements for Obtaining Training

A four-year bachelor's degree is required to become a health information administrator. For the health care technician level, common job titles held by health information technician are: coder, medical record technician, supervisor, and so on. Health information technicians assume roles that support efforts toward the development of computer-based patient record systems and a national information infrastructure. Specific job tasks may be related to the use, analysis, validation, presentation, abstracting, coding, storage, security, retrieval, quality measurement, and control of data, regardless of the physical medium in which information is maintained. A two-year associate's degree is required to become a health information technician.

Accreditation Groups

You may contact the following institution for career or credentialing information. Currently, no certification is required, but for career information, please write or contact the following address:

Careers

American Health Information Management Association
233 N. Michigan Ave., Suite 2150
Chicago, IL 60601-5519
http://www.ahima.org

BLOOD AND AIRBORNE PATHOGENS

OBJECTIVES

Upon completion of this unit of instruction, the student should be able to:

a. List the five classes of organisms that may infect the human body

b. Give examples of several viral and bacterial diseases from your personal knowledge

c. Discuss routes of infection (pathways into the body)

d. Provide information relating to the three categories of medical care workers regarding potential exposure

e. Relate an exposure incident and give the immediate steps to take following exposure

f. List pre-exposure procedures (don't forget education and training components)

g. Discuss processes involved in post-exposure activities

h. Relate the donning of personal protective equipment

i. Give the methods of transmission of the major blood and airborne organisms: HIV, HBV, and TB

SECTION OUTLINE

Introduction to Blood and Airborne Pathogens

Exposure Potential and Prevention

Pre-Exposure Precautions

Exposure Incidents

Post-Exposure Follow-up

Specifics for Bloodborne Pathogen – HIV

Specifics for Bloodborne Pathogen – HBV

Tuberculosis in the Health Care Setting

Suggested Student Activities

Study Questions

Review Study Outline

INTRODUCTION TO BLOOD AND AIRBORNE PATHOGENS

Major Organisms Requiring Precautions

The bloodborne and airborne pathogens presented in this section are by no means all inclusive. Scourges of infectious diseases have racked the world since recorded history. We need only recall the plague that descended upon the Egyptians in Biblical history to realize the broad swaths of destruction and suffering that may be visited upon humankind. The black plague (bubonic plague, caused by a bacterial organism) killed a large percentage of the Europeans several hundred years ago, and smallpox wiped out a large portion of the Native American population with the arrival of Europeans in the early fifteenth century. Much medical progress has been made in the identification of organisms and efficacious treatment of these infectious diseases, but the progress we have made could be undone if cautions are not understood and precautions not taken to ward off these infectious agents.

A large number of virulent pathogens exist that belong to five different categories. The first four categories are bacterial, viral, parasitic, and fungal. The fifth category includes some other pathogens (rickettsiae is an example, and is usually transmitted by the tick vector) that belong to less well defined categories than the four previously listed categories, which comprise the majority of infectious diseases that have plagued humankind. The broad and indiscriminate use of antibiotics that often serve in a palliative role have little therapeutic value when they are used to treat symptoms not caused by bacteria, such as the common cold, which has a viral etiology. This unwarranted use of antibiotics has led to the rise of many bacteria that are resistant to every antibiotic currently in use. Many infections that are difficult to treat rise from hospitalization and contraction of antibiotic-resistant organisms in the facility. It has been said that if you are admitted to the hospital and do not have an infection, you will be issued one before you leave. Hospital-acquired infections are termed *nosocomial* infections. *Iatrogenic* infections are those caused by organisms that gain entry into and colonize the body through the introduction of medical devices used for various treatments. With the proliferation of new medical procedures, some of an elective nature, the rise in these types of infections with resistant strains may cause a local epidemic within a health care facility. It should also be noted that *normal flora*, bacteria that naturally occur in certain parts of the human body, for example in the mouth and the intestine, may be transplanted to another anatomical site, producing an infection. An organism from the body that may be normal in one area may not be normal in another. Protecting yourself against these dangerous organisms is paramount, and most disease prevention efforts are focused on teaching the health care worker to protect himself or herself against a whole host of organisms. Blood and airborne pathogens other than HIV and HBV, as well as environmental organisms that infect large numbers of hospitalized patients, must be prevented through the use of precautions designed to protect both the worker and the patient. Effective and conscientious efforts to avoid becoming infected or infecting a patient will pay dividends in lowering our health care costs as a nation, as well as avoiding needless suffering. In an effort to protect the workers and employees against infection by one of these three organisms, the Infection Control program of each medical facility and educational institution classifies job positions by potential for exposure (discussed in depth in the Infection Control section).

While there are literally thousands of organisms that are capable of causing serious infections in man, only two major organisms associated with the majority of infections by bloodborne pathogens are deemed a status that requires specific training for health care personnel. While the emphasis is on these two organisms, the human immunodeficiency virus (HIV) and the Hepatitis B virus (HBV), we cannot neglect placing attention on other pathogenic (disease-causing) organisms among

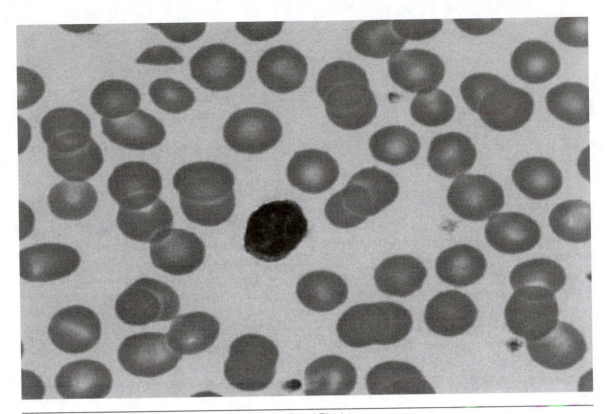

Blood Smear with Red Cells, Lymphocyte (white blood cell) and Platelets

humans. Hepatitis A, which is transmitted through water and food, chiefly, is an important pathogen that may now be prevented through immunization, and hepatitis C, which is bloodborne or sexually transmitted in most cases. Both are becoming increasingly important. However, at this time they are not treated in Occupational Safety and Health Administration's (OSHA) guidelines as "covered organisms" requiring periodic training of the health care worker. Blood is an extremely good bacterial medium, and viruses are intracellular organisms, meaning that they may grow well inside blood cells. An example of a protozoan that grows in blood cells is the malarial organism, of which there are four major strains capable of infecting humans. The strains of malaria organisms, called protozoans, that infect humans are not prevalent in North America currently but are rampant in other parts of the world. There are strains of malaria in the United States that infect birds, but humans have natural immunity against these strains, fortunately. This human immunity to certain animal pathogens and normal flora has seemed to have been breached recently with certain organisms previously unknown to have infected humans. An example is seen in outbreaks (called Severe Acute Respiratory Syndrome (SARS)) in Asia of organisms normally found only in chickens.

Categorization of Medical Care Workers, Faculty and Allied Health Students

Educational institution faculty members and students in programs or course areas requiring direct contact with patients or with their bodily wastes and wastes associated with their care are considered as Category I (high risk). Occupational exposure to HIV, HBV, and TB disease in certain health care professions are considered to be in covered occupational areas falling under federal guidelines. Specific tasks are assigned to workers in these occupational areas, such as those related to nursing care, and are not limited to nurses but to those professionals who perform related duties. The process of categorizing tasks for Categories I,

II, and III relate to the amount of potential for contracting covered infectious diseases relative to the specific tasks, which these workers perform as a portion of their duties. The Infection Control Committee normally categorizes occupational tasks for medical workers as an ongoing process due to the changes in duties and evolution of technology.

There are three categories of health care workers, based on their potential for being exposed to blood, respiratory secretions, and other body fluids in the course of their treatment of the patients and in handling of infectious wastes. Although categorization of health care workers will also be treated in the Infection Control section of this book, it does bear mentioning here, when discussing bloodborne pathogens. Briefly, the three categories of workers are:

Category I

For Category I health care workers, there is a definite possibility of being exposed to blood and airborne pathogens while performing assigned tasks. This category of worker performs procedures in direct patient care and has frequent contact with blood and body fluids on a routine basis. Blood and certain other body fluids carry the most risk of transmitting an infection to the unwary medical worker who comes in contact with an infected patient. All medical workers providing direct patient care are classified as Category 1, despite the fact that barrier devices and personal protective equipment (PPE) are used. Examples of those who work with hospitalized patients in a direct care manner include: nurses, patient care assistants, medical laboratory workers, radiology workers, patient transport personnel, teams such as those that provide infusion services (IV), surgical workers, and a number of others who may be specialized employees in a large and complex facility.

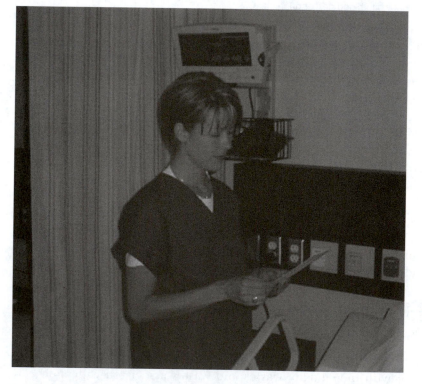

Nurse Providing Direct Patient Care

Category II

In the course of performing Category II tasks, which include procedures performed by custodians and laundry workers, there is a definite possibility that the person will handle blood, blood products, and body fluids. Although barrier equipment will be used, these workers are still classified as Category II. Over the past few decades, medical wastes that were once thrown in ordinary trash bins and dumpsters were required to have special handling by a number of state and federal, as well as some local, ordinances mandating how this possibly infectious material would be disposed of. There are commercial providers that provide collection containers and collect the contaminated material for disposal, usually by burning.

The manner in which these materials are transported is strictly regulated from the collection point to the process of certification that the wastes have arrived at the disposal facility and have been properly disposed of. These disposal facilities are specially designed to provide for safe and effective disposal of waste products that may transmit infections if a person comes into contact with the material. The medical and other biohazardous wastes generated by the health care facility are the responsibility of the generating facility until disposal, ironically. If a shipment is lost, the hospital and not the waste transport company is responsible for ensuring that the wastes are recovered and are properly disposed of according to local, state, and federal laws.

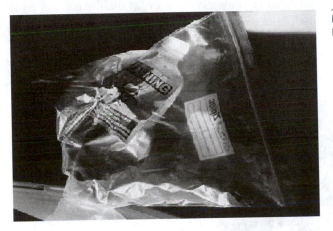

Example of Hazardous Waste Handled by Category II Personnel

Category III

Category III jobs include mainly clerical and secretarial procedures where there is almost no chance of coming into contact with blood and body fluids. Contact with medical patients for these positions does not require direct patient contact or contact with medical equipment and supplies used by patients in these tasks. In some facilities, clerical personnel may be required to accompany the patient and to obtain a history from emergency patients in the treatment areas where they may come in contact with the patient or his body fluids accidentally. In this case, the clerical worker would be treated the same as a worker providing direct patient care.

EXPOSURE POTENTIAL AND PREVENTION

Prevention and Treatment for Bloodborne Pathogens

There is currently no cure for the HIV (sometimes called the AIDS) virus. Hepatitis B infections run their natural course with approximately 90 percent recovering and showing no evidence of the disease after the disease is resolved.

Note: tuberculosis, the most prevalent airborne disease, may be cured in the early stages of the disease by the administration of specific antibiotics in most cases, except those classified as being infected by resistant strains of organisms. However, the emphasis is on prevention, rather than cure, for both blood and airborne pathogens.

Potential Exposure

All medical workers have a responsibility to themselves and the institution to be safety conscious at all times. Using preventive practices should enable the worker to avoid making mistakes that will cause him or her to come in direct contact with blood and body fluids. It is best to avoid exposure incidents, and this is possible by following the policies and guidelines of the institution. If you conscientiously follow these measures, there is very little likelihood of contracting AIDS, hepatitis, or tuberculosis while performing the medical worker's tasks.

Spills of Biohazardous Materials

1. An absorbent material or a specially designed gel should be used to cover the entire spill. The custodial staff will be responsible for the proper removal of the spills and will thoroughly clean the area. Wastes will be disposed of properly.

2. Spill kits designed for biological and hazardous materials cleanup are available and are to be used as required. Kits are usually designed to absorb or contain biohazardous materials for disposal. Following the absorption process, disinfectants are provided to clean the area of any residual material thoroughly.

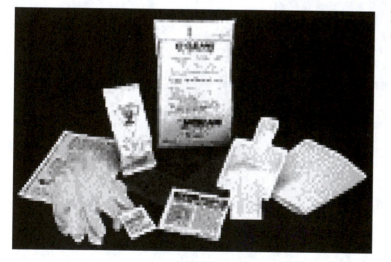

Common Blood Spill Kit for Cleaning of Spills

A large number of commercial kits are available for effectively and safely cleaning biohazardous spills and also dangerous chemical spills. It is a requirement that the facility provide supplies for this purpose. In some of the larger facilities, trained custodial personnel may be dispatched to clean up a hazardous spill properly.

Exposure Determination – Have You Been Exposed

If you believe you have been exposed to a potentially infectious bodily fluid, ask yourself the following questions:

1. **Is medical help needed?** Assess the situation. Is the victim bleeding profusely, or are any bones broken? Serious injury would necessitate calling 911. (Note that in some areas, a 911 number is not available, so you should post the proper number to call in the case of an emergency in the work area. Many health care facilities will have already done this as a

function of the infection control personnel or in some cases, a safety committee. One should always familiarize himself or herself with the proper procedure for reporting an emergency situation.) Primary treatment would focus on keeping the victim comfortable and avoiding further injury by moving them until emergency personnel arrives.

2. **Can the situation be managed without professional help?** If the helper/rescuer has only come into contact with a bodily fluid and has no breaks or cuts in the skin, washing of the affected area(s) with soap and water is sufficient. In case of doubt, or if questions arise, contact the Infection Control Coordinator or seek medical attention in the absence of this person. It is best to seek the advice of a medical professional as early as possible following an actual or potential exposure to infectious body materials. A baseline set of diagnostic tests and a review of the immunization records is always a good idea. A delay in treatment is not advantageous to the exposed person, as early treatment generally leads to a better outcome if the person has been infected.

Typical Hand washing Facility – First Line of Defense against Infection

Pre-Exposure Precautions

To date, there has been no effective vaccine developed to provide immunity against the HIV organism. Several strains of HIV exist, and some strains are similar to those found in animals. For instance, feline leukemia is thought to be a strain almost identical to that of HIV. In some parts of the world, epidemics of both HTLV-1 and HTLV-2 (Human T-Lymphotropic Virus) have occurred. This poses such a risk to our blood supplies that testing of each unit of blood for HTLV-1 and HTLV-2 is performed. Such was the case in the 1990-1991 Persian Gulf conflict, during which massive quantities of blood were collected and tested in order to treat soldiers suffering from tank burns through the administration of fresh or frozen plasma. Immunization where possible when vaccines exist for certain organisms, and training to enable health care workers to avoid becoming infected are the most effective ways to avoid infection.

HBV Vaccination

1. **All employees having occupational exposure to blood or other infectious materials are offered the HBV vaccination at no charge to the employee.** The vaccination is made available within ten working days of initial work assignment. Exceptions are if the employee has previously received the complete hepatitis B vaccination series, if antibody testing reveals the employee is immune, or if the vaccine in contraindicated for medical reasons.

2. Students in occupational areas with potential and likely exposure to blood and airborne pathogens will be required to receive the HBV immunizations or to sign a declination form. This declination form indicates that the student is aware of the risks of not being immunized, but is willing to hold the clinical facility and the educational institute blameless if an exposure results in the contraction of the disease. The student is required to pay for his or her immunizations, and the series of three injections may be provided for the student at cost. Students should receive the first vaccine dose prior to patient-client contact and before performing any tasks, procedures, or activities that involve exposure potential.

3. A prescreening test called an antibody titer may be offered but is not required before receiving a hepatitis B vaccination. If the employee chooses an antibody titer to determine presence of already existing antibodies against HBV, the test is also offered at no charge to the employee. Each employee and student has the right to refuse vaccination by completing a declination form. Those who later decide to be immunized against hepatitis B will be offered the immunization at no cost to the employee, but at cost for the student.

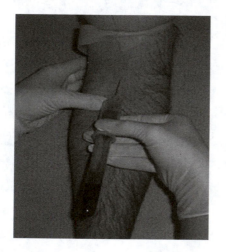

Obtaining blood for antibody titer

4. Vaccination is also offered as a post-exposure follow-up for all instructors, medical workers, or students with an occupational exposure incident (skin, eye, mucous membrane, or parenteral (intravenous, subcutaneous, intramuscular, or mucosal) contact with blood or other potentially infectious materials).

5. Documentation of the immunization status is in each individual faculty member's personnel record as well as a master vaccination file. Documentation of student vaccination is to be maintained in the student's record file and master training file. Any faculty member or student declining vaccination will be counseled on the benefits and safety of the vaccine and will sign a statement to that effect. A simple repeat vaccination when in doubt, or administration of protective antibodies, is a small price to pay for the assurance that you will possibly be protected from a potentially deadly infection.

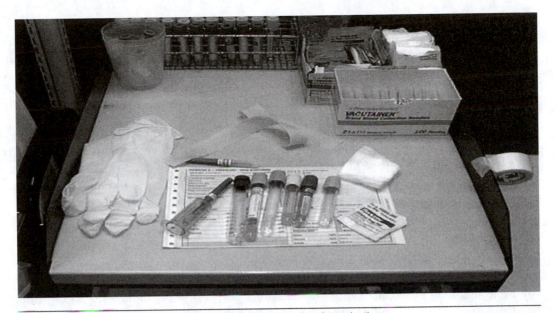

Phlebotomy materials used to collect blood samples for baseline determinations

Pre-exposure Records Storage and Maintenance

For pre-exposure purposes, testing of the employee or student for preexisting conditions is important. If the health care worker is exposed to an infectious agent, records called baseline determinations performed prior to the incident may be compared to those obtained following exposure. Medical records required by the standard governing occupational exposure are maintained as required in the Bloodborne Pathogens Standard previously noted. Student medical records shall be retained for a period of one year after graduation, completion, termination or leaving the educational facility. Faculty medical records and records for medical worker and employees of the medical facility are retained for a period of **thirty years** after the date employment ends for each employee. These records are often accompanied by documentation of training for the employees.

EXPOSURE INCIDENTS

What is an exposure incident?

Any time a layperson or medical worker comes in direct contact with body fluids, or if, after providing treatment, the patient is found to have an infectious disease, the worker or caregiver should be assessed for potential risk of infection. This assessment might require only counseling, but it may include preventive immunization or the collection of a blood sample to determine baseline laboratory values. Later, a second blood sample may be collected to determine if any changes have occurred. The first sample drawn immediately following the incident is called the baseline sample.

1. **Soiled Clothing? Broken Skin? What Should be Done?**
   How much blood is present? A small amount less than the size of a 50¢ piece and that cannot be squeezed from the clothing would not necessitate removal of one's clothing. Extremely bloody clothing should be removed and NOT worn home. One should clean himself or herself carefully and place the soiled clothing in a plastic bag. Clean clothing should be provided for wearing on the trip home.

2. **Washing Bloody Clothing**

Extremely bloody clothing should NOT be washed in commercial washers. It should be soaked in dilute bleach before allowing contaminated water and clothing to enter your washing machine or sink. Very little danger exists from dried blood, but it is important to be very careful, even to the extreme.

3. **Skin Breaks, Rashes, or Lesions**

If skin breaks are present, one should seek medical attention if exposed to blood. If the Infection Control Officer is not present and broken skin or mucus membranes are involved, the employee should go to a physician in either the emergency department or to their own private physician. The educational institution or medical facility is responsible for charges incurred when exposure occurs during duties related to the medical program in which the student is enrolled. Incident reports are initiated at the clinical site and must be supervised by a physician.

4. **Exposure Incident Evaluation and Follow-up**

An Exposure Incident Evaluation and Follow-up Report form should be initiated. These forms will be available in all departments, and additional forms may be obtained from the Infection Control Officer. Counseling will be scheduled for those who have been exposed to infectious materials.

5. **Accidental Exposure**

Accidental exposure to the blood of a suspected or confirmed case of hepatitis B should be followed by:

A. Gamma globulin administration within a few hours of the incident if possible

B. If administered no later than seven days following exposure, immunization to hepatitis B is effective in preventing illness from occurring. This is true of a number of organisms; therefore, if you have been exposed to any organism, it is prudent to seek medical advice so quick treatment may be provided, it indicated.

POST-EXPOSURE FOLLOW-UP (BLOOD OR OTHER POTENTIALLY INFECTIOUS MATERIAL)

When an Exposure is Determined to Have Occurred

A medical worker, faculty member, or student is deemed to have experienced an exposure to possible harmful pathogens if there is a skin break from a needlestick, cut or puncture, or a splash into a mucous membrane. They will be treated as having experienced an accidental exposure. A splash to the eye, nasal mucosa, or mouth might expose the medical worker to infectious body fluids, such as blood or other body fluids containing microorganisms. A cutaneous (skin) exposure due to chapped or abraded skin or other non-intact skin should also be reported as an exposure incident to the medical facility departmental supervisor and the educational institution's Infection Control Coordinator.

Documentation of Exposure

Following the report of an occupational exposure incident, the medical worker, faculty member, or student is required to complete an accident/incident report, available from the Infection Control Coordinator. These forms are organized in such a way that a supervisory

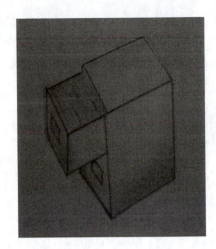

employee will be able to complete all steps necessary immediately following the exposure if the incident occurs when the Infection Control Coordinator or a designee is not on site, such as during the evening or over the weekend. This will insure that all appropriate steps are performed for any employee at any time. Remember, the patient might not agree to have his blood tested, so it is important that a person with a potential exposure make a rational decision. The employee will be offered a confidential medical evaluation and follow-up, which will include the following information:

1. Documentation of the route(s) of exposure, previous HBV and HIV antibody status of the patient(s) (if known), and the circumstances under which the exposure occurred will be gathered.

2. If it is feasible and the source patient can be identified and their permission is obtained, collection and testing of the patient's blood to determine the presence of HIV and/or HBV infections must be conducted.

3. If the patient does not consent to furnishing a specimen, the employer shall establish that legally required consent cannot be obtained. When law does not require the source individual's consent, the blood sample, if available, shall be tested and the results documented. If the source patient is already known to be HIV or HBV positive, then repeat testing is not required.

4. Results of the source individual's testing shall be made available to the medical worker, faculty member, or student, and the affected people will be informed of the applicable laws and regulations concerning disclosure of the identity and infectious status of the source individual.

5. The exposed or student's blood shall be collected as soon as possible and tested after consent is obtained from the exposed person.

6. If the medical worker, instructor, or student consents to baseline blood collections but does not give consent at that time for HIV serologic testing, the sample shall be preserved for at least ninety days. If within the ninety days of the exposure incident the faculty member or student elects to have the baseline sample tested, such testing shall be done as soon as it is feasible.

7. The educational facility and the medical facility shall ensure that the health care professional responsible for the medical worker's, instructor's, or student's hepatitis B vaccination is provided a copy of the regulation for *Occupational Exposure to Bloodborne Pathogens*.

8. The institute shall ensure that the health care professional evaluating an employee after an exposure incident is provided the following information:

   A. A copy of the regulation for *Occupational Exposure to Bloodborne Pathogens* in order for the individual to insure that he or she understands the risks involved and that the treatment is adequate.

   B. A description of the duties for a medical worker, instructor, or student as they relate to the exposure incident will be available to determine if the employee was performing a procedure outside the scope of his or her training that could have been avoided.

   C. Documentation of circumstances leading to the exposure incident, including the route of exposure, will be provided. Statistical evidence indicating more than one occurrence under the same conditions would possibly lead to modification of employee training.

   D. Results of the source individual's blood testing, if available, is to be provided with the source individual's consent. The source individual may be asked to provide a blood or bodily sample but can refuse to do so.

   E. All medical records relevant to the appropriate treatment of the employee, including vaccination status, are the responsibility of the facilities to maintain. The records should be available to the counselor who is performing preliminary processes to document the exposure and to determine the risk to the employee.

9. The facilities shall obtain and provide the employee with a copy of the consulting health care professional's written opinion within fifteen days of the completion of the evaluation. The health care professional's written opinion for hepatitis B vaccination shall be limited as to whether the vaccination is indicated and if the medical worker, instructor, or student received such vaccination. NOTE: An employee who declined HBV immunization and is exposed may be immunized within a few days of the incident. This will usually provide protection to the employee, as will gamma globulin administration containing antibodies against the virus.

10. The health care professional's written opinion for post-exposure evaluation and follow-up is limited to the following information:

    A. The medical worker, faculty member, or student should be informed of the results of the evaluation.

    B. The faculty member, medical worker, or student is to be told about any medical conditions resulting from exposure to blood or other infectious materials that require further evaluation and treatment if clinically indicated

11. NOTE: All other findings are confidential and are not included in the written report and are to be written and provided to the exposed medical worker.

SPECIFICS FOR THE BLOODBORNE PATHOGEN – HIV

The human immunodeficiency virus (HIV) causes a disease called Acquired Immunodeficiency Syndrome (AIDS). A syndrome is a group or collection of symptoms and signs associated with a particular disease. The etiology, or study of the causes of the disease, provides grounds for disagreement among many medical specialists. As an example, two theories being espoused are that the organism originated with the hunting and eating of the green monkey of Africa, or that the disease originated with the administration of polio vaccine made from the kidneys of rhesus monkeys. Neither theory has been proven to date. Signs that can be seen as manifestations of the disease and symptoms (which relate how the patient feels) are well documented and predictable. With proper precautions, the health care worker is at no more risk of contracting AIDS than the layperson.

The AIDS virus, or human immunodeficiency virus (HIV) has two strains called HTLV-1 and HTLV-2. Symptoms associated with AIDS are caused by the presence of a virus that commonly attacks blood cells of the immune system, leaving the victim susceptible to a number of opportunistic infections. Symptoms will depend on the site of infection and the organism involved. Initial symptoms may be insidious or mild, with nonspecific symptoms like those associated with a flu-like illness. Signs and symptoms may include lymphadenopathy (enlargement, tenderness), anorexia, chronic diarrhea, weight loss, fever, and fatigue. Later stages will reveal Kaposi's sarcoma, manifested by red-brown to purple lesions of the skin and mucous membranes.

AIDS has been found worldwide and was first identified in the United States in 1981. However, the disease may have been present for some years before sufficient occurrences, diagnostic technology, and documentation existed to investigate the disease as an important malady. Some reports indicate that the blood component, serum, was saved from an adolescent who died with an undiagnosed and wasting disease in the late 1960s. Tests performed on this preserved blood sample indicate that there may have been antibodies developed against the human immunodeficiency virus at that time. The disease is now raging in a number of areas of the world. Efforts to eradicate the disease have not been effective to date, often because of political views in some developing countries, even by heads of states.

Humans are now recognized as reservoirs of the HIV. A reservoir may be an environmental habitat, such as water or soil, or a living organism, like humans. The transmission or passing of the AIDS virus from one person to another has been found in blood, semen, saliva, urine, tears, and tissue. But to date, there have been no documented cases of transmission from contact with fluids other than blood, semen, and vaginal secretions. In adults, the virus is most often spread through sexual contact or by sharing needles, although early in the history of the disease before testing for the virus or antibodies was routinely performed on blood donor samples, transfusions resulted in a large number of infections. Most infected children acquired the virus from infected mothers during pregnancy. Some cases have occurred as the result of transfusions of blood or blood products, such as the blood factors necessary to treat patients suffering from hemophilia. It is possible that HIV may spread by getting blood from an infected person into open cuts, abrasions, the mouth, or the eyes of another person.

AIDS is not spread by coughing, sneezing, hugging, or by contact with eating utensils, faucets, or toilet seats. It is possible, however, that AIDS may be spread through kissing, if a person infected with the virus has mouth-to mouth contact with someone who has vigorously brushed his teeth and has minute bleeding of the gums. AIDS may be transmitted in a similar manner as hepatitis B, so learning about the spread of one of these organisms will enable the health care worker to protect himself or herself against both, as the precautions for both HIV and HBV are similar. Although sweat, tears, urine, and vomitus (if containing blood) HAVE transmitted HIV, NO transmission is known to have occurred through vectors such as mosquitoes, fleas, ticks, other insects, or animals at this time. A possibility of transmission through animal and arthropod vectors is remote but periodically investigated on the chance that this may eventually occur. Such a possibility would greatly raise the possibility and even the probability that large numbers of people would become infected.

The incubation period, or the time required for the organism, a virus, to grow and to reproduce to a level where symptoms and signs appear, is unknown and therefore may also be variable in length. Asymptomatic people are known to have harbored the virus for more than ten to fifteen years. Some who have been diagnosed have been successfully treated for a number of years and are living relatively normal lives due to advanced and improved treatment developed over the intervening years since the first cases of AIDS were documented. In transfusion-related cases, the incubation period has most often been about two years, but fortunately, with routine testing of blood supplies, the number of transfusion-related cases has practically disappeared.

The length of the stage or period of time between HIV infection and possible transmission to another person is unknown. It is believed that the disease may be transmitted prior to the appearance of symptoms and that it persists even after successful treatment has alleviated the initial symptoms. It should be noted that a person who has been successfully treated may appear normal while continuing treatment yet may be able to infect the unwary person who comes in contact with the infected person. Therefore, preventive measures in relation to sexual practices and performance of medical procedures should always be taken.

Prevention and control of the human immunodeficiency virus go hand in hand. Since most cases are transmitted sexually or by shared using of drug paraphernalia, these practices must be modified or curtailed by those who are positive for the AIDS virus. A good rule to follow is to avoid indiscriminate sexual contact with new partners whose background is unknown, and to avoid sharing IV drug items. In the health care facilities and when treating patients at the sites of accidents, scrupulously careful cleaning and disinfection of blood and body fluid spills are necessary to avoid the spread of the virus. Cleaning practices should include protection for the person responsible for cleaning the area, such as where medical procedures have been performed. Protective aprons or other clothing impervious to liquids, such as safety aprons, should be worn over the clothing normally worn for work, along with reusable gloves that are in good condition and that are cleaned between usages. Surfaces and objects contaminated with blood or body fluids that may contain blood (e.g., vomitus or urine) must be cleaned with detergent and water and disinfected immediately. The most effective disinfectant readily available is 10% bleach sodium hypochlorite (Clorox). The AIDS virus is often found in conjunction with other infectious organisms because of the immunocompromised condition of the patient seeking treatment. The AIDS virus along with other potentially dangerous organisms may be found in body fluids even when there are no symptoms to suggest infection is present. A person with an HIV infection has a weakened immune status and is vulnerable to a host of opportunistic infections.

Wear disposable gloves when handling blood (nosebleeds, cuts) or bloody items (surfaces or clothing), particularly if you have open cuts, rashes, or sores on your hands. Even a torn cuticle is a portal for the entry of microorganisms. Use caution when handling needles and other "sharps." Avoid contamination of eyes and mouth by touching them with soiled hands.

After contact with any bodily fluid, the hands should be washed as quickly as possible. Even if gloves were worn, the hands should be washed thoroughly and vigorously with running water and

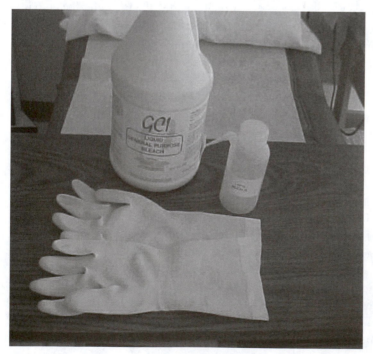

Reusable Gloves for Cleaning Body Fluids Spills

soap for at least thirty seconds, ensuring that the webbing between the fingers is also scrubbed. Remove rings and other jewelry in order to do a more thorough job of washing hands and arms. Particular care should be taken to wash around the cuticles of the nails, and to rub the hands together to produce friction. It might be noted that there now is a sentiment that antibacterial soap may lead to the increase of antibiotic resistant organisms. There is no substitute for ordinary hand soap, warm water, and friction in washing all parts of the hands, including the cuticles.

To keep workers and patients safe from accidental infection, use disinfecting solutions that are effective against viruses, fungi, bacteria, and other organisms that may be encountered in the medical treatment areas. A number of commercial products are available as disinfectants, but the most effective and cheapest method for decontaminating nonfood contact surfaces is a diluted 1:10 bleach (Clorox) solution. Sodium hypochlorite is the active ingredient in bleach, but it must be used properly in order to achieve maximum results. You should saturate the area and allow it to air-dry before wiping to complete the cleaning process. Prepare bleach solution fresh daily as the bleach loses its effectiveness after a few hours.

SPECIFICS FOR BLOOD BORNE PATHOGEN – HBV

The disease hepatitis B is the second important bloodborne pathogen which is also considered a "covered' disease that several governmental agencies deem important enough to mandate training of health care workers on an ongoing and periodic basis. The causative organism is the Hepatitis B virus (HBV) and is spread much in the same manner at the human immunodeficiency virus covered in the previous section.

The symptoms for HBV is similar to that of HIV with the general exceptions of nausea and jaundice (yellowing chiefly of the skin and eyes) in HBV cases. Anorexia (loss of appetite), tiredness, nausea, and vomiting, often accompanied by arthralgia (joint pain), and sometimes a rash are often present. Jaundice is most often present in adults and is not typically found in young children. Symptoms will vary widely from person to person, with some patients having almost no symptoms at all while others become seriously ill. Again, a person with hepatitis may exhibit almost no signs, yet be capable of infecting another through exchange of bodily fluids during sexual acts and/or the sharing of needles and blood products.

Hepatitis B is found throughout the world, and the disease is rampant in many areas where medical care and immunization is not readily available. The only known reservoir for HBV is the human body, but unlike HIV, the HBV organism may persist in dried body fluids for up to ten days, it is estimated. Transmission of the disease has occurred through a number of routes or portals of entry into the body. Hepatitis Surface Antigen (HbsAg) refers to the actual viral particles so this procedure tests directly for the organism, unlike those tests in which the antibody response to the

Face Shield

virus is measured. These viruses have been found in virtually all body fluids, from tissue secretions to wound excretions, but only blood and blood products, semen, and vaginal fluids, as in HIV, have been found to transmit the disease. It can be spread person-to-person from blood finding its way into open skin cuts or abrasions of another person. Splashing of blood and other body fluids into the eyes of another person may cause contraction of the disease, as well as sexual contact. Transmission from a mother to her baby is common when the mother is HBsAg positive. Accidental inoculation through needlesticks or shared razors and toothbrushes has been documented on rare occasions. Fecal-oral transmission has not been demonstrated despite being associated with hepatitis A, another important disease that is more easily spread than hepatitis B but does not have the important medical ramifications as HBV infections. The incubation period for the Hepatitis B virus is about 45 to 180 days, with an average of a 60 to –90-day period elapsing from exposure to the onset of symptoms of the disease. The amount of inoculum or dose (number of organisms or materials containing the virus entering the body) accounts for the differences of time before symptoms appear, as larger doses of inoculum most often result in the quicker manifestation of signs and symptoms.

Preventive measures are similar to those for HIV. Cleaning and disinfecting an area where blood and body fluid spills have occurred before an unprotected person comes into contact with the material is most effective in preventing spread of the organism. Surfaces and objects contaminated by blood, blood products, or body fluids must be cleaned with detergent and water and then disinfected.

The Hepatitis B virus, along with other infectious germs, may be found in most body fluids even where no symptoms are present. A number of people (about 10 percent) who are infected with the Hepatitis B virus become carriers and are capable of transmitting the organism after symptoms have subsided. Approximately 10 percent of those who contract hepatitis B become carriers for life and may not donate blood for transfusions. These carriers also may appear healthy, but they are

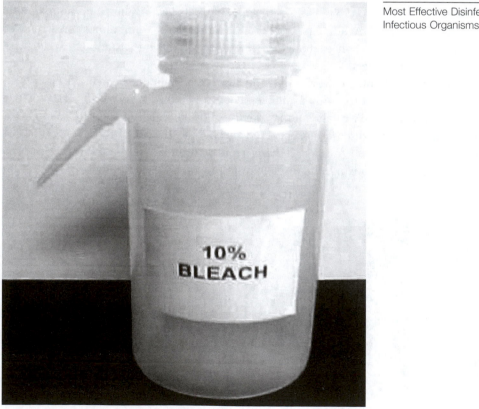

Most Effective Disinfectant against
Infectious Organisms

able to infect any of their sexual partners. It must also be noted by the student that there are more than sixty organisms that may be transmitted sexually or by other sharing of body fluids. Many of them have a lifetime impact on the lives of those who contract an infection from these organisms. Also, many of these organisms are reportable and require surveillance. All people suffering from a significant list of infections and their partners are required to reveal sexual contacts in order for governmental agencies to contact those at risk of having contracted the infection.

Proper cleaning of work areas is of paramount importance. In order to clean and disinfect an area properly, and while treating patients, disposable gloves are mandatory when handling blood or injuries accompanied by bleeding, or bloody and body fluid-contaminated items, work surfaces, or clothing. Open cuts, rashes, or sores on the hands require special precautions when removing the gloves and when washing the hands.

Most Effective Disinfectant against Infectious Organisms

Extreme care should be taken when handling needles or sharp instruments and supplies. Hand-washing immediately following contact with any body fluids is required even when gloves are worn. It is possible that the outside of the gloves may come into contact with portions of the hands. To reiterate, wash hands thoroughly and vigorously with soap and running water for a minimum of thirty seconds. Also, please note that hands should be washed BOTH before donning gloves, and after removing them, after disinfecting, or after treating a patient with injuries or illness of an unknown etiology.

The disinfecting solution mentioned previously, bleach) and water at a 1:10 ratio, is extremely effective against almost all organisms, including viruses as well as bacteria. Follow the same procedure as for HIV. In addition, generously saturate the area with the solution and let the surface air-dry. DO NOT RINSE.

REMINDER: Prepare solution fresh daily as the bleach loses its potency within a few hours. Some medical facilities use materials other than bleach and use additional procedures for disinfecting and surfaces within the clinical areas. Policies for these facilities are published in a facility's policy and procedure manual and will be assured of being effective by a committee such as the Infection/Exposure committees prior to adoption.

Treatment for hepatitis B is not currently available, so prevention is of the essence. Prophylaxis, meaning "to prevent disease" from occurring, is the most effective manner of halting spread of this disease along with conscientious cleaning and use of aseptic techniques in the treatment of patients. Immediately following a probable exposure, hepatitis B immune Globulin (HBIG), containing antibodies against the organism, is available for post-exposure treatment. If HBIG is to be used, it should be given as soon as possible, and always within seven days following exposure. Exposure through needlestick injuries would be of the most concern and would give the most potential for transmitting the organism from a patient to the health care worker. Blood splashes to the eyes, or blood or other body fluids contaminating cuts, rashes, and abrasions on the hands would also give cause for concern.

These situations where blood or other potentially infectious materials occur should be carefully evaluated and the source patient considered for testing if available to determine if blood came from an infected patient. Remember, a patient cannot be forced to agree to have his blood collected and tested. Prevention of hepatitis has been readily available for more than twenty years. In health care facilities and other agencies where a high likelihood exists for coming in contact with hepatitis B, the employer provides the hepatitis B vaccine, as previously discussed. Although a worker may decline the immunization, it is highly recommended for people considered at high risk for contracting this illness, particularly for health care workers. Immunization for hepatitis B leaves few side effects and is the most effective way to avoid contracting the illness. Pre-hospital health care personnel, such as emergency workers, are also included in the high risk category. These workers are required either to undergo the three-dose immunizations or to sign a declination form stating that the risks are known but that the worker does not wish to be immunized. Indiscriminate sexual encounters and sharing of drug needles must be avoided at all costs if the rate of infection is to be controlled.

Hepatitis B infections are often accompanied by hepatitis C viral infections. While only approximately 10 percent of hepatitis B-infected people become chronically infected, hepatitis C has more long-term effects. One serious long-term effect of hepatitis C is the statistical increase in liver cancer among those who were infected even decades earlier. Often the contraction of hepatitis B and hepatitis C occurs simultaneously, along with several other lesser-known viruses proven to cause hepatitis (most common are the delta and echo varieties).

TUBERCULOSIS IN THE HEALTH CARE SETTING

Introduction

Prior to the development of antibiotics effective against the TB organism, treatment consisted of isolation in a sanitarium where patients stayed until their sputum no longer carried the organism. This sometimes occurred when the lungs calcified and effectively walled off colonies of the TB organism. Isolation was the only treatment available, and often patients were kept in the sanitariums for years before they were released to live among the uninfected population. The focus on treatment was to help the patient become as healthy as possible through adequate nutrition and the provision of fresh air. When the patients no longer exhibited overt symptoms, they were often released into the general population until another episode of illness occurred. When relapses occurred, patients were readmitted. Symptoms were treated in the sanitariums and patients were removed from the general population to prevent spread of the organism, much as lepers were placed in colonies early in the history of civilization. Ironically, the causative organism for leprosy is the same genus as that for tuberculosis, *Mycobacterium leprae*, and certain parts of the world still have colonies of people infected with leprosy.

While a number of airborne pathogens exist, and the medical worker or student is exposed to many organisms that may be transmitted through the respiratory tract, TB is the only disease currently included in the governmental agency guidelines for airborne pathogens requiring specific protection against the organism. *Mycobacterium tuberculosis* is the name of the organism that causes this disease.

Tuberculosis is caused by a bacillus (rod-shaped bacterium) that is more difficult to treat than many bacterial organisms, and different strains also occur in both birds and cattle, to which humans are also susceptible. A diagnostic skin test is performed to determine if the patient has developed a reaction against this particular organism, and if the skin test is positive, a chest X-ray is done to determine if the person is an active stage of the disease. While antibiotics are effective except in the more resistant strains of *Mycobacterium tuberculosis*, the administration of antibiotics for treating uncomplicated cases of TB requires daily isoniazid and rifampin doses for two months, followed by four months of additional self-administration of these antibiotics. There is an 80 percent mortality rate for multidrug resistant strains of the organism.

Symptoms and signs of the disease, including fatigue, fever, and weight loss, may occur early in the illness. During the advanced states of the disease, cough, chest pain, hemoptysis (spitting up of blood), and hoarseness may be prevalent. The disease is found worldwide, but most often it occurs in crowded areas of cities and in facilities where people are housed in close proximity to each other. The disease most commonly infects the respiratory system but may become systemic in the blood, affecting any of the organs in the body. For example, the disease may also affect the gastrointestinal and genitourinary systems, as well as bones, joints, nervous system, lymph nodes, and the skin.

The main reservoir for tuberculosis is humans, and next in importance in some instances are cows through their milk, followed sometimes by birds that live in close proximity to humans. There are a number of similar organisms thought to be harmless that have recently been implicated in cases of pulmonary fibrosis mimicking TB and have produced lesions. Cleanliness and sanitation of public facilities, inspection of cattle by governmental agencies, and control of bird roosting and nesting in buildings may do a great deal toward alleviating conditions that give rise to larger and more prevalent reservoirs for the organisms. Secluding those suffering from tuberculosis while symptoms are acute is the most effective process for avoiding the spread of the organism.

Transmission of the disease is primarily through airborne droplets from sputum of people with infectious tuberculosis. Repeated and close exposure to an infectious case often leads to infection of contacts, including family members. When a family member is diagnosed with tuberculosis, the other family members should be tested and given prophylactic treatment if necessary. Often, a person is infected and lives among the general population for a period of time before signs and symptoms become noticeable. The organism may incubate for a period ranging from four to twelve weeks before the victim is alerted by symptoms to seek medical treatment, and by then a number of people who have come in close contact with him may be at risk for contracting the disease.

A person who is infected by the bacterium causing tuberculosis may transmit the disease as long as he or she is harboring the organism. As a general rule, the person is considered to be able to communicate the disease to others as long as the infectious tubercle bacillus can be isolated from the sputum. Improvement of sanitary conditions and wearing of personal protective equipment (PPE) are the best methods for preventing and controlling the spread of tuberculosis. Treatment of those who have come in close contact with a person who later develops symptoms of the disease requires surveillance, diagnosis, and early treatment of all who may have been exposed to the organism.

Good work practices, such as effective hand washing, providing filtered ventilation if available, and good housekeeping practices, should be maintained as provided for in the Infection Control manual. Organisms found in sputum may survive for days on inanimate objects, necessitating the practice of good and regular cleaning of surfaces and objects used in patient care. The medical worker should wear a mask when a patient may cough or sneeze in his face. All health care workers and students in the health professions are to be fit tested and provided with HEPA filter masks when treating patients who are under respiratory precautions status as well as those having symptoms of respiratory diseases. Patients under respiratory precautions must wear a mask when

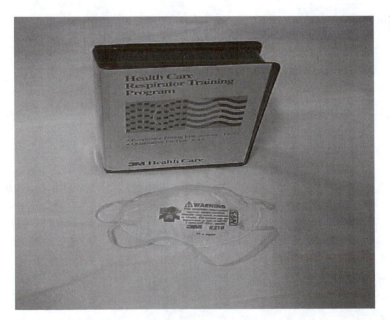

HEPA Mask Fit Test Kit

being transported about the facility, as sputum may harbor the organism for several days and infect the unprotected worker.

Workers who may be required to perform direct patient care should be fit tested for an individualized HEPA mask. For both students and medical workers, routine tuberculin skin tests to determine if an unknown exposure has occurred are required prior to entering a clinical facility. This is done as part of the physical examination of health care students and new employees in medical facilities. OSHA regulations require testing twice per year to determine if a medical worker or student has been exposed to the *Mycobacterium tuberculosis* organism. Medical facilities will not allow anyone to work in direct contact with patients unless the worker has been tested for the disease or for recent exposure. A recent exposure will usually yield positive results on the PPD skin test.

Centers for Disease Control and Prevention – Guidelines for Preventing the Transmission of Tuberculosis in Health Care Settings

The CDC's (Centers for Disease Control and Prevention) "Guidelines for Preventing the Transmission of Tuberculosis in Health Care Settings" (1994) provides for post-exposure reporting and follow-up for TB exposure in a medical area where there is a potential for exposure. The requirements for HEPA respirator training and education, as well as the use of personal protective equipment are addressed in this document. These guidelines are to be in effect until OSHA acts on the *Occupational Exposure to Tuberculosis*; Proposed Rule 29 CFR 1910.1035. Changes may be required at that time.

Types of Workplaces Covered by These Guidelines

People are more susceptible to tuberculosis when living in unsanitary conditions. Those confined to crowded areas with poor ventilation are at greater risk of contracting tuberculosis than others in less-cramped and better-maintained facilities or homes. The following work sites have been identified as being likely to house patients with active tuberculosis. They are considered as workplaces with an inherent potential for exposure to the TB disease.

1. Health care facilities, such as hospitals and clinics

2. Rehabilitation facilities

3. Correctional facilities

4. Homeless shelters and battered spouse facilities

5. Long-term health facilities

6. Drug treatment centers

7. Any other facility where groups of people are congregated in close contact with each other. For example, travelers to parts of the world where tuberculosis is endemic often contract the disease if proper precautions are not observed.

What is Exposure Potential?

An exposure potential is defined as an exposure to the inhaled or exhaled air of a person suspected of having TB disease and confirmed by skin test and X-ray. Certain high-hazard procedures performed on an individual with suspected or confirmed TB disease have a high potential for producing infectious airborne organisms through respiratory secretions. Specific procedures that place the medical worker at greatest risk are those involving the giving of aerosolized medication treatments, and assisting in or performing bronchoscopies, sputum inductions, intubations, suctioning procedures, and autopsies.

Workers Most at Risk for Occupational Exposure

As patients from all walks of life come into health care facilities, any contagious infection could present itself in a medical facility. All medical workers or people with direct or indirect patient care are considered at risk for contracting TB, even those who have responsibilities not directly related to medical procedures but that merely place the person in close proximity to the infected person. Examples include, among others: physicians, nurses, physician's assistants, respiratory therapists, radiography technologists, laboratory workers, morgue workers, EMS personnel, corrections personnel, students, and medical course instructors (CDC, 1990).

Physical Examination for Pre-Exposure

1. Each medical worker, student, and faculty member in a covered occupational area should have a tuberculin skin test at the time of employment or prior to assignment to a clinical area for training or performance of medical procedures. If the worker, student, or faculty member previously showed a positive reaction to the TB organism, determination must be made by X-ray that the person is no longer contagious and likely to transmit the organism to patients or coworkers. The person with a positive test must have completed adequate therapy prior to assuming duties in a medical treatment facility, with appropriate documentation of having met these requirements.

2. Any covered medical worker, faculty member, or student with a history of Bacillus of Calmette and Guerin (BCG) vaccination should also have the tuberculin skin test as required in all other cases. This treatment is often practiced in other countries.

3. A covered medical worker, faculty member, or student who shows a first time positive reaction to the skin test must receive medical clearance by a physician before further contact with patients or coworkers. This clearance must be in writing and filed appropriately as required by the medical facility or educational institution. Personnel found to have active TB disease should be also offered HIV antibody testing, as TB often occurs in immunocompromised people.

4. Covered faculty members and students with a **documented** history of a positive skin test (PPD) or adequate treatment of latent or active disease are not required to obtain further

testing unless signs and symptoms of active TB disease develop. It is often required that people in this category be routinely screened on a periodic basis to determine if the disease has returned to an active status. Initial and follow-up tuberculin skin tests should be administered and interpreted according to current CDC guidelines. A copy of this manual should be present in each health care facility.

5. Repeat testing of PPD-negative medical workers, faculty members, and students should be conducted periodically in order to identify people whose skin tests convert to a positive reading. The frequency of repeat testing is risk-dependent. Routinely, the schedule for people performing high-risk procedures is every six months, as required by OSHA.

6. Initial and periodic tuberculin skin tests are offered to covered faculty members at no cost to the employee. However, students are responsible for the cost of their skin tests.

Post-Exposure Follow-up Procedure

In order to determine the immune status of a patient that may indicate an earlier exposure or immunization, obtaining a baseline status is of the utmost importance. A person may have developed immunity to a disease-causing organism by vaccination or exposure to the disease, and he or she would show a positive reaction to testing for antibodies to that organism. The definition to exposure to tuberculosis, for instance, is determined to have occurred when any worker is exposed to a patient or client who exhibits symptoms of active disease or who tests positive even at a later time for the disease.

1. An accidental exposure is defined as an exposure in which the medical worker was unaware that a risk was present. Often, newly admitted patients who arrive with other symptoms will later be determined to have active TB. An exposure may occur in any clinical facility or work site where patients or clients are under treatment. The high-risk areas for exposure potential were listed earlier.

2. Immediately upon determining that an accidental exposure involving a covered medical worker, faculty member, or student has occurred, the clinical instructor or departmental supervisor must be notified as well as infection control coordinators of both the educational facility and the medical facility where the exposure occurred.

3. The exposure incident is to be documented in writing on appropriate forms provided with copies to the authorized person at the clinical or work site, the instructor, and the educational facility's infection control coordinator. Forms will be available at both the educational institute and the clinical site. Documentation pertinent to the incident is to be prepared the day of the incident and must be filed with the Infection Control Coordinators at both facilities within 24 hours of the incident.

4. The instructor, medical worker, or student is to be counseled immediately after the exposure incident and referred to his or her family physician or health department for appropriate therapy. **Baseline testing should be performed as soon as possible following an exposure incident. The educational institution is responsible for the cost of post-incident treatment for instructors and students as most, if not all, state governments specify it.**

5. Any instructor, medical worker, or student in a covered occupational area with a positive skin test upon repeat testing, or after exposure, should be clinically evaluated for active tuberculosis. If active tuberculosis is diagnosed, appropriate therapy should be initiated according to CDC guidelines or established medical protocol.

6. Any instructor, medical worker, or student in a covered occupational area with a positive skin test, upon repeat testing or exhibiting signs and symptoms of TB, is to be prohibited from having patient or client contact until he or she is cleared by a physician. This clearance is not

obtained until after further testing and/or by initiation of appropriate therapy as necessary based on test results.

7. If an instructor or student in an occupational area covered by guidelines is found to have a clinically confirmed case of TB, the following procedures are to be followed. All workers, instructors, and students who have had close contact with the infected person will be advised to have a PPD skin test. A negative result must be obtained prior to reentering the clinical area. As described in #6 above, the person must be medically cleared for further participation in the clinical area or any courses in the classroom areas. A person exposed to tuberculosis and who has a documented history of positive skin tests and radiographic findings must obtain a current chest X-ray to assess the status of the person relative to his infectious status.

8. Treatment regimens outlined by current CDC guidelines and a timetable for repeat testing shall be established and compliance documented. Changes should be heeded.

Required Personal Protective Equipment (PPE)

Personal protective equipment in sufficient quantity will be supplied by the clinical facility to enable the medical worker, student, or instructor to protect himself or herself from exposure to contagious diseases. Training will be provided in classroom activities as well as during orientation to clinical facilities for both medical workers and students. The costs of the required training and the necessary PPE to perform tasks in the safest manner possible is borne by the medical facility.

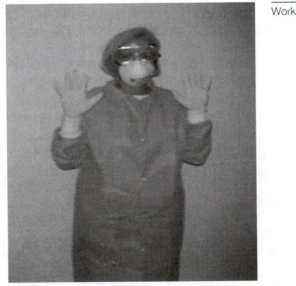

Worker Wearing PPE

Gloves, Masking, and Gowning

When are gloves worn?

Gloves should be worn during many aspects of patient care, particularly under the following conditions:

Likelihood of contact with patient's blood or other body fluids except for sweat

When collecting or transporting a specimen

If cleaning up spills of bodily fluids

When transporting or handling soiled bed linens or towels

If you have open cuts, sores, or chafing of skin of the hands and arms

Procedure for donning gloves

Wash hands before putting on gloves, sterile or non-sterile.

Check the physical conditions of the gloves – look for discolorations, stickiness, cracks, holes, and tears.

Choose properly fitted gloves without wrinkles.

If wearing a gown, the gloves should cover the cuffs of the sleeves of the gown.

Remove gloves by grasping the cuff of one glove with the other gloved hand, then pull the glove over your hand, allowing it to turn inside out; place the ungloved index and middle fingers inside the cuff of the glove, turning the cuff downward and pulling it inside out and over the glove already removed. (Instructor should demonstrate and allow students to practice process.)

Gowns as Barriers against Contamination

Gowns are used to protect the caregiver from becoming infected while providing procedures for the patient. Gowns may be sterile or non-sterile, as determined by the procedure being performed. Normally, sterile gowns are worn to protect the patient from contamination when an invasive procedure is being performed. Moisture-resistant gowns may be used if there is a danger of splatter of infectious materials from the patient. These gowns must be removed prior to leaving the patient's room when they are used for performing procedures involving body fluids. Gowns that have been used in the performance of medical procedures are considered contaminated materials and should not be worn in general areas of a hospital or other health care facility. All overgarments, such as protective gowns and overshoes, are also to be removed prior to leaving the facility and are not to be worn in public areas.

Procedure for Gowning

1. Wash the hands before donning a gown (roll up sleeves of undergarments before putting on gown).

2. Unfold the gown so the opening is at the back.

3. Put both arms into the sleeves of the gown.

4. Make sure uniform is covered at the neck by adjusting the gown at the neck.

5. Tie the straps attached to the gown at the neck with a bow that is easily undone (adhesive may be used).

6. Reach to the back at the waist and pull the edges of the gown together, then overlap one edge over the other; tie a simple bow at the waist (adhesive may be used).

Note: A gown that has become wet with body fluids, sweat, or any other liquids should be replaced during the procedure to prevent contaminating clothing and skin of the care provider.

Removing a gown

1. First, remove gloves properly and discard in appropriate container.

2. Wash hands effectively.

3. Pull sleeves off by grasping and pulling at each shoulder.

4. Turn the sleeves inside out as you remove them from your arms.

5. Hold the gown inside out and away from the body by the inside of the shoulder area.

6. Roll up the gown with the inside out, and discard in appropriate waste container.

7. Wash hands.

Masking

Face masks may be worn to protect the caregiver from patients who have respiratory infections or may protect patients who are vulnerable to infectious organisms that may be transmitted by the caregiver. A mask that has been used for thirty minutes or one that has become damp is not effective. The most common filter masks are discarded after use. Respirator masks for use with TB patients and others with highly contagious respiratory infections require a fit test before they are effective for use with these patients. Many facilities fit test each employee and ensure that a supply of these masks is available when needed. Employees should be instructed during orientation as to the type of mask that is appropriate to the work area where assigned.

Procedure for Donning Face Mask (Not Respirator Type; See Next Section for Respirators)

1. Wash hands.

2. Obtain a face mask from supply container or area.

3. Do not lay the mask on a contaminated or wet surface.

4. Pick up mask by elastic bands or tie strings; do not touch area that will cover face.

5. Place mask over nose and mouth; elastic bands should be pulled around the ears and those with strings should be pulled over the ears and tied behind the head with a bow.

6. Ensure coverage of both mouth and nose.

7. For lengthy procedures, the mask may need to be replaced after thirty minutes of use.

8. Discard mask in appropriate container following use.

9. Properly clean area and discard all used supplies in the appropriate containers.

10. Wash hands before leaving patient area.

Personal protective equipment (PPE) is used as follows:

A. When treating patients with highly suspicious symptoms or confirmed cares of contagious diseases

B. When treating patients who are confirmed as having active TB disease. Use of high efficiency particulate air (HEPA) Safety and Health (NIOSH)-approved N-95 respirators is enforced for medical workers when entering a patient who has a confirmed case of TB's hospital room.

C. HEPA (filter) respirator fit testing for each medical worker, faculty member, or student must be conducted to insure an effective fit for the facial features and a face seal prior to use of the equipment. This is required only if the HEPA respirator is to be used in lieu of other types of available respirators.

D. The person using the respirator should check the respirator seal for a good seal each time the respirator is to be used before entering a patient's room.

E. Disposable or reusable HEPA or other NIOSH-approved respirators may be used. Reusable respirators must be stored to maintain the form-fit according to the manufacturer's instructions and cleaned appropriately following contact with a patient. If a respirator is assigned to an employee, it is the responsibility of the employee to maintain it.

F. Medical workers, instructors, and students with a documented previous respiratory disease or other disorder causing respiratory impairment/decreased pulmonary function may use alternate methods of protection and should be provided for by the employer. This documentation must be by a physician and be in writing.

G. Medical workers, instructors, and students with a certified respiratory impairment preventing the use of a HEPA or other respirator should not be assigned to a known TB case or to a patient who has highly suspicious symptoms. An alternative assignment is usually made according to the facility's policies and procedures.

H. The educational facility is to provide PPE for demonstration and practice lab activities. The clinical or work site may provide PPE for faculty members and students during rotations. If the PPE is not provided for actual patient-client contact, it is the responsibility of the educational institution to provide it at no cost to faculty members and at cost to students.

Education and Training Required for Faculty and Students

Education and training for faculty and students are required to enable these personnel to protect themselves in a medical environment where highly contagious patients may be treated. This education and training is to be relevant to the areas in which these personnel will be working. Students may be required to purchase some of the supplies and equipment needed. Supplies and equipment will be furnished to the instructors at the expense of the educational institution, and the types of supplies and equipment required for training will be specified in program outlines.

1. Each medical worker, instructor, and student is to receive education and training on tuberculosis as part of the blood and airborne pathogens section of instruction, as required by law. Medical workers receive training and education during their orientation at medical facilities and also receive annual updates. Instructors shall receive annual refresher training throughout their tenure. The educational facility's infection control coordinator is responsible for monitoring and evaluating effectiveness of this education and training process, assuring that appropriate documentation has been achieved.

2. Training will be documented as specified in the institute's Exposure Control Plan. This plan is written to include guidelines from OSHA, NIOSH, and CDC, as well as any other state or federal governmental entity that has input. Each student will have the appropriate documentation relative to compliance with the training needs as outlined by the institutional committees, accreditation officials, or statutory bodies.

Training and Education Will Contain the Following Elements

This specific section on training for prevention of contracting TB requires that certain standards be met. A formal class most practically accomplishes this. This should be a class in which both didactic presentations and laboratory exercises are included, emphasizing the need for both information as well as practical application of measures designed to prevent the contraction of tuberculosis.

1. Minimum requirements designed for effective training and education of the health care worker for blood and airborne pathogens will include the following:

   A. Mode(s) of Transmission
      The mode is the method by which a disease is passed on to another. The mode may be mechanical through equipment or person-to-person.

   B. Pathogenesis
      Pathogenesis refers to where and how the development of a disease progressed from its inception.

   C. Diagnosis and assessment of TB

      a. Skin test (tuberculin) to be read after 48 hours
         The body reacts to the antigen (organism) causing the disease by forming a raised and discolored lump at the site of injection. This reaction indicates that the body has been exposed to and has made antibodies against the TB organism (also remember BCG, which may give false positive results)

      b. X-ray of the chest
         A radiograph is taken of the lungs to show any processes caused by infection, which would appear as milky areas sometimes with harder calcified areas easily visible.

   D. Latent infection stage is compared to the active disease state. The latent stage is the period where the disease is quiet or not active and during which an infected person is showing no manifestations of disease.

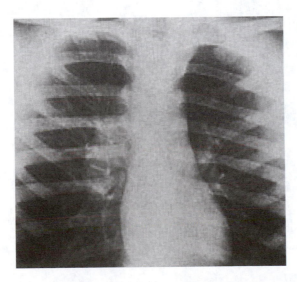

Radiograph of Lung - Tuberculosis

E. Signs, symptoms of tuberculosis - Fatigue, fever, and weight loss may occur early in the illness. Cough, chest pain, hemoptysis (spitting up of blood), and hoarseness may be prevalent during the advanced stages of this disease.

F. Possibility of reinfection in patients with positive PPD
A reinfection by the causative organism is possible following an initial infection that has been controlled or eliminated by drugs.

G. Potential for occupational exposure and transmission of TB
The number of cases is growing in the United States, and there is a high probability of being exposed to a patient with tuberculosis in the course of one's duties in a medical facility or when working with clients in high-risk populations.

H. Routines that reduce risk of exposure or transmission of TB
These include use of personal protection, both work practice and engineered controls.

I. Written policies and procedures to prevent the contraction of TB by those exposed to infected patients or others will be promulgated. Policies and procedures should be available for all employees and students in each facility. Properly maintained equipment and supplies for use of students, faculty, and staff will be included to minimize the risk to other health care professionals.

J. Proper and complete documentation of previous exposure incidents
A legal requirement exists for documenting all exposure incidents within 24 hours of the incident. Medical advice and treatment will be provided in order to afford the exposed person(s) an opportunity to receive adequate protection and treatment.

K. Purpose of PPD testing; significance of positive result
PPD testing entails the inoculation of non-vital organisms under the skin of the person being tested. If the person has been exposed to the TB organism, antibodies present in the body will attack the injected site and produce a visible response. A raised, reddened and hardened area is indicative of antibodies against the TB organism. A positive PPD test indicates that the person has been exposed but may not be in an active stage of the disease.

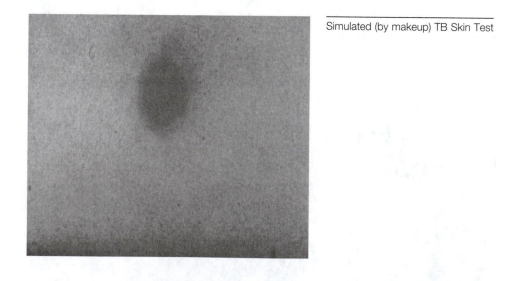

Simulated (by makeup) TB Skin Test

L. If the skin test is positive, evaluation of the PPD test conversion is followed up
A positive PPD test requires that a chest X-ray be performed to determine if the person

needs antibiotic therapy. Until the definitive tests are done and the status of the individual is determined, the worker is not to be in direct contact with patients.

M. Determination of necessary drug therapy for an active tuberculosis case
In the past, isolation in sanitariums was the treatment for TB. Effective antibiotics are now available, and often they must be given for a protracted period of time. The antibiotics suggested by the U.S. Public Health Service are isoniazid (INH) and rifampin (RIF) for a period of twenty weeks, and then daily INH and ethambutol administrations until sputum cultures have remained negative for one year. Patients on this treatment regimen must be monitored for compliance.

N. Increased risk of TB in HIV or AIDS patients or with other disease states
The statistical chance for coming into contact with patients who are in the active stages of both TB and AIDS is significant. However, the risk of contracting the disease is almost nonexistent if proper precautions covered in this section are taken.

O. Immunosuppressive disease or medication increases risk level of contracting TB
Both diseases and medications prescribed for certain diseases may adversely affect the body's immune response, removing the protective state that normally helps the body to avoid contracting infections. Conditions affecting the immune status are discussed in the infection control section of this book.

P. Follow confidentiality practices in assessment and treatment of faculty, medical workers, or students who become actively infected with the disease
Confidentiality must be practiced when treating people with TB. However, the person who has been exposed to the disease also has the right to know the status of the person to whom they were exposed but is not allowed by law to learn the name of the source. Additionally, the source patient cannot be forced to submit to testing in many states.

Q. The educational facility's and clinical site's policies on voluntary duty reassignment must be available and followed
Students or medical workers may be reassigned to non-patient work until the status of their test results is completed following exposure to or treatment for TB.

R. Published options for immunocompromised faculty, students in health care
Immunocompromised people may perform work in certain areas where infected patients are being treated. When symptoms have abated, or when the disease is in remission or has been resolved, the faculty member or student may return to the clinical area as appropriate according to policy.

S. All faculty, staff, students, and health care professionals who present with a positive TB skin test must be evaluated as to their respective conditions. The probability that one of these people might pose a risk to patients and other workers must be weighed before the worker may return to a work area.

SUGGESTED STUDENT ACTIVITIES

List: Name the three major *covered* organisms for bloodborne and airborne diseases. List the modes of transmission for each of the three blood and airborne pathogens.

List the protective equipment necessary for full protection when splatter of body fluids is likely or even possible that must be provided.

Immunization/vaccination availability for the three blood and airborne pathogens include what steps?

Perform: After demonstration by instructor, the student should be able to:

1. Properly don gloves, both sterile and non-sterile

2. Assist in setting up a sterile field

3. Employ face, eye protection, - including goggles, shield, HEPA mask fit to ensure proper protection

4. Put on protective clothing, including gown, mask, overboots, gloves, and remove same appropriately

5. Discuss proper disposal of needles and sharps

6. Demonstrate proper technique for removing and disposing of broken glass

7. Simulate cleaning a biohazardous spill by using a spill kit

Student Activity

Demonstration of effectively putting on and taking off gloves

1. Place gloves on both hands, using the proper size. Avoid the use of heavily powdered gloves because of the congealing of the materials during the following procedure.

2. Don the gloves as demonstrated by the instructor. Properly fit gloves to hands, tightening around the ends of and between the fingers.

3. Have the instructor apply a small portion of foamy shaving cream into the palm of one hand.

4. Put a drop of dark-colored food dye into the center of the mound of shaving cream.

5. Rub and knead the hands together, mixing the two materials. Cover the entire surface of the gloves, front and back. Try not to get any of the combination onto wrists and hands.

6. Practice removing the gloves without getting any of the dye onto the hands during the process. This is good practice for donning and removing gloves and illustrates the possibility of becoming contaminated during the removal of the gloves.

7. In your own words, answer the questions in the next section.

STUDY QUESTIONS

The following questions will require some critical thinking by the student. Not all questions will be directly covered in the preceding material; some require a synthesis of what you have studied. Think through the questions before looking for the answers.

1. Name some common ways that health care workers are exposed to bloodborne pathogens. Consider cleanup procedures, assisting with surgery, disposing of used equipment, assisting with invasive medical procedures, as well as others you can think of.

2. How are most health care workers exposed to airborne pathogens? Consider collection of specimens, cleaning equipment, patient coughing, and handling materials from the patient's room for this type of exposure.

3. People with hepatitis B and C may have no symptoms for up to how many years?

4. How do hepatitis B and C, along with HIV, spread most easily?

5. What does the acronym OPIM mean?

6. What is the first step you should do if you are exposed to OPIM?
Consider treatment, cleaning wound, incident report, and so on.

7. What vaccine is offered free of charge to health care workers who may potentially become exposed to infectious diseases (bloodborne)?

8. What should you do if your clothing becomes contaminated with blood?

9. Describe preventive measures to avoid exposure. Tailor them to the work situation.

10. What agencies provide guidelines and requirements for training to protect oneself against blood and airborne pathogens?

11. What is the single most important thing you can do to protect yourself from infection?

12. What types of patients may transmit an infectious blood or airborne disease?

13. Which of the following patients are considered a risk with whom to work:
those that look suspicious; those that are known IV drug users; those that have a history of HIV; those who look sick and unclean; those known to have had multiple sex partners; those who have had blood transfusions; any patient?

REVIEW STUDY OUTLINE, BLOOD AND AIRBORNE PATHOGENS

Each student should be prepared, after completing the section, to discuss and understand each area fully as follows. This section provides a recapitulation of the previous sections and combines both blood and airborne pathogens material.

Protection Against Blood and Airborne Pathogens

Practices and Precautions for the Allied Health Worker

Allied health care workers and prospective medical care providers must be given information on specific bloodborne and airborne diseases. This is necessary in order to enable the medical worker to make informed decisions for protecting himself or herself from contracting a disease in the course of treating patients. This section is designed to inform the potential student in health care provider professions the information on specific airborne and bloodborne diseases necessary in enabling the student to make informed decisions about protecting himself or herself from contracting an infectious disease. Students and health care workers who practice the precautions outlined in this book will face little possibility of becoming accidentally infected. Two of the practices necessary for self-protection components are:

1. **Personal Protection**

    A. Protective Equipment
    This principally entails wearing appropriate protective garments like respirators while providing care to patients who are known to be or are potentially infectious. Wearing appropriate protective clothing and devices protects the patients and self against cross-contamination from workers and students who have had contact with other contagious patients.

B. Work Practice and Engineered Controls

Although a province of Infection Control, to be discussed in the next section of this book, the use of **work practice** as well as **engineered controls** to provide for optimum protection is included in the area of self-protection. Work practice controls relates to the practices of the medical care worker to minimize risk of contamination. It is related to what the worker does rather than what he or she uses. One example of a work practice control is washing the hands before donning gloves and washing the hands following performance of a procedure. Engineered controls relates to the hardware or equipment used for minimizing the risk of or for immediate treating of an exposure. An example of an engineered control would be the eyewash stations at each sink in labs and certain work-stations. The categories of engineered controls and work practice controls are covered more extensively in one of the following sections on Infection Control/Exposure Control.

2. Immunizations

An immunization is the *most specific* way of protecting oneself. There are no immunizations to date for certain infectious diseases. While great strides have been made in the past few decades to rid the world of certain epidemics, there are no vaccines against certain organisms, such as the HIV organism. Often, as is the case with the HIV organism, there are a number of strains for which no effective immunizations against all the strains have been developed. Even when immunizations are available to prevent infection by certain organisms, medical workers must continue to protect themselves. While immunization is specific against certain infectious organisms, there are numerous organisms other than the three major blood and airborne pathogens found in a large number of infectious diseases.

Exposure to Infectious Organisms

Exposure incidents occur when a medical worker is exposed to infectious patients or materials that may be contaminated by infectious organisms. Exposure incidents are usually the result of a failure to follow protocol while performing medical procedures, an exposure to a patient who is newly admitted or may have no symptoms, or an exposure to materials contaminated while performing a procedure. Take these steps if you are exposed, in the following order:

1. Contact people

    A. Clinical preceptor as soon as incident occurs

    B. Instructor from educational facility as soon as possible

2. Documentation

    A. Documentation should begin as soon as incident occurs

    B. Baseline immune status of exposed worker and status of patient, if available

    C. Medical evaluation of exposed worker

3. Laboratory Testing

    A. Baseline testing of exposed person – testing of a worker or student before the person begins to perform medical procedures. This will allow the investigator of an incident to determine if a condition was preexisting.

    B. Immune or disease state of source patient may be known prior to an exposure incident. The patient may decline to be tested when a worker is exposed to the blood or OPIM from the patient.

Liability and Responsibility

Both personal liability and responsibility are present in the treating of patients. We must take proper protective measures to protect ourselves and our patients, as well as our families and all of society, to prevent devastating epidemics.

1. As health care workers, and by extension this applies to medical students, we bear responsibility to break the cycle of infection so we may protect our families, other patients, and ourselves.

2. As allied health care providers, we will be faced with many unknown situations that could possibly put our families, our patients, and ourselves in danger.

3. The goal for teaching blood and airborne pathogens is to inform you as to decisions you will make on personal protection and available immunizations.

4. The health care facility is responsible for providing protective equipment and scheduled training to equip the student and employee to properly protect themselves against becoming infected.

Terminology

A set of terms common to all medical areas has evolved and must become part of the language of the medical worker in order for the worker to stay well informed and to operate safely in medical environments.

The following terms will be discussed for the use of the allied health student:

1. COVERED BLOODBORNE DISEASES

    A. HIV /AIDS

    B. Hepatitis B

2. COVERED AIRBORNE DISEASE

    A. Tuberculosis

3. NON-COVERED DISEASES COMMONLY SEEN IN MEDICAL PRACTICE

With the exception of meningitis, which may be viral, fungal, or bacterial, the others are exclusively viral. Inoculation against many organisms is possible, with some notable exceptions, including the various strains of herpes and meningitis. The covered organisms, or those where OSHA mandates training for the employee of a health care facility, are HIV, hepatitis B, and tuberculosis. However, these are by no means the only diseases requiring precautions by health care workers. NOTE: For some types of meningitis, immunization is possible.

Other Diseases That Require Precautions

(Note: these diseases are for the most part viral in nature. Meningitis may be fungal, bacterial, or viral).

Shingles (Herpes zoster)

Meningitis (various viruses, bacteria, and occasionally fungal or parasitic)

Measles (viral, number of varieties)

Mumps (viral, infection of parotid glands)

Chickenpox (Herpes zoster, may predispose patient to shingles in later life)

Herpes (viral, number of strains, may be oral, genital, or rarely other body sites)

Human papilloma virus (more than 100 strains, leads to cervical cancer in some cases)

Mononucleosis (90 percent of cases caused by Epstein-Barr virus; cytomegalovirus rarely involved)

Other Communicable Diseases with Worldwide Impact

With world travel available for almost everyone, diseases once confined to other continents often become a reality in the United States. In addition to Hepatitis B and Tuberculosis, as well as HIV, other diseases are equally important, but are not transmitted as frequently in medical settings, as the hepatitis, TB, and HIV organisms are. It is important for the health care worker to be able to recognize certain signs manifested by infectious diseases, and to refer the victim for health care. Most of these diseases are preventable through adequate vaccination, but visitors and immigrants from other countries may unwittingly expose the health care worker and the general population to organisms easily transmitted from one person to another. Spreading disease may also be used by bioterrorists to accomplish goals for themselves and the group with which they are affiliated. All health care workers have an important role to play in preventing a widespread infection rate, called an epidemic. Several of these diseases common in other parts of the world are as follows:

Anthrax

Anthrax is caused by an organism called *Bacillus anthracis*. It occurs in both the respiratory and cutaneous forms, with the respiratory type being most dangerous to the victim. Originally the disease was known as the 'hide-handlers' disease, as the organism is often found in the wool or hair of animals used for food or other animal products. If the organism is found in the organs and body cavities of the human victim, it causes effusions and hemorrhage, along with extreme exhaustion called prostration. In the cutaneous variety, one may find large fluid-filled vesicles called carbuncles.

Cutaneous variety of anthrax (NIAID, Biodefense Research, World Health Organization)

Chicken pox

Chicken pox is also called varicella, after the organism causing the disease. It was once a scourge of young children, as the majority of youngsters 'caught' the extremely contagious organism. Immunization has now caused this disease to be somewhat rare in the United States.

A disease caused by a similar organism is that of shingles, also manifested by blister-like lesions that may occur on almost any part of the body, but follows major nerve trunks, the tissue that is affected by this disease.

Rubella or Measles

There are several varieties of rubella, caused from the virus of the family Rubivirus. While the disease may be dangerous for anyone, it is most dangerous when contracted by a pregnant person, as it may cause birth defects. Babies are now immunized in this country by a combination immunization, which provides protection against measles, mumps, and rubella.

Small pox

Small pox is extremely contagious and has been associated with wide spread epidemics. In the United States, the majority of our Native Americans died from this disease, brought from Europe early in the colonization of the United States. After a massive world-wide vaccination program began by the World Health Organization in the late 1960's, no new cases have been reported. Stock cultures of the organism exist throughout the world, for research purposes only. However, stocks of organisms that fell into the hands of bioterrorists could initiate another epidemic, as vaccination is no longer performed on a wide-spread basis.

Transmission of Organisms

The definition of transmission of organisms is the route by which microorganisms are transmitted. There are four main routes of transmission:

1. Contact

    A. Direct contact is the direct physical transfer between a susceptible host and an infected or colonized person and occurs when the medical worker has come into direct contact with a patient who is or later is found to have a contagious disease. This entails direct contact with the contagious patient.

    B. Indirect contact refers to transmission of an organism through personal contact of susceptible host with a contaminated object that has been used personally by the infected patient. Transmission through indirect contact requires personal contact of the susceptible host with a contaminated object. This type of exposure may also involve workers not in direct contact with the infected patient. Implements and materials used in care of the patient that have become infected may be improperly handled for processing or disposal and may infect the person handling them. Examples would be a laundry worker who is laundering bloody linens or a custodian who is picking up regulated waste which has been contaminated in the course of being used for a medical procedure.

    C. Droplet contact – spread of disease-causing organisms by the spraying of droplets from the mouth.

2. Common Source Transmission
    This type of transmission refers to the transmission of disease through the use of contaminated items that are commonly in use in medical facilities. These items could include food, iced beverages, water, drugs (prescription as well as illicit), blood and blood products, as well as dirty supplies and equipment.

3. Airborne
    Airborne transmission refers to dissemination of the organisms in droplets of sputum, dust, saliva, or blood in minute particles, blown about the environment.

4. Vectorborne Transmission
    Vectorborne transmission is disease transmission via contact with an infected vector, which most often are insects, flies, ticks, and snails. Ticks and mosquitoes are found worldwide and are extremely important vectors for many diseases. As a matter of interest, ticks are not included in the insect family, but are found in the same classification as spiders, and are blood-sucking arachnids. Mosquitoes are flies from the *Culicidae* family of insects and are important vectors of viruses as well as parasites, including the well-known malarial diseases. In some countries, snails and plants are also important reservoirs for various organisms.

Common Terms Associated With Transmission of Disease

1. Blood and body fluids (include OPIM; other potentially infectious materials) – All body fluids are potentially capable of carrying pathogenic organisms. Universal Precautions states that infection is transmitted chiefly through only blood, semen, vaginal secretions, and sputum. Other body fluids that are blood-tinged may transmit organisms.

2. Contamination – The condition where organisms are on the surface or within a material or an object is called contamination. The material or surface may have been sterilized or disinfected previously but due to having been exposed to a person or other materials, it is no longer deemed clean; it is contaminated.

3. Source of an infection – This is the initial place or medium from where the organism was transmitted to a human, animal or plant.

4. Host – The host is the organism where the pathogen derives its nourishment and then reproduces before being transmitted to another organism that may become diseased.

5. Origin – Where was the organism originally found or developed, before being able to survive and to infect organisms? The term is similar to the "source," and in some cases the origin is unknown, such as in the case of the HIV organism. Despite this, theories usually exist.

6. Autogenous infection – Autogenous infection is self-inoculation of disease-causing organisms to receive attention.

7. Respiratory Precautions – Patients or people exhibiting a positive PPD, chest X-ray, or symptoms suspicious of tuberculosis will be placed on respiratory precautions. People treating them or visiting them will adhere to the appropriate wearing of protective equipment while in the room with the patient. Also remember that there is a second type of isolation called *reverse isolation*. This type of isolation is used to prevent exposure of a patient with low levels of immunity from being infected by health care workers, visitors, and any equipment and supplies that may be brought into the patient's room.

Types of Precautions

1. Universal Precautions

2. Standard Precautions

3. Personal Protective Equipment (PPE)

4. Disinfection

5. Sterilization

6. Decontamination

7. Immunization

Is There a Difference between Universal and Standard Precautions?

Sometimes these terms are used synonymously. *Taber's Cyclopedic Medical Dictionary*, 20th Edition (pp.1751, 2266), gives the following (paraphrased by the author) definitions for each. In general, the chief difference lies in the intention of the guidelines, both developed by the Centers for Disease Control and Prevention. Standard precautions were developed to reduce the spread of infection in hospitals and other health care facilities, while universal precautions focus on protection of the workers with occupational exposure to blood and airborne pathogens (disease-causing organisms).

Standard Precautions

The term standard precautions refers to guidelines that have been recommended by the CDC to reduce the risk of the spread of infection in hospitals. These precautions include hand washing, gloves, mask, eye protection, gown, and apply to blood, all other body fluids, secretions, excretions (except sweat), non-intact skin, and mucous membranes of all patients and are the primary strategy for successful nosocomial infection control. (Nosocomial infections are those that the patient acquired during a visit or a stay in the hospital, not outside the hospital.)

Universal Precautions

Guidelines established to protect workers with occupational exposure to bloodborne pathogens, such as hepatitis B and HIV, are called universal precautions. OSHA Bloodborne Pathogens Standard (1991) mandated these "universal blood and body fluid precautions," for workers in all U.S. health care settings, such as the use of gloves, masks and gowns. The CDC originally recommended them in 1985.

Pre-Exposure Precautions

Work practice and engineered controls are important methods by which to combat infection of workers and cross-contamination of other patients in multiple patient cases.

1. Personal Protective Equipment and Work Practice Controls include:

    A. Hand washing routinely before donning and after removing gloves

    B. Using disposable gloves for medical tasks, reusable gloves for cleaning purposes

    C. Wearing disposable surgical face masks; removal when wet; one time use

    D. Using goggles or face shields when splashing of blood and body fluids likely

    E. Wearing special clothing including aprons to prevent saturation of clothing

2. Immunization and Vaccination

    A. PPD (tuberculin skin test)

    B. Hepatitis B vaccine

    C. MMR (Mumps, Measles, Rubella), Tetanus if applicable

    D. Multiple Patient Situations

        a. Responsibility for protecting patients from exposure by transmission from sources used in treatment of another patient

        b. Immunodepressed patients

            aa. May be related to age

            bb. Often related to disease conditions that compromise the patient's ability to fight infections

            cc. May be related to medications that suppress the immune system

    E. Guidelines for Infectious Exposure
       Guidelines to follow should be in place as precautions for possible exposure to infectious diseases in the following situations:

        a. Classroom Lectures and Lab Practice

            aa. Utilizing appropriate supplies and equipment

            bb. Practicing clinical applications in labs

            cc. Rehearsing case studies and relating appropriate acting

        b. Clinical Rotations

            aa. Preceptors in the workplace monitor appropriate practices relative to protection against blood and airborne pathogens

Post-Exposure Incident – Procedures to Follow

1. Post-exposure considerations

   A. What is an exposure incident?

   B. Who to contact, and when?

      a. Clinical preceptor

      b. Instructor

   C. What paperwork is required to be completed?

   D. What lab work should be done?

   E. Guidelines for Infectious Exposure
   Guidelines to follow should be in places precautions for possible exposure to infectious diseases in the following situations:

      a. Classroom and Lab Exercises

      b. Clinical Rotations

   F. Treatment for affected patient(s) and worker(s)

Disposal and Decontamination

   A. Disposal of equipment

      a. How to dispose of contaminated waste properly

      b. How to mark containers for disposal

      c. How to store containers for disposal

      d. How to transport contaminated materials (including linens)

   B. Non-disposable equipment

      a. How and when to clean

      b. How and when disinfecting or sterilization is needed

   C. Disposal of needles and sharps

      a. Always use caution

      b. Do not recap needles

      c. Do not bend or break needles

      d. Use puncture-resistant containers

INFECTION CONTROL FOR HEALTH CARE FACILITIES

OBJECTIVES

Upon completion of this unit of instruction, the student should be able to:

a. Understand the role of the medical facility in protecting the medical workers and the patients

b. List examples of work practice controls

c. List examples of engineered controls in the typical medical care facility

d. Discuss methods to interrupt pathways for infection to enter the body

e. Provide information relating to the three categories of medical care workers regarding potential exposure

f. Relate an exposure incident and give the immediate steps to take following exposure

g. List pre-exposure procedures (don't forget education and training components)

h. Discuss processes involved in post-exposure activities

i. Relate steps for the donning of personal protective equipment

j. Give the methods of transmission of the major blood and airborne organisms: HIV, HBV, and TB

SECTION OUTLINE

Introduction to Infection Control

Exposure Potential and Prevention

Pre-Exposure Precautions

Exposure Incidents

Post-Exposure Follow-Up

Specifics for Bloodborne Pathogen – HIV

Specifics for Bloodborne Pathogen – HBV

INTRODUCTION TO INFECTION CONTROL

What is infection control and why is it important? There are definite correlations to the previous section, in which we discussed blood and airborne infections. The blood and airborne pathogens section was focused mainly on the individual. Infection control programs focus on the institution, for the protection of the individual worker as well as the patient. Infection can be defined as the invasion and multiplication of any organism that has the potential to harm the body of a human or other organism. Infection control for a medical facility is one of the most important facets of the holistic approach to delivery of health care. Most human diseases either are or were the result of an infectious process where pathogenic organisms invaded and set up residence in the human body. In some disease states, an infection may have subsided or have been overcome, but the damage done leaves lasting problems for the victim, leaving them with permanent problems that may shorten or limit enjoyment of life. The focus in this section is to acquaint the medical worker or student with the methods used by most health care institutions to protect their workers and patients from infection. A simulated Infection Control/Exposure Control Plan for a fictitious hospital has been developed and presented in this section.

Infection Control and its Relationship to Health Care Facilities

All personnel employed in the health care environment are required to have a basic knowledge and understanding of disease and disease transmission. This knowledge is focused toward protection of both the patient and the health care worker. A number of issues related to infection control are common to all categories of health care workers in order to accomplish the goal of preventing oneself and his or her assigned patients from becoming infected through exposure to pathogens.

According to a documentary by the *Chicago Tribune* of July 2002, a number of startling charges were made related to infection control in hospitals.[1] Infection control is designed to protect both patients and workers, but even in this day with increased availability of products and services designed to do just this, there are many breaches of established policies in many hospitals. This article states that approximately 75,000 patients die needlessly each year due to dirty hospitals, and that the most effective and simple way of preventing the spread of pathogens, hand washing, is practiced by only about 50 percent of physicians and nurses as they go from patient to patient. The most helpless of patients, infants, neonates, the elderly, and immunocompromised or weakened patients, are at the greatest risk of developing a hospital-acquired infection. Pioneers who more than a century ago recognized the importance of hand washing, such as the Hungarian physician Ignaz Philipp Semmelweis, showed that simple hand-washing could lower the infection rate, but it is still not being conscientiously practiced, even with the requirement for documentation of both work practice and engineered controls. Many people use the restroom, never wash their hands, then prepare and/or eat food and shake hands with others immediately afterward.

---

[1] Michael J. Berens, "Lax Procedures Put Infants at High Risk: Simple Actions by Hospital Workers, Such as Diligent Hand-Washing, Could Cut the Number of Fatal Infections," (Tribune Investigation: Unhealthy Hospitals) *Chicago Tribune*, 22 July 2002.

When Hand Washing is Required

Hand washing, a work practice control, is the simplest and most basic procedure to prevent the spread of organisms. You are exposed to many organisms while at work, and the most effective way to prevent spread of organisms from another person or object to you, or from you to a patient, is by proper hand washing. Hands that are chapped or have open cuts or even torn cuticles open you to the possibility of becoming infected. Hand washing facilities are located near all work areas in health care facilities and should be utilized in the following situations:

- Before you start your work shift and upon completing your work

- Before eating and drinking, and then before returning to work

- After using restroom facilities

- After returning from other areas of the facility

- After transferring equipment and supplies from one area to another

- After blowing your nose, coughing, or sneezing

- Before and following performance of any procedure upon or for a patient

- After handling equipment or supplies in a patient's room

- After handling dressings and patient specimens

- Following the changing of a patient's bed or used towels

Official Agencies Responsible for Policies Related to Infection Control

Many governmental agencies work with state and local governments to foster effective infection control in medical care, agricultural processes, and manufacture of products that may release both organic and/or toxic chemicals. There is no doubt that these organizations are achieving great strides in protecting the health of the public, as evidenced by an expanding life span in the United States and other developed countries. Some of the organizations include, but are not limited to: National Institute of Health (NIH); Centers for Disease Control and Prevention (CDC); Clinical Laboratory Improvement Amendments (CLIA); Environmental Protection Agency (EPA); Federal Drug Administration (FDA); Occupational Safety and Health Administration (OSHA); and a whole host of state and local agencies that are often funded in part by the larger federal agencies. FEMA, the Federal Emergency Management Agency, to a lesser extent works to provide safe water and sewage disposal during natural and man-made disasters and to contribute to the good health of the population of the United States. Most often, governmental offices and a number of national and international organizations, such as the American Red Cross and the Salvation Army, to name two, work during disasters to provide healthful living conditions for those displaced from their homes, or whose homes have been damaged so as to cause unsafe living conditions. We must realize that since the black plague devastated Europe in the mid-fourteenth century, developed nations have done a great deal to control the spread of infectious diseases. Basic sanitation can go a long way toward preventing these diseases on both a local and a global basis.

History of Infection Control

Several centuries ago, scientists discovered that many diseases were caused by very small living organisms called germs. In the nineteenth century, a French chemist and bacteriologist named Louis Pasteur contributed to the founding of the modern science of microbiology. His greatest endeavors were related to the fields of bacteriology and immunology, the study of the body's reaction to disease. He discovered that diseases could be killed by excessive heat of approximately

140°Fahrenheit, or 60°Celsius for a half hour. Milk is rid of harmful bacteria by this process, and it is called "pasteurization" after the developer of the process. Everyone is exposed to numerous organisms and toxic chemicals daily, and without good health, the body is unable to combat the potential onslaught from these environmental dangers.

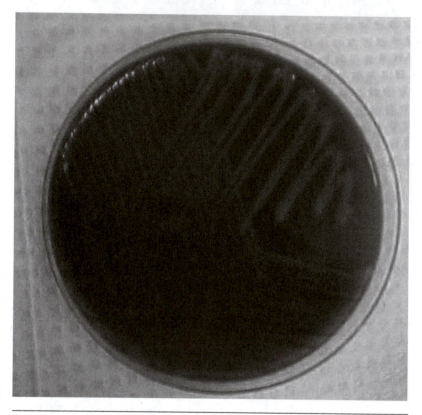

Petri Dish With Bacterial Colonies

Another contributor to the field of bacteriology is Joseph Lister, a British surgeon. Lister determined that germs (bacteria only) could be killed by carbolic acid. It was determined at this time that many deaths in hospitals were related to the unclean conditions of the health care facilities. Lister demanded that surgical wounds be kept clean and the air in the operating rooms be kept clean and circulating. The number of deaths related to complications from surgical procedures diminished dramatically when these changes were instituted. These practices eventually found their way to the battlefield, and the number of soldiers who had amputations in military facilities benefited from the knowledge of microorganisms. During the U.S. Civil War, many deaths were caused by infection rather than the severity of the wound. Following this war, practices developed during the internecine struggle, such as transportation of the wounded by ambulance for treatment behind the lines, often in a house or other building, or a tent, were adopted for use in civilian facilities. The model for this treatment persisted into World War I, and from this modest beginning, evolved into rapid treatment in sanitary facilities for the wounded soldier.

Engineered Controls

Engineered controls refers to equipment manufactured for the purpose of enabling workers to protect themselves as preventive measures, as well as to react to an exposure incident. Engineered controls include but are not limited to all hardware such as hand washing facilities, eyewash stations, sharps disposal containers, laundry hampers that are impervious to dust and liquids, and are used for transporting and storage of both clean and soiled linens, and sterilizers, to name a few. These control devices are designed for use in the areas where treatment is being performed. It is much easier to maintain asepsis (clean or sterile work area) when devices are near at hand for cleaning and disposal of soiled wastes that may be impregnated by body fluids, particularly blood.

Engineered controls are designed for ease of use and effectiveness in preventing the spread of diseases to both the patients and the health care workers. When building a health care facility, much planning is done to provide for air exchange, transport of waste throughout the facility, and removal of waste. Waste is separated into routine office type waste materials that may be safely disposed of in regular waste and waste that may be biohazardous and must be discarded in a manner such that all organisms are destroyed. Incineration by commercial companies is the most common method for destroying these potentially infectious materials.

Work Practice Controls

In general, this type of control includes but is not limited to hand washing, cleaning of work areas with bleach or other prescribed disinfectants, and sterilizing of reusable items. Precautions consist of a number of common medical practices that are employed during the performing of tasks and procedures in the treatment of patients. Work practice controls are tailored to suit the procedure being performed. It is not necessary to be fully garbed in personal protective equipment in order to perform a simple, noninvasive procedure or one that requires little or no direct physical contact with the patient.

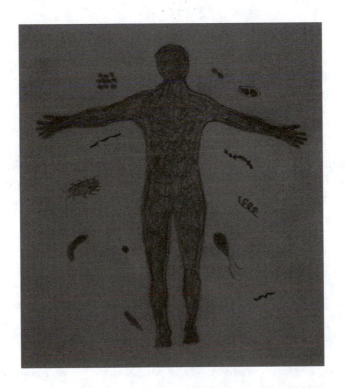

Humans are Exposed to and Harbor Many Organisms

Recent data appears to support a change in the initial requirement for using running water and germicidal soap for cleaning of the hands. The use of waterless germicidals obtained from

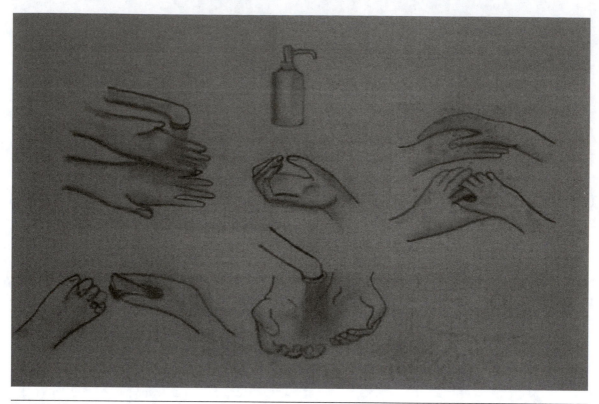

Hand Washing Procedure

dispensers located strategically around the medical facility has been shown by some research to be much more effective in reducing the number of bacterial contaminants remaining on the hands, when a comparison of hand washing under a faucet and use of the germicidals that do not necessitate rinsing of the hands following application is made. However, this is not widely practiced to date. As more research of both the products used and the effectiveness of the procedure of using the waterless hand cleansing technique, policies may change in many, if not all, medical facilities. A substantive change in the procedure for cleaning hands would have to be approved by the Infection Control Committee, after evaluating the research performed on the subject.

After learning of the risk involved in handling infectious materials and exposure to an infected patient, many students are initially frightened of the possibility of becoming themselves infected. The purpose for training students and health care workers, even experienced ones, of methods that may be employed to protect oneself is to avoid this unwarranted fear. Students and medical workers who conscientiously follow guidelines and policies established through research, experience, and plain caution seldom, if ever, become unwittingly infected. It is when one lets his or her guard down, or violates infection control procedures willfully or out of ignorance, that one becomes infected. This is why incident reports are filed when an exposure occurs so the infection control authorities may investigate and possibly change certain procedures. Most normal, day-to-day activities by the health care worker with direct patient responsibilities requiring close contact will not place the person providing care under any undue risk. Standard and reasonable care will protect the health care worker from contracting organisms harbored by a patient under most circumstances. Patients who provide most risk to caretakers are usually in isolation, where contact is carefully monitored. The following table describes a number of simple procedures that are performed on a regular basis in all medical facilities, from physicians' offices, to treatment rooms, to surgical suites. Precautions that should be taken for the various levels of patient contact, when providing certain services, are outlined here. The beginning student often is overwhelmed when told of the risks of treating people with illnesses, but with the proper training, continuing education, and correct use of both engineered controls and work practice controls, there is little danger to the worker as he or she performs the duties required of the position. Training is provided relative to the job performed and should be an ongoing process, with updates at least annually.

WORK PRACTICE CONTROLS/POTENTIAL RISKS FOR COMMON PROCEDURES

Procedure	Hand Washing	Gloves	Gowns	Mask	Eyewear
Talking to Patient					
Performing Blood Pressure	X				
Hands Soiled, Body Fluids	X				
Examining, not touching body fluids, mucous membranes	X				
Simple intradermal or intramuscular injection for non-isolation patient	X	X			
Touching body fluids, broken skin, lesions, contaminated equipment	X	X			
Performing phlebotomy	X	X			
Performing finger or heel stick	X	X			
Inserting IV catheter	X	X			
Going from patient to patient	X	X			
Suctioning (danger of splatter)	X	X			
Handling soiled linen (include gown if materials saturated)	X	X			
Surgery, other operative procedures if splatter of body fluids probable	X	X	X	X	X

Sample Infection Control Policy Manual for a Hospital

The following section is a sample of the infection control manual of a small hospital and covers all of the main areas addressed by an infection control committee. The major categories of a sample infection control manual from a small hospital indicates all of the major components required to be considered by the Infection Control Committee for a health care institution. Some infection control manuals are entitled "Exposure Control" and include caustic, radiologic, and hazardous materials other than biological materials related to treatment of patients. Infection or exposure control manuals should be available for employees in all work areas of a medical facility.

Sample Infection Control Manual

Infection or exposure control manuals should be available for employees in all work areas of a medical facility.

Employee Instruction Sheet

An employee instruction sheet is often incorporated into the orientation process for all new employees, and updates are provided annually or as needed. This is a sample instruction sheet with which the employee should familiarize himself or herself. These instructions are often placed in clinical areas of the facility for quick access by employees.

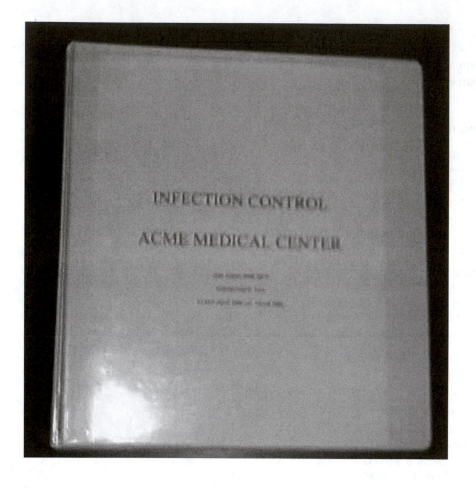

Universal Precautions are used to minimize the potential for spread of organisms and should be practices with every patient. This term indicates that these precautions should be practiced with every patient to indicate a potential risk for being infected by any patient. The health care worker must realize that the physical appearance of health in a patient does not ensure that the patient is infectious for a variety of organisms. Work practice controls for common medical procedures assess the potential risk for tasks related to direct patient contact. Practicing these simple work practice controls will remove much of the possibility of contracting disease from patients. The medical worker must overcome the anxiety and even fear associated with treating patients who have contagious diseases and realize that conscientious practice of good hygiene will protect him or her almost completely. Universal Precautions is designed to protect the worker by having the medical worker treat each patient as though he or she were contagious. Universal Precautions considers blood and certain body fluids as being potentially a source of infection, and issues guidelines for handling procedures and disposal of these fluids. Another category designed by CDC to protect the medical worker is called Standard Precautions. Standard Precautions are guidelines by CDC that recommends practices to prevent nosocomial (hospital-acquired infections), while Universal Precautions are mandated by OSHA, requiring training of health care workers in all medical facilities, chiefly confined to bloodborne pathogens.

Practices Related to Universal Precautions

1. To prevent exposure of the skin and mucous membranes to blood or other body fluids, health care workers should routinely use appropriate barrier precautions.

2. Wear gloves when touching blood and body fluids, mucous membranes, or non-intact skin of all patients; for handling items or surfaces soiled with blood or body fluids; and for performing venipuncture and other vascular access procedures.

3. Change gloves after contact with each patient.

4. Wash hands immediately after removing gloves.

5. Wear gowns or aprons during procedures that are likely to generate splashes of blood and/or body fluids.

6. Wash hands and other skin surfaces immediately and thoroughly if contaminated with blood or other body fluids.

7. To prevent exposure of mucous membranes of the mouth, nose, and eyes, wear masks and protective eyewear or a face shield during procedures that are likely to generate droplets of blood or other body fluids.

8. To prevent needlestick injuries, needles should not be recapped, bent or broken by hand, removed from disposable syringes, or otherwise manipulated by hand.

9. Disposable syringes and needles, scalpel blades, and other sharp items should be disposed of in puncture-resistant containers: these containers need to be located as close as practical to the use area.

10. Reusable large-bore needles should be transported to the reprocessing area in puncture-resistant containers.

11. All health care workers should take precautions to prevent injuries caused by needles, scalpels, and other sharp instruments or devices during procedures, when cleaning used instruments, during disposal of used needles, and when handling sharp instruments after procedures.

12. Although saliva has not been implicated in HIV transmission, resuscitation bags or other ventilation devices should be available to minimize the need for emergency mouth-to-mouth resuscitation in areas where the need for resuscitation is predictable.

13. Health care workers with exudative lesions or weeping dermatitis should refrain from all direct patient care and from handling patient care equipment until the condition resolves.

14. Pregnant health care workers are not known to be at a greater risk for contracting HBV than nonpregnant health care workers. However, if the mother is infected, the infant is at risk of infection resulting from perinatal transmission. Because of this risk, pregnant health care workers must be familiar with, and strictly adhere to, the precautions for minimizing the risk of HIV transmission.

15. Workers with skin rashes or breaks, and those known to be infected or to be in an immuno-compromised condition, are kept from duties requiring direct patient contact.

Infection Control Program

Purpose

The purpose of the Infection Control Program is to prevent, control, and evaluate the incidence and spread of nosocomial (hospital-acquired) infections and to address patient care and employment issues related to prevention if in contact with blood or other potentially infectious materials, or hazardous materials related to daily operations of the facility. To accomplish this goal, the hospital shall comply with institutional policies, federal and state legislation, OSHA's Final Bloodborne Pathogen Standard and Centers for Disease Control and Prevention guidelines, as well as institutional and departmental regulatory agencies. It is essential that all employees involved with patient care conscientiously follow accepted techniques and take necessary preventive measures in order to protect both the health care worker and the patient.

Duties of the Infection Control Committee

1. To provide a committee that can give direction to and strengthen the clinical aspects of infection control throughout the facility.

2. To provide inservice and continuing education programs for all employees on an ongoing regular basis. Challenges brought about by new pathogens must be met and explored as they occur.

3. To establish and enforce written infection control policies and procedures for all departments and to maintain a sanitary environment hospital-wide.

4. To establish various isolation procedures and precautionary measures and promote their proper use through surveillance, observation, and other means.

5. To have an effective system of surveillance and reporting of infections to the appropriate governmental agencies.

6. To establish criteria for nosocomial infections based on national guidelines provided by the CDC, JCAHO, FDA, EPA, and others as appropriate, and approved by the hospital Infection Control Committee.

7. To report all communicable diseases on a regular basis to the local health department, and to assist in providing information required to determine the source of disease.

8. To provide an effective employee health program for all employees with regular testing for communicable diseases, and to make reasonable decisions regarding reassignment when health of employees would jeopardize safety of patients.

9. To make recommendations and take appropriate action to limit further spread of any dangerous pathogen through isolation, quarantine, and so on, as appropriate based on informed decisions by the Infection Control Committee.

10. To prevent and control the spread of nosocomial infections when possible.

11. To participate in special studies as needed, including the review of antibiotics and the appropriate use of antibiotics.

12. To enforce the Exposure Control Plan through any means necessary to insure compliance with the program.

13. To enforce the Tuberculosis Control Program through testing and treatment of infected employees.

EXPOSURE CONTROL PLAN

The Infection Control Committee and the medical facility are committed to provide a **safe** working environment and believe employees can make knowledgeable decisions about any personal risks of employment when they are provided with current and correct information. The Exposure Control Plan is established to include policies, procedures, and responsibilities of both departments and individual employees. It is designed to develop an informed awareness in employees of potentially infectious materials in the workplace and to train employees to protect themselves appropriately, as well as to provide safe working conditions by providing for workers' safety and welfare. This plan is reviewed and updated annually, and a copy of the plan is available for all employees in their respective work areas. Employees who are not provided a copy or who are unable to locate a copy should contact the Infection Control Coordinator as soon as possible. All employees are to have access to current and pertinent safety information and appropriate personal protective equipment through their supervisory staff. The periodic training program for employees of this facility is designed for the benefit and protection of all of our employees and is the most important aspect of teaching the employees about protecting themselves against becoming infected in the course of duty. It is the responsibility of each individual worker to take advantage of this training, and also to report breaches of these policies to the highest level of this facility's management.

This Exposure Control Plan is a guide for all employees to protect them and their patients and to minimize risks associated with being in the proximity of bloodborne and airborne pathogens. The plan details how the medical facility or educational facility will meet responsibilities under OSHA Standard 19 C.F.R. Section 1910.1030.

Objectives of Exposure Control Plan

1. To protect the health care worker who reasonably would be expected to come into contact with human blood and other potentially infectious materials in the course of normal duties for the position from bloodborne and airborne infections.

2. Voluntary vaccination of workers, at the employer's (the hospital's or clinic's) expense, is a requirement. This vaccination could prevent a majority of hepatitis B infections in the workforce and reduce the risk of transmitting hepatitis B infections to other workers and patients. This will serve to decrease the total number of HBV infections both locally and nationally, greatly aiding the facility and the country in avoiding needless medical expenses and lost work days due to industrial accidents, such as exposure.

3. Engineered controls, work practices, and personal protective equipment will serve to reduce the occupational risks of both HIV and HBV for all employees. Engineered controls refer to actual hardware furnished by the facility in order to enable the worker to protect himself or herself.

4. Workers with reasonably anticipated exposure to blood and other potentially infectious materials in the performance of Category I and II tasks will be identified and trained with procedures to avoid becoming infected.

Work Practice Controls refer to activities by workers to avoid contracting disease. Proper washing of the hands is one of the most effective means by which a person can avoid becoming infected when working in a health care facility.

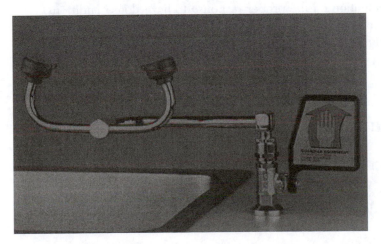

Example of Work Practice Controls – Proper Washing of Hands

Responsibility/Accountability

1. The Infection Control Officer has been designated as the hospital's Exposure Control Plan Coordinator and works in conjunction with all departments of the hospital. Resources with pertinent information from departments such as the clinical laboratory will be utilized to accomplish the goals of the institution to minimize risk and disease rates.

2. The employer is responsible for development and implementation of the Exposure Control Plan. (Also see #4 in this section.)

3. The Infection Control Committee is responsible for ensuring the implementation and compliance of the Exposure Control Plan.

4. The employees are responsible for complying with policies, procedures, rules, and regulations specified by the Infection Control Committee. Employees should be provided with periodic updates, particularly when job requirements change, or if new procedures are instituted that may provide a greater possibility of exposure to biohazardous materials.

Scope of Involvement

The Exposure Control Plan is introduced to all employees during the orientation and employee update program and is scheduled at least on an annual basis. Often pertinent and applicable handouts will be provided to the employee for personal use and familiarization. The importance of the Exposure Control Plan is stressed to all personnel. This orientation attempts to acquaint the employees of all departments with requirements of the institution related to protection of workers and patients and to ensure the worker is aware of his personal responsibility for adhering to the policies and procedures set forth by the Infection Control Committee. There will be an annual update, and changes in policy will be communicated to the health care worker in a timely fashion. Technological changes in the workplace and research leading to more effective medical practice will be communicated to the medical worker as soon as feasible. A copy of the Infection Control/ Exposure Control manual will be available for all employees for reference. The custodial or housekeeping departments should have ready access to supplies and equipment to remove hazards associated with spills of blood and body fluids quickly. It is paramount that these workers also be knowledgeable in order to deal with a hazardous situation.

Procedures for handling biohazardous conditions that may pose a threat to the health care worker or the patient and his family or other visitors will be available at each workstation. Steps to perform prior to the arrival of the housekeeping staff will be available, along with supplies for a quick response to the condition. Employees will be trained and updated periodically, and new employees will be provided with orientation on the proper response to hazardous conditions.

Materials needed for effectively cleaning up a biohazardous spill would include an absorbent material, such as a pad, as previously pictured. A container for broken glass and a germicidal for disinfecting the area would also be required.

MAJOR ELEMENTS OF THE EXPOSURE CONTROL PLAN

The Exposure Determination

All routine and reasonably anticipated job-related functions will be classified to ensure that all Category I and II tasks are properly identified. This exposure determination is made without regard to use of personal protective equipment. Category I, II, and III tasks must be identified and

Spilled Blood is a Major Hazard in Health care Facilities

outlined by the Infection Control Committee and made available for all employees at regularly scheduled assemblies. Manuals will be located in all sections for employees' convenient access. Each job title has been assigned a risk category for blood or body fluid exposure depending upon the tasks to be performed in that job, categorized by the potential for exposure to infectious or biohazardous materials. Protective equipment and supplies will be provided as needed for the various categorical tasks.

Task List

A task list shows related tasks and procedures where occupational exposure potential has been determined. New tasks and equipment will require additions to the task list on a continuous basis and employees should refer these changes to the Infection Control Committee for appropriate documentation. Employees who assume additional duties, or whose essential duties change through new assignments or position transfers, will be oriented as to the risks they may encounter in a timely manner.

Universal Precautions

Universal Precautions will be observed to prevent contact with blood or other potentially infectious materials (OPIM). When differentiation between body fluid types is difficult or not possible, **all** body fluids will be considered potential infectious materials.

Engineering and Work Practice Controls

Engineering and work practice controls will be used to eliminate or minimize employee exposure. Where occupational exposure remains after institution of these controls, personal protective equipment shall also be used.

Engineering controls shall be examined and maintained or replaced on a regular schedule, to ensure their effectiveness, by each department head and through the performance improvement program. Managers, supervisors, and the employee routinely replace supplies or broken engineering controls. This is accomplished by ordering supplies on units and work orders to the Engineering Department or Materials Management. Nursing, Environmental Services, and ancillary department staff are responsible for assessing needle boxes for fill level, closing them securely, and disposing waste appropriately in a large biohazard container. A new replacement is then obtained and put into place.

Engineering Controls

These include leakproof, puncture-resistant sharp containers appropriately labeled. Contaminated needles and other contaminated sharps shall not be bent, recapped, or removed unless a one-handled technique is used. Shearing or breaking of contaminated needles is prohibited. Sharps containers are accessible in all areas where procedures are performed requiring the use of needles. These boxes are to be replaced when they are filled near to the top. The filled sharps containers will be sealed and placed in a clearly designated area for appropriate pickup and transport to an area where a commercial biohazard disposal company may remove them to a disposal room, in clean and dirty utility. In the Intensive Care Unit (ICU), sinks are located in each ICU room, medication station, dirty and clean utility. In the ER, there are sinks in each exam room, patient bathrooms, and in the dirty and clean utility rooms. On the OB Nursery Unit, sinks are in each patient room, medication room, dirty utility room, in the labor rooms, the employee bathroom, and in the neonatal and regular nurseries. In the Rehabilitation Department, in the Whirlpool Clinic, Rehabilitation Ward, and in Respiratory Therapy, sinks are present in the bathroom. In the Operating Room, there are physician scrub sinks, a sink in the sterilizer area, and a sink in the doctors, nurses' lounge. Recovery Room has a sink, and in the Outpatient Clinic, a sink is located in the storage area as well as the bathrooms. In Radiology, sinks are present in each procedure room. In the Lab, there are sinks present in the cleaning room and each departmental work area. In the Pharmacy, sinks are present in the drug room where medications are compounded. In the Special Procedures Department, sinks are located in each patient room, dirty utility rooms, clean utility rooms, and in all areas of the kitchen and where food is stored prior to be taken to the kitchen for preparation. In Central Supply/Sterilizing, there is a sink at each workstation.

Sinks are located in all patient rooms, as well as dirty and clean utility rooms located in patient areas and near the nurses' stations. Throughout the institution, sinks are available in all visitor and employee bathrooms, with antiseptic soap provided for hand washing. Antiseptic hand cleaner or towelettes may be used whenever clean, running water is not available but will not be used as a substitute. The hand cleaners or towelettes are a temporary solution for cleaning hands, when ongoing tasks prevent the immediate opportunity to wash hands or when there is an exposure requiring immediate attention.

Work Practice Controls

1. When employees are to perform procedures that create splashing, spraying, or splattering of blood or other potentially infectious materials, they will do so in a manner that reduces the risk of exposure. Blood specimens are opened using sponges to minimize contamination or plastic shields or boxes are used to reduce splashing. Specimens are to be centrifuged with the lid firmly closed to reduce risk of infection and are remote from areas used for washing equipment or for waste disposal. Thorough cleaning of sinks and surrounding areas with a disinfectant is required before hand washing. These are responsibilities of both housekeeping and the individual workers.

2. Employees should wash their hands immediately after removal of gloves or other personal protective equipment. This equipment will be disposed of properly, as is required if PPE is contaminated with blood or other potentially infectious materials (OPIM).

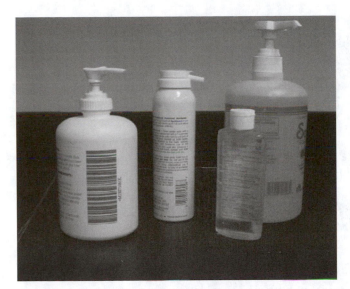

Examples of Hand washing Supplies

3. Employees will wash their hands and any other skin with antiseptic soap and water, or flush mucous membranes with water immediately following contact of such body areas with blood or OPIM. Hand washing facilities and supplies are available and conveniently located throughout the facility. In areas where no sink is available, alternate waterless hand cleaners are obtainable but are not used as a substitute. If towelettes or other cleaning measures have been employed, hands will be thoroughly washed as soon as feasible with soap and running water.

4. Eating, drinking, applying cosmetics or lip balm, or handling contact lenses are prohibited where there is a reasonable likelihood of occupational exposure.

5. Specimens of blood or other potentially infectious materials shall be placed in a container preventing leakage during collection, handling, processing, storage, and prior to transport or shipping. Shipping specimens/containers to other facilities should be labeled and treated with Universal Precautions.

6. Properly trained personnel will transport gross tissue specimens and other specimens from surgery and will deliver the specimen(s) to the pathology department of the laboratory.

7. Specimens requiring transport within the facility will be collected in the appropriate containers provided and will be transported in closed containers placed in leakproof bags or Styrofoam boxes. For accountability, specimens will be labeled as to source of specimen, name and identifying number of the patient, and the time and area where the specimen was collected.

8. Biomedical repair uses decontamination procedures for all equipment to be serviced. If decontamination resources are not available, then biomedical engineering uses biohazard labels and informs the service employee receiving the piece of equipment. In some cases, the departmental employees where the equipment is normally used are responsible for cleaning the equipment prior to presenting it for servicing.

9. Food and drink shall not be kept in freezers, refrigerators, shelves, cabinets, or on countertops with stored blood or other potentially infectious materials. Refrigerators, freezers, and cabinets will be labeled as to what is allowed to be stored in them. Periodic inspections will be accomplished to enforce this requirement.

10. Cleaning processes for heavily contaminated reusable items will be performed prior to performing decontamination or sterilization procedures.

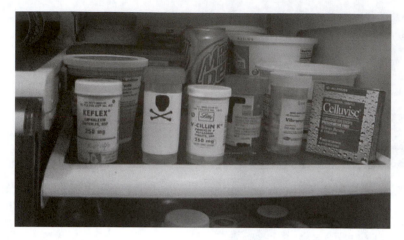

Refrigerator – Mixed Food, Medications Storage

11. The area where the equipment was serviced must have visible disposable parts and trash discarded, and the area decontaminated following completion of the process.

12. If outside contamination of a primary container occurs, the primary container shall be placed inside an additional container without attempting to clean the primary container.

Transport Container for Biohazardous Materials

Personal Protective Equipment

Note: All Personal Protective Equipment Must be Removed Prior to Leaving a Work Area

1. Gloves are worn when an employee anticipates the possibility of contact with blood, other potentially infectious materials, mucous membranes, and skin lesions or rash when performing venous or arterial puncture procedures or when handling contaminated items or surfaces.

2. Personal protective equipment (PPE) is the most effective line of defense in protecting employees from contact with blood and other potentially infectious material. Where occupational exposure remains following initiation of safe work practices and engineering controls, PPE must be used. PPE includes gloves, gowns masks, protective eyewear, face shields (used when potential for splatter of blood or body fluids is present), and ventilation. Each department manager is responsible for ensuring that these requirements are met. **All PPE used at this facility will be provided without cost to employees.** PPE will be chosen based on the anticipated exposure to blood or other potentially infectious materials. (Refer to table provided previously.)

3. Disposable gloves shall be replaced if they become contaminated or torn, punctured, or their integrity as a barrier is breached. Disposable gloves will be discarded after use into the appropriate container. Those saturated with blood or body fluids will be disposed of as regulated waste (red bag with biohazard label). Glove wearing follows aseptic technique, hand washing, and universal precaution guidelines. Utility gloves may be decontaminated for reuse, but must be discarded if they are cracked, peeling, torn, punctured, or exhibit signs of deterioration.

4. Masks, eye protection, or face shields such as goggles or glasses with solid side shields should be worn whenever splashes, spray, spatter, or droplets of blood or other potentially infectious materials may be generated.

5. Gowns, aprons, and other protective body clothing shall be worn in occupational exposure situations, such as handling saturated bed linens. Surgical caps or hoods and/or shoe covers or boots shall be worn in instances when gross contamination from medical procedures is reasonably possible.

6. Each department manager shall enforce the requirement to use appropriate PPE except in rare and unusual cases where the employee temporarily and briefly declines to use PPE in order to better and in a more timely fashion execute a procedure. Ordinarily, this would be a case where PPE would have prevented the delivery of health care or posed an increased hazard to the safety of the worker or coworker. When the employee makes this judgment, the circumstances shall be investigated and documented in order to determine whether changes can be instituted to prevent such occurrences in the future.

7. Each department manager shall ensure that appropriate PPE, in the appropriate sizes, is readily available in the various work areas and is provided at no cost to the employees. Hypoallergenic gloves, glove liners, or powderless gloves will be available to those employees who are allergic to latex gloves or the powder used in these gloves.

8. All PPE will be cleaned, laundered, or disposed of by **this institution** at no cost to the employee. The employer will make repairs and replacements at no cost to the employees.

9. All garments that are penetrated by blood shall be removed as soon as possible. **All PPE is to be removed prior to leaving the work area**. Employees will not wear PPE as they travel to their homes, even if no stops are made enroute.

10. When PPE is removed, it shall be placed in an appropriately designated area or container for storage, washing, decontamination, or disposal as appropriate for the item.

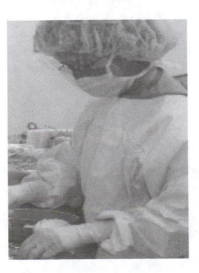

Hospital Employee With Mask, Goggles, Head Cover, and Gloves

11. Employees are required to wear surgical caps or hoods and shoe covers or boots when contamination by blood might normally occur in procedures, such as orthopedic surgery or vaginal delivery.

12. Employees must wear face and eye protection when there is a probability of splashing, spraying, or splattering of blood or other potentially infectious materials due to type of procedure being performed. Shields *with masks* are the most effective barriers against splashing and spraying.

13. Ventilation devices for resuscitation are provided for use in strategic areas throughout the institution. These devices include the various sizes of bag-valve masks and pocket masks for use when performing CPR in an emergency situation.

Housekeeping

The work site is maintained in a clean and sanitary manner. The Environmental Services Supervisor, chief of Housekeeping and Custodial Services (with input from the Infection Control Committee) shall

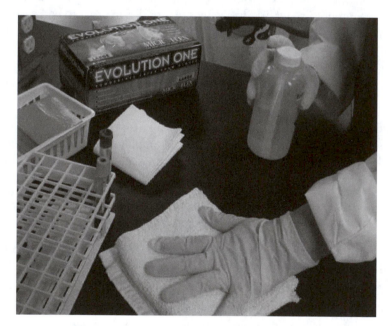

Housekeeping Decontaminating Work Counters

implement a posted schedule for cleaning and method of decontamination for all work areas and common areas in the facility. Written policies and procedures with schedules for cleaning and decontamination are followed that are specific for locations within the hospital. Clinical workers are to be trained by the hospital in the appropriate cleaning procedures to protect themselves as well as to provide a safe and clean work environment for the patients and medical workers and staff. Records of this training, and when job descriptions change, are to be maintained in the workers' files for a specific period of time.

1. All equipment and environmental and working surfaces shall be cleaned and decontaminated by acceptable practices after contact with blood or other potentially infectious materials. Departmental policy and Universal Precautions policy is followed.

2. The housekeeper shall wear appropriate personal protective equipment during cleaning of blood or other potentially infectious materials and during decontamination procedures.

3. Initial cleanup of blood or other potentially infectious materials shall be followed with the use of an approved hospital disinfectant chemical germicide that is tuberculocidal or a solution of 5.25 percent sodium hypochlorite (household bleach) diluted at a 1:10 ratio with water. The

Proper Removal of Broken
Glass for Protection

Environmental Services Department follows recommended dilution and concentration for use of any commercially provided hospital disinfectant.

4. The Environmental Services Department routinely cleans the waste cans, bins, pails, etc., and decontaminates as soon as feasible after contamination occurs.

5. Universal Precautions policy is followed for removing broken glass possibly contaminated with blood/body fluid. **Do not vacuum glass!**

6. Equipment contaminated with blood or other potentially infectious materials shall be checked routinely and decontaminated prior to servicing in the Biomedical Repair department or shipment to the manufacturer for upgrade or maintenance.

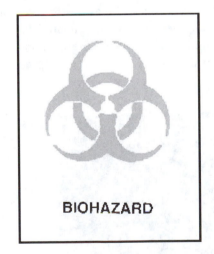

BIOHAZARD

7. Regulated waste shall be placed in containers that are closable and constructed to contain all contents and prevent leakage of fluids during handling, storage, transport, or shipping, and labeled or color coded. All waste receptacles are emptied facility-wide by housekeeping (with gloves on) on a regular basis, at least once per day. If a waste receptacle becomes full after

housekeeping has cleaned the area, the staff from that area will empty the waste receptacle into the appropriate collection bin with gloved hands.

8. Tags shall be used to identify hazards. Tags shall contain the word "BIOHAZARD" or a symbol.

9. Physical Plant Operations department will ensure that biohazard labels are affixed to all containers of regulated wastes, including those that are to contain red biohazard bags. Refrig-

Enclosed Laundry Cart

erators and freezers containing blood or other potentially infectious materials and other containers used to store, transport, or ship blood or other potentially infectious materials will be properly labeled.

10. Contaminated laundry shall be handled as little as possible with a minimum of movement and disturbance during transport of the linen. Contaminated laundry shall be bagged and not sorted or rinsed prior to complete and appropriate cleaning. All linen shall be considered contaminated through Universal Precautions even if not grossly visible. When contaminated

Waste Receptacle Designed for Discarding Biohazardous Wastes

with blood/body fluids, it is handled with gloves and additional personal protective equipment if needed, including a waterproof apron. The laundry facility does practice the use of Universal Precautions.

11. Red bags or red containers may be substituted for labels or containers of infectious waste. **Red bags will not be used for anything but disposal of regulated waste.**

12. All employees shall be informed of the meaning of various labels, tags, and color-coding system during orientation and annual training.

13. Blood products that have been released for transfusion or other chemical use are exempted from these labeling requirements. However, the Blood Bank employs strict handling procedures for blood product components for testing, and for units of blood prepared for transfusion.

Vaccination/Immunizations

Depending on institutional policies, immunization requirements may vary among institutions depending on types of patients treated. These are done at the employer's expense. Almost all, if not all, facilities require a minimum of the following:

Hepatitis B Vaccination

1. Refer to the Hepatitis Control Program for your institution. The hepatitis B vaccination (HBV) shall be made available after receiving training prior to initial duty assignment to all employees who have occupational exposure unless the employee has previously received the HBV series, antibody testing has revealed the employee is immune, or the vaccine is contraindicated for medical reasons.

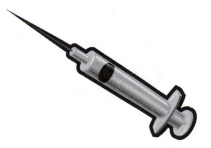

2. If the employee initially declines the HBV vaccine but at a later date decides to accept the vaccine, it will be made available to the employee at that time. Employees who choose to decline the HBV immunization must sign a declination form.
   If a routine booster dose of the hepatitis B vaccine is recommended by the U.S. Public Health Service at a later date, such booster doses shall be made available by the employer.

3. Infection control and employee health maintain current review of CDC's guidelines. Subscription to American Hospital Association (AHA) and Georgia Hospital Association (GHA) keeps the institution informed as to pertinent issues related to infection control. This hospital also keeps abreast by membership in Association for Professionals in Infection Control and Epidemiology (APIC). Infection control maintains resources with local public

health through surveillance, reporting, and adhering to any guidelines published by the state public health department.

The hospital laboratory is accredited by the College of American Pathologists (CAP) and State Department of Human Resources or other agencies as applicable.

POST-EXPOSURE EVALUATION AND FOLLOW-UP

Written policies and guidelines to follow in reporting and receiving immediate treatment following possible or actual exposure will be posted in each clinical area. Following a report of an exposure incident, the employee shall have a confidential medical evaluation through the emergency department and follow-up with the infection control officer or his or her designee.

1. The route of exposure, HBV and HIV status of the source patient, if known, and circumstances under which the exposure occurred shall be documented.

2. The source individual's blood should be tested as soon as possible after patient consent is obtained for HBV and HIV. The results of the testing shall be made available to the exposed employee, and the employee shall be informed of applicable laws and regulations concerning disclosure of the identity and infectious status of the source patient.

3. The exposed employee's blood should be collected as soon as possible and tested after consent is obtained. Provided the employee agrees to a baseline blood collection but does not give permission at the time to have HIV testing performed, the sample shall be preserved in an approved manner for ninety days. If, within ninety days of the exposure incident, the employee elects to have the baseline sample tested, this testing shall be done as soon as possible.

4. The health care professional's written opinion for post-exposure evaluation and follow-up shall inform the employee of the results of the evaluation, and any medical conditions resulting from exposure that require further evaluation or treatment.

Note: Refer to the Hepatitis B program and HIV policies for more information.

Training and Education of Employees

1. Exposure Control Plan
   The Exposure Control Plan is available for review by all employees of this institution. Copies will be maintained in all administrative offices, employee health, infection control, and hospital-wide in the infection control manuals distributed to all major departments for easy access by individual employees.

2. Scheduled Orientation Training
   All employees whose duties entail exposure to blood or other potentially infectious materials (particularly with body fluids) shall participate in a training and education program during orientation and will be updated annually as necessary, and if the job requirements change.

3. Infection Control and Employee Health
   All new employees will be shown a video or PowerPoint presentation that is current with any recent developments covering the hazards associated with exposure to blood and the procedures employed when observing Universal Precautions. This orientation includes information

on infection control and employee health benefits available to personnel, and a professional who is responsible for keeping abreast of changes and has input into the Exposure/Infection Control Committee available to answer questions as an expert resource. The employees receive a brochure on Universal Precautions for reference on the job.

4. Annual Inservice

   All employees are required to attend an annual inservice and continuing education update that includes infection control with resources for questions. Each department has specific orientation by a supervisor from the area where the employee will be assigned. Departmental orientation will include infection control and Universal Precautions as well as other hazards that may be a danger to the employee.

5. Change of Position

   When an employee changes position requiring new and/or different exposures to blood, he or she will be oriented to the specific tasks of the department where the employee will be working. Along with education for risks of exposure and appropriate Universal Precautions, the employee will be oriented to the location of supplies and equipment needed to protect the employee.

The Training Program Should Contain the Following Elements

1. A general explanation of the epidemiology and symptoms of HBV and HIV. Explanations of the differences in the symptoms for infections by the two organisms will be stressed.

2. An explanation of the modes of transmission of HBV and HIV will be provided. Personal as well as work-related exposure will be discussed.

3. An explanation of the employees' infection control program and the duties and responsibilities of the employer and employee will be outlined.

4. An explanation of the use and limitations of methods of control that may prevent or reduce exposure including Universal Precautions, engineering controls, work practices, and personal protective equipment will be provided in a brochure to the employee.

5. Information on the HBV vaccine, including its efficacy, safety, and the benefits of being vaccinated will be provided, and employees will be advised of their right to decline immunization.

6. An explanation of the procedure to follow if an exposure incident occurs, method of reporting the incident, and the medical follow-up that will be made available, as well as the contact person for emergency treatment for exposure will be provided.

7. An explanation of signs, labels, tags and/or color-coding used to denote biohazards, and a picture card (the back of ID badge) will be introduced so the employees will not unknowingly become infected because they are unaware of the meaning of various signs and labels.

8. The training records shall include the dates of the training sessions, the contents or a summary of the training, the names and qualifications of people conducting the training, and the names and job titles of all people attending the training session. Employees will be required to provide a signature as evidence that the training was received.

9. The records must be maintained for three years from the date on which the training occurred. Employee training records for bloodborne pathogens shall be provided upon request to employees or an employee representative who may have legal standing to provide assistance to the employee. Representatives of any governmental agency regulating requirements related to infection control and prevention may also review these records.

Record Keeping Security

Medical records for pre-exposure physical examinations and any medical records compiled during an examination following an exposure incident shall be maintained in accordance with OSHA Standard 29 CFR 1910.20. These records shall be kept confidential and must be maintained for at least the duration of employment plus thirty years.

These records shall include the following:

1. The name and social security number of the employee

2. Copy of employee's HBV vaccination status, including the dates of vaccinations

3. Copy of all results of examinations, medical testing, and follow-up procedures

4. A copy of information provided to the health care professional, including a description of the employee's duties as they relate to the exposure incident, and documentation of the routes of exposure and circumstances of the exposure

5. Training records shall be maintained for three years from the date of training. The following information shall be documented:

   A. The dates of the training session

   B. Outline describing the material presented

   C. Names and qualifications of people conducting the training

   D. Names and job titles of all people attending the training sessions

6. All employee records shall be available to the employee

Hazard Communication

Information concerning the hazards of materials used in the workplace will be communicated to employees by means of a comprehensive hazard program. Even very simple materials normally found in the workplace may, if proper care is not exercised, pose a threat to the health of the user of the materials. This shall include the availability of Material Safety Data Sheets (MSDS) and any changes in materials used that may pose different or additional risks to the patient or worker. The Exposure Control Plan will be reviewed at least annually at the beginning of each fiscal year for effectiveness and possible updating. The annual update will include a review of the general employee instruction sheet containing elements of Universal Precautions, as outlined previously. Updated information from any regulatory agency will be presented at this time.

Introduction to Blood and Airborne Pathogens

As we saw in the Section Two, Blood and Airborne Pathogens, there are three organisms associated with the majority of infections by blood and airborne pathogens. Infection Control is not limited to the Blood and Airborne Pathogens, but it includes all organisms, bacterial, viral, protozoal, and

fungal, that may invade the human body and cause infectious processes. However, the major pathogens that are considered "covered organisms by agencies of the federal government receive the most attention in Infection Control/Exposure Control documents. While protecting the medical worker against blood and airborne pathogens, the work practice and engineered controls protect the worker and the patient against many other organisms. In the case of a patient undergoing a surgical or other invasive procedure, the transfer of "normal flora" that is harmless in one part of the body to another where the organisms may be injurious can occur through careless practices. Inordinate numbers of these types of incidents would warrant an investigation by the Infection Control Committee in order to combat the problem.

Potential Exposure

The following questions apply if you believe you have been exposed to a potentially infectious bodily fluid:

1. Is medical help needed?
   Assess the situation. Is the victim bleeding profusely, or are any bones broken? Serious injury would necessitate calling 911. The victim must be kept comfortable and prevented from doing further injury by moving about.

2. Can the situation be managed without professional help? If the helper/rescuer has only come into contact with a bodily fluid and has no breaks or cuts in the skin, washing of the affected area(s) with soap or water is sufficient. In case of doubt, or if questions arise, contact the Infection Control Coordinator or seek medical attention in the absence of the

Infection Control Officer. It is best to err on the side of caution when such an incident arises.

Actual Exposure

An actual exposure occurs when a worker or patient has in actuality been exposed to an infectious patient, as in the case of tuberculosis or meningitis, or to blood and other body fluids that actually came into contact with the worker. What would be the appropriate action to take when the following situations occur? What should a medical worker do for: Soiled Clothing? Broken skin? Burns or severe injury? The Infection Control Committee drafts policies and procedures as to the procedure to be followed in order to ensure that all requirements have been met for the protection of the worker or the patient.

1. How much blood is present, and did the blood contact the worker in a way that might leave the worker vulnerable? Examples of vulnerability would be a splatter into the eyes, nose and mouth, or onto the body with an accompanying injury to the worker that might cause contact with an open wound. Once the worker or patient is determined to have had an actual exposure incident, proceed to step #2. If possible, cleanse the blood or bodily fluid from the worker or patient as soon as possible.

2. Is the worker's clothing bloody? A small amount the size of a 50¢ piece that cannot be squeezed from the clothing would not necessitate removal of one's clothing. Extremely bloody clothing should be removed and NOT worn home. A worker should clean himself or herself carefully and place the soiled clothing in a plastic bag. Clean clothing should be provided for wearing home. Extremely bloody clothing should NOT be washed in commercial washers. The clothing should be soaked in dilute bleach before allowing contaminated water and clothing to enter your washing machine or sink. Very little danger exists from dried blood (with the exception of hepatitis B virus), but it is important to be careful, even to the extreme in any case involving blood.

3. Are any skin breaks present? Skin breaks may include a situation seemingly so insignificant as a torn cuticle. When skin breaks are present, the worker or patient should be immediately referred for medical attention. If the Infection Control Officer is not present and broken skin or mucus membranes are involved, one should go to a physician in either the emergency department or to his or her own private physician. The educational institute or medical facility is responsible for charges incurred for treatment or evaluation in the case of a student. Most educational facilities have accident insurance to cover the cost of a student's treatment when he or she is exposed in the workplace.

4. How should the exposure be documented? The facility will have a protocol to follow in order to fulfill policies of the facility. An exposure incident report form will be initiated, and the exposed employee or student will be given instructions regarding follow-up responsibilities. These forms are available in each departmental manager's office. The Infection Control Officer is responsible for insuring the availability and validity of the forms. These forms will be approved annually and will be revised as necessary. Individual and confidential counseling will be scheduled for those who have been exposed to infectious materials. The counselor may be the attending physician designated by the facility or the Infection Control Officer.

5. Accidental exposure to the blood of a suspected or confirmed case of hepatitis B should be investigated according to the following steps. If the status of the patient whose blood came in contact with the worker is unknown and no sample for testing is available or consent for testing cannot be achieved, the patient will be treated as though he were contagious.

A. Evaluation by a health care professional for documentation and treatment will be accomplished as soon as feasible.

B. Gamma globulin will be available and will be administered within several hours of the incident.

C. Within seven days, immunization for hepatitis B is effective in preventing illness from the disease. This may be true for certain other organisms, and the Infection Control Officer or the attending physician will decide on the necessity for immunization.

Spills

1. An absorbent material should be used to cover the entire spill. A satisfactory type of absorbent material will be procured upon approval by the Infection Control Committee and will be readily available for application as needed. The custodial staff will be responsible

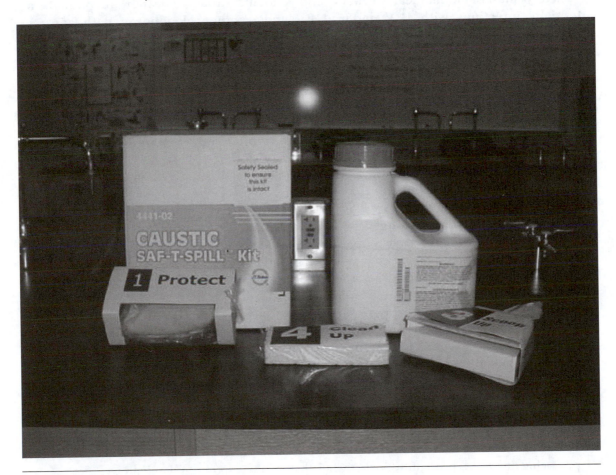

Spill Kit for Caustic Agents

for the proper removal of the spills and will provide thorough cleaning of the area. Wastes generated though use of spill-absorbent materials will be disposed of properly, in accordance with policies established by the Infection Control Committee and local and state ordnances.

2. Spill kits designed for biological and hazardous materials cleanup are to be used as required. Policy and procedure manuals, augmented by MSDS, contain specific instructions on proper

use of spill kits in order to minimize risks to the worker and to facilitate effective removal of the hazardous materials.

3. When large-scale industrial spills occur, it is necessary for professional teams to be called in to protect the population at large, as well as to prevent damage to the environment. Every community has a rapid response team, and if the task is too large for this local team, help is solicited from both the state and federal governments to prevent further damage by providing rapid and expert help.

HBV/HIV Guidelines Under the Regulatory Standard

The following guidelines are a combination of the recommendations of the CDC (Centers for Disease Control and Prevention), OSHA, and the OSHA Bloodborne Pathogen Standard.

Faculty members, medical workers, and students should consider all patients as potentially infectious with HIV and/or HBV and/or other bloodborne pathogens (in accordance with CDC guidelines). Adherence to the infection control guidelines and Universal Precautions or Standard Precautions, as outlined in this manual, will greatly lessen the potential for contamination of faculty members or students in the workplace.

HBV Vaccination

1. **All employees having occupational exposure to blood or other infectious materials are offered the HBV vaccination at no charge to the employee.** The employee may elect to decline the opportunity for hepatitis B immunization but must sign a waiver stating that the availability of the preventive measure was explained, and that the employee is aware of the dangers of not being vaccinated. **The vaccination is made available within ten working days of initial work assignment** unless the employee offers proof of having previously received the complete hepatitis B vaccination series or antibody testing. Acceptable proof will also include documentation of an immune status, or reveal the vaccine is contraindicated for medical reasons, such as allergies or an immunocompromised medical condition. These medical conditions may serve as a bar to employment in certain areas requiring direct patient contact and contact with blood and body fluids (OPIM). There are provisions for declining the HBV vaccination with the employee being required to receive counseling before signing a declination form, documenting that the employee is aware of the risk and will hold the facility blameless if subsequently infected in the course of his or her duties.

2. Students in covered occupational areas will be offered the vaccination series at cost, and the series will be completed prior to performing medical procedures in a medical facility.

3. Students should receive the first vaccine dose prior to patient/client contact and before practicing any tasks, procedures, or activities that involve exposure potential.

4. A prescreening test may be offered but is not a prerequisite for receiving hepatitis B vaccination. If the employee selects the testing, it shall also be offered at no charge to the employee. Each employee has the right to refuse vaccination while reserving the right to obtain it at a later date (at no charge to the employee) in the event the employee or student changes his or her mind or if an exposure incident occurs.

Post-Exposure Follow-up (Blood or OPIM)

Vaccination is also offered as a post-exposure follow-up for all faculty members or students with an occupational exposure incident (skin, eye, mucous membrane, or percutaneous contact with blood or other potentially infectious materials). Documentation of the vaccination program (using HBV immunization record form, or a declination statement form found in the section entitled "Forms and Letters") will be filed in each individual faculty member's personnel record as well as a master vaccination file maintained in administrative records of the hospital. Documentation of student vaccination is to be maintained in the student's record file at the school overseeing the student's educational progress and in a master training file maintained by the In-Service Training Office. Any faculty member or student declining vaccination should have been counseled on the benefits and safety of the vaccine and shall have signed a statement as specified in the section of the Infection Control Manual pertaining to Hepatitis B Vaccine Declination (Mandatory).

Note that these requirements are written from the perspective of both an educational institution as well as a health care facility. Often a dual role exists when a student is performing clinical work under medical supervision in an affiliated medical facility. It is usually most advantageous to seek documentation and treatment at the facility where the incident occurs. If the faculty member or student has a percutaneous (needlestick, cut, or puncture) or mucous membrane (splash to the eye, nasal mucosa, or mouth) exposure to body fluids (blood or other infectious materials) or has a cutaneous exposure when the individual has chapped or abraded skin or otherwise non-intact skin, it shall be reported as an exposure incident to the faculty member and/or the institute's Infection Control Coordinator.

Following the report of an occupational exposure incident, the faculty member or student should complete an accident/incident report. The employee will be offered a confidential medical evaluation and follow-up, which will include the following information:

1. Documentation of the route(s) of exposure, previous HBV and HIV antibody status of the patient(s) (if known), and the circumstances under which the exposure occurred.

2. If possible and source patient (who is infected) can be determined and grants permission, collection and testing of patient's blood to determine presence of HIV and/or HBV infections by a procedure to determine either antibodies or antigens shall be done.

3. If the patient refuses permission to submit a specimen and to be tested, the employer will determine and note that the legal requirement for consent cannot be obtained. If the source individual's consent is not required by law, his blood, if available, will be tested and documentation of the results provided to the exposed employee, as well as being filed. When the source patient has a previous positive test or tests, a new determination is not needed.

4. Results of the source individual's testing shall be made available to the faculty member or student, and the faculty member or student shall be informed of the applicable laws and regulations concerning disclosure of the identity and infectious status of the source individual. It is rare that the identity of the patient will be revealed.

5. Blood of the exposed faculty member or student shall be collected as soon as resources are available and tested after consent is obtained. All procedures relating to testing of the exposed person's blood sample will be documented.

6. If the faculty member or student allows baseline blood collections but does not give consent at that time to have HIV or HBV serologic testing, the sample should be adequately preserved for at least ninety days. Within the ninety days of the exposure incident, the faculty member or student may elect to have the baseline sample tested, and appropriate testing shall be done as soon as feasible.

7. The educational facility or health care institution will ensure that the health care professional responsible for the faculty member or student's hepatitis B vaccination is provided a copy of appropriate regulations for occupational exposure to bloodborne pathogens as determined by the institution. Documentation of the treatment or counseling by the professional will be accomplished by making the worker or student aware of his or her vulnerability to the organisms.

8. The educational facility or health care institution will provide to the health care professional evaluating an employee after an exposure incident the following information:

    A. Copies of appropriate institutional and legal regulations for occupational exposure to blood and airborne pathogens indicating the instruction and training of the student or the medical worker, and records of physical examinations and immunizations will be provided upon request.

    B. A written description of the faculty member or student's job-related duties and his or her activities leading up to the incident will be provided.

    C. Route(s) of exposure and circumstances under which the exposure occurred will be documented. Steps will be taken to prevent repeat occurrences if an error of omission or commission has occurred. The Infection Control Committee and other administrative entities as required will be provided details of the exposure.

    D. The results of the source individual's blood testing, **if performed**, will be provided. There is no requirement to furnish the name of the source individual.

    E. All medical records relevant to the appropriate treatment of the employee including vaccination status, which are the institute's responsibility to maintain, will be verified. If immediate treatment is indicated, such will be expeditiously performed, either by the facility where the incident occurred, or at the exposed person's request, by his or her personal physician.

    F. The institute shall obtain and provide the employee suffering the exposure with a copy of the consulting health care professional's written opinion within fifteen days of the completion of the evaluation. The health care professional's written opinion for hepatitis B vaccination shall be limited to whether the vaccination is indicated and if the faculty member or student received such vaccination.

Documentation of Post-Exposure Follow-Up

The health care professional's written opinion for post-exposure evaluation and follow-up shall contain the following information:

1. That the faculty member, medical worker, or student has been informed of the results of the evaluation, and pertinent information regarding testing procedures given

2. That the faculty member, medical worker, or student has been told about any medical conditions resulting from the exposure to blood or other infectious materials and if further evaluation or treatment is required

3. Findings of a personal nature and either related to or unrelated to the exposure incident should remain confidential and will not be included in the written report

4. Medical records required by the standard governing occupational exposure should be maintained as outlined in a document normally entitled the "Bloodborne Pathogens Standard"

5. Student medical records shall be retained for a period of one year after graduation, completion, termination, or leaving the educational institute. Faculty medical records shall be retained for

a period of thirty years plus the length of employment, the same as those for medical workers of the medical facility

AIRBORNE PATHOGENS – TUBERCULOSIS

Purpose of policy

This document is an outline of post-exposure reporting procedures for follow-up after a documented exposure incident. This material is excerpted from CDC's "Guidelines for Preventing the Transmission of Tuberculosis in Health Care Settings" and is from a 1994 document. OSHA periodically updates these guidelines and makes them available for public consumption.

Compliance With Official Tuberculosis Guidelines

Tuberculosis is a respiratory infection that has experienced an resurgence in prevalence over the past few years. The *Mycobacterium tuberculosis* organism causes the infection and is an organism for which humans as well as cattle are reservoirs. Birds may also carry a species of the *Mycobacterium* organism. Beginning many years ago, governmental inspections of cattle herds have been used in an effort to stem the tide of TB infections. Thousands of new cases of TB are reported in the United States each year. Hundreds of health care workers have been infected or exposed to the tuberculosis organism. Resistant organisms are increasing, and in 1993 OSHA issued guidelines utilizing the 1990 CDC guidelines for treating both suspected or confirmed cases of TB. Since the early 1980s, more and more cases of TB in conjunction with HIV infections due to an immunocompromized (low level of immunity) condition are occurring, and this has impacted the development of new and more effective protocols for treatment.

The health care worker should learn to recognize the symptoms of tuberculosis. Situations exist where there is the potential for exposure to TB by health care workers, but those with the greatest risk of contracting and transmitting TB are those with suppressed immune systems. A number of diseases may cause suppressed immune systems, including those with autoimmune diseases, such as lupus and rheumatoid arthritis, among a host of others. People who are HIV positive and elderly patients are other prime targets for tuberculosis infections, as well as residents of long-term care facilities. Anyone who is in close contact with groups of closely congregated people, particularly in institutional settings, is at risk for developing tuberculosis.

Symptoms of Tuberculosis

Patients with TB may have any or all of the following signs and symptoms: productive cough (coughing up mucus or other fluid) and/or coughing up blood, weight loss accompanied with loss of appetite, lethargy and weakness, night sweats, and fever. A good rule of thumb is that anyone with a suspicious productive cough may be infected with the tuberculosis organism. With an airborne disease such as TB, the medical worker may not realize that the patient he cared for was infected. Diagnosis requires a skin test, which also determines previous exposure even if the disease was not contracted, and a chest X-ray to reveal lesions that may have healed as fibrosis or calcification of the lungs.

Approved HEPA Mask Fit Test

When a medical care worker is in a situation where the potential exists for exposure to exhaled air of a person with suspected or confirmed TB, OSHA requires that the worker be provided a National

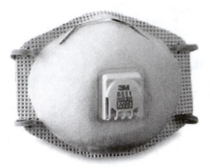

3M Particulate Respirator, N95 HEPA Mask

Institute of Occupational Safety and Health (NIOSH) approved N-95 or high efficiency particulate air (HEPA) respirator. The workers are required to wear an N-95 or HEPA respirator when performing procedures for a patient who is in isolation due to possible respiratory infection with the tuberculosis organism. Medical workers must be fit tested for these masks by the use of a hood and nebulized saccharine, or by one of the newer automated systems designed to efficiently test workers for proper fit.

Preventive Measures against Contracting TB

Anyone working in high-risk areas or with high-risk people is susceptible to contracting the organism causing TB. Correctional institutions, shelters for the homeless, long-term care facilities for the elderly, and drug treatment centers often harbor people with TB on a higher rate of prevalence than the general population. A steady flow of fresh air is essential in avoiding contracting of TB, as well as taking precautions when working with all patients. In our country's medical history, TB sanitariums were built usually on mountains where a steady flow of supposedly clean air was available, prior to the development of definitive antibiotics to combat the disease. Workers should take all recommended infection control precautions, including hand washing and the use of personal protective equipment. People who have been diagnosed with tuberculosis and who need treatment usually require that employees treating them observe respiratory precautions (the patient and the health care worker may both wear masks). Employing of barrier devices, such as pocket masks or bag-valve masks for rescue breathing or resuscitation, is important. Properly dispose of contaminated equipment and materials, and decontaminate all surfaces, clothing, and equipment as outlined in the Infection Control Manual should be observed. These guidelines are to be in effect until OSHA acts on the specific *Occupational Exposure to Tuberculosis*; Proposed Rule 29 CFR 1910.1035. Changes will be required at that time. As earlier outlined, the specific requirements for HEPA respirators/PPE and training and education were addressed in these guidelines.

1. **Definitions**

    A. Workplaces with Inherent Exposure Potential to TB Disease

        a. Health care facilities

        b. Corrections facilities

        c. Homeless shelters

        d. Long-term health facilities

        e. Drug treatment centers

        f. Ambulances/EMS vehicles

B. Potential for Exposure

Exposure potential is defined as an exposure to the exhaled or expired air of a person with suspected or confirmed TB disease. Exposure to a high-hazard procedure or an individual with either suspected or confirmed TB disease increases the potential for contracting TB. Coughing and sneezing patients who have the potential to generate potentially infectious airborne respiratory secretions – through procedures such as aerosolized medication treatment, bronchoscopy, sputum induction, endotracheal intubation, suctioning procedures, and autopsies – increase the risk of transmitting the organisms.

Workers in Health Care Facilities at Risk for Occupational Exposure

In 1990, the CDC gave the following description of health care workers at great risk for occupational exposure to the TB organism: "all persons with direct or indirect patient care or client responsibilities. Examples include, but are not limited to: physicians, nurses, assistants, technicians, laboratory workers, morgue workers, EMS personnel, corrections personnel, students, [instructors]."[2]

Allied health students, medical workers, and allied health faculty members in program or course areas previously addressed are to be considered as Category I (high risk) for the occupational exposure to TB disease and are to be considered as in a covered occupational area.

Testing and Surveillance Procedures

1. All allied health students and faculty members in a covered occupational area should have a tuberculin skin test at the time of employment or prior to assignment to clinical or work site area. This applies unless a previously positive reaction can be documented or after completion of appropriate preventative therapy or adequate therapy can be documented.

2. Any covered faculty member or student with a history of Bacillus of Calmette and Guerin (BCG) vaccination should also have the tuberculin skin test as in #1.

3. Any covered faculty member or student who exhibits a first time positive reaction to the skin test must be cleared by a physician prior to further contact with students or patients/clients. These students may be placed in alternate training positions until clearance is received from a health care professional, such as a physician. Clearance must be documented in writing. Personnel with documented, active TB disease should also be offered HIV antibody testing, as often the two occur simultaneously.

4. Covered faculty members and students with a **documented** history of a positive skin test (PPD) or adequate treatment of latent infection or active diseases are to be exempt from further testing unless signs and symptoms of TB disease develop. Periodic chest X-rays are performed in most cases in order to determine if the employee has become active for the disease.

5. Initial and follow-up tuberculin skin tests should be administered and interpreted according to current CDC guidelines. Students and employees who work in high-risk areas are encouraged to be tested twice per year.

6. Periodic retesting of PPD-negative faculty members and students should be conducted to identify people whose skin tests convert to a positive status. The schedule for retesting is

---

[2] Centers for Disease Control, *Guidelines for Preventing the Transmission of Tuberculosis in Health Care Settings with Special Focus on HIV-Related Issues*, 1990.

risk-dependent, but for people performing high-risk procedures, retesting is done every six months. In general, other covered faculty and students should be tested annually.

7. Tuberculin skin tests (initial and periodic) shall be offered to covered faculty members at no cost to the employee. Students are responsible for the cost of their skin tests, with the initial test being required before the student is able to have any contact with patients.

Post-Exposure Follow-Up Procedures

1. An accidental exposure is defined as coming into contact with a patient exhibiting symptoms of tuberculosis or with items with which the patient came in contact and later tested positive for tuberculosis. An exposure may occur in any clinical facility or work site where patients or clients are under treatment. The high-risk areas for exposure potential were listed previously in this section.

2. Immediately upon identification of an accidental exposure involving a covered faculty member or student, the clinical instructor or instructor's supervisor shall be notified as well as the technical institute infection control coordinator and the authorized contact person at the clinical or work site.

3. The exposure incident shall be documented in writing with copies given to the authorized person at the clinical or work site, instructor, and institute's infection control coordinator. Incident forms for accidental exposure are available at the clinical site as well as the educational institution. Initial documentation is to be prepared the day of the incident and must be filed with the Infection Control Coordinator within 24 hours of the incident.

4. The affected instructor or student is to be counseled immediately after the exposure incident and referred to their family physician or health care clinic for follow-up and therapy if necessary. Baseline testing should be performed as soon as possible after the incident. The educational institution or medical facility is responsible for the cost of a post-incident follow-up for covered faculty members, medical workers, and students.

5. Any faculty member or student in a covered occupational area with a positive skin test upon repeat testing or after exposure will be required to be clinically evaluated for active tuberculosis. If active TB is diagnosed, appropriate therapy should be initiated according to CDC guidelines or established medical protocol.

6. Any instructor or student in a covered occupational area with a positive skin test upon repeat testing or exhibiting signs and symptoms of TB is not to have patient or client contact until such time as he or she is cleared by a physician after further testing and/or by initiation of appropriate therapy.

7. If an instructor or student in a covered occupational area is found to have clinical TB, all students or instructors within the immediate class or course shall be advised to have a PPD skin test to be cleared for further participation in the class or course. Any person exposed, as above, with a documented history of positive PPD skin tests may be recommended for a prophylactic chest X-ray.

8. Appropriate treatment protocols shall be followed per CDC guidelines and a timetable for repeat testing should be established.

Personal Protective Equipment (PPE) – HEPA or Approved N-95 Respirators

1. Personal protective equipment (PPE) shall be utilized as follows:

   A. Known or highly suspicious patient or client cases

a. HEPA or high efficiency particulate air respirators or NIOSH-approved N-95 respirators are to be provided and used by faculty and students when entering a patient's hospital room when the patient is positive for or is highly suspected of having active TB disease.

b. HEPA (filter) respirator fit testing for each faculty member or student must be conducted to insure a reliable fit and face seal prior to use of the equipment. This is required only if the HEPA respirator is to be used in lieu of other types of respirators.

c. The user should fit-check the respirator seal each time he or she uses the respirator, and prior to entering a patient's or client's room.

d. Disposable or reusable HEPA or other N.I.O.S.H. approved respirators may be used. Reusable respirators must be stored to maintain the form-fit following careful cleaning after patient contact.

B. A covered faculty member and student with a respiratory disease or other disorder that would cause respiratory impairment/decreased pulmonary function may be required to be certified as capable of using an approved respirator by a physician. This certification must be in writing. The student may also be assigned patients in another area or alternate duties if he is unable to wear an appropriate mask or respirator.

C. A covered faculty member or student with a certified respiratory impairment that would prevent the use of a HEPA or other respirator should not be assigned to a known TB case or to a highly suspicious patient/client. An alternative assignment should be made.

D. Personal protective equipment is to be provided by the educational facility or the clinical site for demonstration and practice lab activities. The clinical or work site may provide PPE for faculty members and students during rotations. If the PPE is not provided for actual patient/client contact, it is the responsibility of the institute to provide it at no cost to faculty members and to students at their cost.

E. In the instances where a patient has been placed in reverse isolation to protect the patient from visitors and workers who might infect him, and for those who might transmit organisms to workers and visitors, protective equipment appropriate for the type of infection the patient has contracted will be provided by the facility. Special rooms are usually provided in health care facilities for patients who must be protected from visitors in the case of reverse isolation, or to protect the health care workers and visitors from exposure. These rooms are actually two rooms, one being at the entrance for donning personal protective equipment and to remove the equipment and dispose of it upon leaving the main room.

BLOOD AND AIRBORNE PATHOGENS – TUBERCULOSIS

Education and Training

1. Each medical worker, allied health care student, or faculty member will receive education and training regarding tuberculosis as part of the blood and airborne pathogens module during initial orientation.

   A. Annual refresher training will be provided appropriate to the tasks performed in the job description and again if job requirements change.

B. The educational institute infection control coordinator will be responsible for monitoring and evaluating effectiveness of this education and training process.

Documentation of Training

1. Training will be documented as specified in the institute's Exposure Control Plan.

   A. The following topics are to be included but are not limited to:

      a. The Risk of TB in HIV or AIDS Patients or Other Immunosuppressive Disease

      b. Mode(s) of Transmission

      c. Signs and Symptoms of Tuberculosis

      d. Diagnosis and Assessment of TB

      e. The Purpose of PPD Testing and Significance of a Positive Result

      f. Pathogenesis

      g. Principles/Practices that Reduce Risk of Exposure/Transmission

      h. The Potential for Occupational Exposure and Transmission of TB

      i. Review of Written Policies and Procedures

      j. Principles of Drug Therapy for Active Tuberculosis

      k. Process and Steps in the Medical Evaluation of a PPD Test Conversion or Following Signs and Symptoms of TB Disease (Faculty and Students)

      l. Confidentiality Secondary to Assessment and Treatment of Faculty or Student Who Develops TB Disease.

      m. Principles of Preventive Therapy in Latent Infection

      n. The Possibility of Reinfection in People with a Positive PPD

      o. Latent Infection Stage Compared to the Active Disease State

      p. The Institute's Policy on Voluntary Duty Reassignment Options for Immunocompromised Faculty Members and Students in Covered Occupational Areas

Causative Organism

The causative organism is a bacillus (rod-shaped bacterium), *Mycobacterium tuberculosis*.

Symptoms

Fatigue, fever, and weight loss may occur early in the illness. A productive cough with chest pain, hemoptysis (spitting up blood), and hoarseness may be prominent during later stages of the disease.

Occurrence

Occurrence is worldwide, but widespread in underdeveloped countries and crowded facilities.

Reservoir

The organisms reside in humans and sometimes cattle and birds. Some varieties of the organism previously thought to be harmless to man have been found to cause pulmonary disease resembling tuberculosis with the *Mycobacterium tuberculosis* species.

Route of Transmission

Transmission is through airborne droplet from sputum of people with cases of infectious tuberculosis. Close exposure for long periods of time to an infectious case may lead to infection of contacts.

Incubation Period

About four to twelve weeks may elapse between infection and appearance of a positive tuberculin skin test or lesions in the lungs. The length of time before signs and clinical findings are present may depend on the immune status of the victim. Those with HIV infections and other immunocompromising conditions may cause a weak or negative reaction to the PPD skin test.

Period of Communicability

As long as the infectious tubercle bacilli are isolated from the sputum, the infected person is contagious. In the past, before effective antimicrobial agents were developed, the only treatment was for isolating the patients and affording them adequate clean, fresh air. Many TB sanitariums were therefore located in isolated mountainous regions.

Prevention and Control Measures

1. Hand washing, filtered ventilation, and good housekeeping practices should be maintained according to policies prescribed by the Infection Control Committee.

2. Wear a mask when providing care to patients that may cough or sneeze in the face of those caregivers providing service.

3. Regularly scheduled tuberculin skin tests will monitor the possibility of unknown exposure. OSHA guidelines require medical workers to have TB skin tests twice per year.

4. Sanitize facilities where groups of people are gathered for extended periods of time.

STUDY GUIDE

Bloodborne and Airborne Pathogens

1. INTRODUCTION

A. Give the potential allied health care provider information on specific bloodborne and airborne diseases to allow an informed decision on:

1. personal protection

2. need for immunization

B. Give information on how to handle exposure incidents.
   As allied health care providers, we may be faced with many unknown situations that could possibly put ourselves, our families, and our patients in danger. This session

will introduce for thought the transmission of diseases that are or could be lethal to us as health care providers. The goal of this section is to inform you as to decisions you will have to make on personal protection and immunization available for you to employ.

2. TERMINOLOGY

Discuss the following terms:

DISEASES	TRANSMISSION
HIV /AIDS	Source
Hepatitis	Host
Tuberculosis	Contact transmission
Meningitis	Airborne, direct, and indirect transmission
Mumps	Droplet transmission
Measles	Blood and body fluids
Chickenpox	Contamination
Herpes	Source

PRECAUTIONS

Universal Precautions

Personal protective equipment (PPE)

Disinfection

Sterilization

Decontamination

Immunization

3. ROUTES OF TRANSMISSION

Definition: Route by which microorganisms are transmitted. There are four main routes of transmission:

A. CONTACT

   a. Direct contact – direct physical transfer between susceptible host and an infected or colonized person

   b. Indirect contact – personal contact of the susceptible host with a contaminated object

   c. Droplet contact – spread of disease-causing organisms by the spraying of droplets from the mouth

   d. Autogenous infection - self-inoculation of a disease-causing organism

B. COMMON SOURCE TRANSMISSION – applies to disease transmitted through contaminated items: (for example, food, water, drugs, blood, dirty equipment)

C. AIRBORNE TRANSMISSION – occurs by dissemination of either droplet nuclei or dust particles in the air containing the infectious agent

D. VECTORBORNE TRANSMISSION – disease transmission via contact with an infected vector (for example, tick or mosquitoes)

4. PRE-EXPOSURE PRECAUTIONS

The following are considerations to reduce the contamination by, or the contraction of, infectious diseases.

A. EQUIPMENT

    a. Hand washing

    b. Disposable gloves

    c. Disposable surgical face masks

    d. Goggles

    e. Special clothing

B. IMMUNIZATION AND VACCINATION

    a. PPD (tuberculin skin test)

    b. Hepatitis B vaccine

    c. MMR (Mumps, Measles, Rubella)

    d. Tetanus

    e. Influenza vaccine

    f. Polio vaccine

C. MULTIPLE PATIENT SITUATIONS

    a. Responsibility to other patients from possible exposure through your transmission from another source (e.g., gloves and equipment)

    b. Considerations for the elderly and very young
      (a) possible immunodepressed

D. GUIDELINES FOR INFECTIOUS EXPOSURE

Guidelines should be in place to follow for precautions to possible exposure to infectious diseases for the following situations:

    a. Classroom and Lab Exercises

    b. Clinical Rotations

The following precautions should be stressed:

    a. Universal Precautions

    b. Standard precautions

    c. Respiratory precautions

5. POST-EXPOSURE INCIDENT

A. What is an exposure incident?

B. Who to contact, and when?

a. Clinical preceptor

b. Instructor

C. What paperwork do I fill out?

D. What lab work should be done?

6. DISPOSAL AND DECONTAMINATION

A. Disposal equipment

a. How to dispose of property

b. How to mark containers

B. Non-disposable equipment

a. How and when to clean

b. How and when disinfecting or sterilization is needed

C. Disposal of needles and sharps

a. Always use caution

b. Do not recap needles

c. Do not bend or break needles

d. Use puncture-resistant containers

7. SPECIFIC INFORMATION

A. Hepatitis B (HBV)

B. HIV/AIDS

C. Tuberculosis

8. DEMONSTRATION AND LAB EXERCISE

A. Gloves

B. Eye protection

C. Disposable mask

D. Protective clothing

E. Disposal of needles and sharps

9. SUMMARY

A. Different types of blood and air-transmitted diseases

B. Modes of transmission

C. Protective equipment

D. Immunization/Vaccination

STUDY QUESTIONS

Bloodborne and Airborne Pathogens

1. **Matching**

Wearing of gloves is an example of:	Personal protection
Using hand washing facility	Immunization
HBIG	Engineered controls

Multiple Choice

2. Universal Precautions are used with:

   a. Patients known to be infected

   b. Patients known to have hepatitis

   c. All patients who come for treatment

   d. Only patients who look sick

3. An example of an exposure incident is when:

   a. A patient exposes himself or herself

   b. Patients known to have hepatitis come into the medical office

   c. A patient coughs violently in the waiting room of the medical clinic

   d. A medical assistant is splattered by blood

4. The MOST EFFECTIVE and SPECIFIC means for avoiding a disease is:

   a. Washing hands

   b. Wearing gloves

   c. Being immunized against organism

   d. Avoiding people

5. HIV/AIDS is:

   a. Caused by a virus

   b. A blood borne pathogen

   c. Caused by a bacterium

   d. All of the above

   e. a and b

6. To prevent transmission of diseases, reusable medical instruments should be:

   a. Disinfected

   b. Sterilized

   c. Isolated

   d. Immunized

7. Tuberculosis is usually spread by:

   a. Vectors

   b. Food, drugs, water

   c. Sputum/mucous

   d. Blood

8. Hepatitis B is usually spread by:

   a. Vectors

   b. Food, drugs, water

   c. Sputum

   d. Blood

9. If used properly, which of the following destroys ALL organisms?

   a. Decontamination   b. Personal protective equipment

   c. Disinfection   d. Sterilization

10. Which of the following is NOT one of the main routes for transmission of organisms?

   a. Direct contact – direct physical transfer between host and infected or colonized person

   b. Droplet contact – spread of disease-causing organisms by spraying of droplets from mouth

   c. Autogenous infection – self-inoculation of a disease-causing organism

   d. Immunosuppressed person – more easily transmits diseases to others

   e. Indirect contact – personal contact of the susceptible host with a contaminated object

11. Vectorborne diseases in the United States are transmitted chiefly by:

   a. Birds   b. Food

   c. Fish   d. Ticks

12. Pre-exposure precautions refer to:

   a. Hand washing   b. Sterilization

   c. Decontamination   d. Avoiding sick people

13. The following are considerations to reduce the contamination by, or the contraction of infectious diseases.

   a. Hand washing   b. Disposable gloves

   c. Disposable surgical face masks   d. Special clothing

   e. All of the above

14. Immunizations and vaccinations are available for all of the following except:

   a. HIV   b. hepatitis B

   c. MMR (Mumps, Measles, Rubella)   d. Polio

   e. All of the above

15. Which group(s) is(are) more susceptible to "catching" infections?

   a. Elderly patients   b. Very young patients

   c. Immunosuppressed   d. All of the above

   e. a and c

16. Respiratory precautions would most likely be used for:

   a. Meningitis   b. Tuberculosis

   c. HIV   d. hepatitis B

17. Disinfection or sterilization is needed for which of the following?

   a. Disposal of needles and sharps   b. Face masks

   c. Metal surgical instruments   d. Puncture-resistant containers

18. The most effective and practical way of preventing contraction of diseases in everyday life would include:

    a. Protective clothing

    b. Gloves

    c. Hand washing after visiting the restroom

    d. Avoiding contact with people

19. Most serious infectious diseases are contracted through contact with:

    a. Semen and vaginal secretions

    b. Blood

    c. Workplace practices

    d. Food and water

    e. a and b

20. Which of the following would NOT be a way of avoiding the contractions of an infectious illness?

    a. Personal protective equipment

    b. Reporting all exposures

    c. Work practice controls

    d. Universal Precautions

ANSWER KEY TO STUDY QUESTIONS

1. **Matching**

Wearing of gloves is an example of:	Personal protection
Using hand washing facility	Engineered controls
HBIG	Immunization

2. c.   All patients who come for treatment

3. d.   A medical assistant is splattered by blood

4. c.   Being immunized against an organism

5. e.   a and b

6. b.   Sterilized

7. c.   Sputum/mucous

8. d.   Blood

9. d.   Sterilization

10. d.   Immunosuppressed person – more easily transmits diseases to others

11. d.   Ticks

12. a.   Hand washing

13. e.   All of the above

14. a.   HIV

15. d.   All of the above

16. b.   Tuberculosis

17. c.   Metal surgical instruments

18. c.   Hand washing after visiting the restroom

19. e.   a and b

20. b.   Reporting all exposures

REGULATORY AGENCIES GOVERNING HEALTH CARE

Centers for Disease Control and Prevention (CDC)

The Centers for Disease Control and Prevention (CDC) operates under the auspices of the Department of Health and Human Services. It is recognized internationally as the lead federal agency for protecting the health and safety of people at home and abroad, providing credible information to enhance health decisions and promoting health through strong partnerships. CDC serves as the national focus for developing and applying disease prevention and control, environmental health, and health promotion and education activities designed to improve the health of the people of the United States. CDC is located in Atlanta, Georgia. Its stated mission for the twenty-first century is: ***Healthy People in a Healthy World – Through Prevention.***

Through decisive courses of action, collecting the right information, and working closely with other health and community organizations, CDC has been putting the latest health research and development to practical use in attacking important health problems since 1946. CDC's 8,500 employees operate from offices throughout the country and play a key role in protecting the public from the most widespread, deadly, and mysterious threats against our health today and tomorrow. CDC's mission is broad based, and correlates its efforts with a multitude of state and federal agencies to promote health and quality of life by preventing and controlling disease, injury, and disability. CDC seeks to accomplish its mission by working with partners throughout the nation and world to determine threats that might enter the United States. Therefore, approximately 120 members of the CDC team are assigned to overseas duties in at least 45 countries. As a part of their efforts to prevent disease, it is necessary that the agency monitor health and detect and investigate health problems here and abroad. So CDC conducts research to aid in prevention, to develop and implement safe and effective health policies, and to provide guidance and training to personnel involved in patient care.

Infectious diseases with the capability of disrupting lives throughout the world must be investigated and treatment as well as preventive protocols developed. With global travel, there are no safe havens where "new" diseases cannot strike. By assisting state and local health departments, CDC works to protect the public every day by identifying the sources for certain infectious organisms. One recent example of this is the effort to identify the sources of various strains of anthrax that were mailed to governmental officials and others. Through advanced technology, CDC has the capability to identify the organism as well as to compare it with known strains in an effort to apprehend the purveyor of the organisms.

Practical application of technology developed at CDC is provided to governmental agencies in the United States as well as around the world. CDC even becomes involved in such mundane areas as pollution and congestion in the air we breathe; contamination in our water supply; and unsafe conditions in our daily workplaces. CDC works with national, state, and local organizations as well as others to help protect communities from dangerous environmental exposures, including chemicals, biohazardous agents, radiation, and pollution, to name a few. CDC utilizes many public outlets, including publications and the media, to spread its message that everyone is responsible for the health of self and community.

Future Challenges That CDC Faces

Improving People's Health by Putting Science into Action

Preventing Violence and Unintentional Injury

Meeting the Health and Safety Needs of a Changing Workforce

Utilizing New Technologies to Provide Credible Health Information

Protecting Individuals against Emerging Infectious Diseases including Bioterrorism

Eliminating Racial/Ethnic Health Disparities

Fostering Safe and Healthy Environments

Working with Partners to Improve Global Health

The Occupational Safety and Health Administration

The Occupational Safety and Health Administration (OSHA) has a mission to save lives, prevent injuries, and protect the health of America's workers in a variety of settings. To do this, federal and state governments must work in partnership with the more than 100 million working men and women and their 6.5 million employers who are covered by the Occupational Safety and Health Act of 1970.

OSHA works with state agencies with a total of approximately 2,100 inspectors, including several hundred more support staff to field complaints, formulate standards, and provide expert advice in the writing of these standards. There are more than 200 offices spread across the United States. This staff investigates incidents in which accident(s) or death(s) have occurred. Almost every worker in the United States falls under OSHA's jurisdiction (with some exceptions, such as miners, transportation workers, many public employees, and the self-employed). Other users and recipients of OSHA services include: occupational safety and health professionals, the academic community, lawyers, journalists, and personnel of other government entities.

OSHA develops improved quality of efforts and determines violations and risks through surveying of both employers and employees. Workplace inspections are one of OSHA's major activities, and because voluntary efforts to improve working conditions ultimately depend on strong enforcement, surveys are based on the inspection process. OSHA's new standards for public service are based on what is learned from these surveys, from meetings with employee and employer groups, and from focus group discussions with workers from many plants and industries across the country.

Environmental Protection Agency

The Environmental Protection Agency (EPA) compiles and continuously modifies a strategic plan to cover all of the environmental factors that impact upon the health of the citizens. This plan is a broad-based plan for taking the EPA into the twenty-first century and achieving critical public health and environmental protections for the American people. The EPA also provides access to materials the agency uses for reference information about the definition, origin, source, and location of environmental data. This office touches upon virtually all aspects of life, so the EPA impacts the medical field in almost every area of operation. Since the EPA is involved with bioterrorism, including both chemical and biological threats, medical facilities are often called upon to test patients for many types of hazardous materials. This also includes biochemical testing of the effects of these materials and organisms on victims of disasters. Areas of expertise available to communities for responding to health threats include:

Chemical Emergency Preparedness and Prevention Office

Chemical Testing and Information Gathering

Community-Based Environmental Protection

Emergency Response Notification System (ERNS) – database contains information on notifications of oil and hazardous substance releases that have occurred throughout the United States

Federal Emergency Management Agency

Federal Emergency Management Agency (FEMA) is part of the Department of Homeland Security's Emergency Preparedness and Response Directorate. This federal agency has almost 3,000 full-time employees. They work at FEMA headquarters in Washington, D.C., and at regional and area offices across the country, the Mount Weather Emergency Operations Center, and the National Emergency Training Center in Emmitsburg, Maryland. FEMA also has nearly 4,000 standby disaster-assistance employees who are available for deployment after disasters, both natural and man-made. FEMA often works hand-in-hand with other private and public organizations that are part of the nation's emergency management system. These partners include state and local emergency management agencies, twenty-seven federal agencies and American Red Cross. This information was excerpted from FEMA's website (http://www.fema.gov).

The Clinical Laboratory Improvement Act (CLIA)

Since the medical laboratory is the single most-used department of the medical facility for diagnosing disease, the most extensive regulative legislation has been aimed at the medical laboratory over particularly the past few decades. The Clinical Laboratory Improvement Act of 1988 (CLIA '88) has drastically altered the management and use of the physician's office laboratory as well as private and hospital-based laboratories. CLIA '88 was not the first effort of the federal government into the regulation of the clinical laboratory. The Clinical Laboratory Improvement Act of 1967 (CLIA '67) regulated laboratories that engaged in interstate commerce. This law pertained to approximately 12,000 mainly commercial and hospital laboratories. Except for a few states, laboratories located in physicians' offices or other small health care facilities were largely unregulated prior to CLIA'88. Technology changes in medical laboratory diagnostic testing will require newer versions of the Clinical Laboratory Improvement Act.

Federal Drug Administration (FDA)

America has been drafting legislation designed to protect consumers from unsafe food and medicine since 1785, when the colony of Massachusetts passed a "general food adulteration" law. The first law in the United States against toxic medications and preparations was passed in 1927 and was titled the Caustic Poison Act. During this same year, Congress created the Food, Drug, and Insecticide Administration and the name was changed in 1930 to the Food and Drug Administration (FDA). The FDA has regulatory authority over all food and drug processing and distribution. It has a great deal of clout in providing for our health and exceeds that of other consumer protection agencies. The FDA has the authority to back its findings with regulatory action, even to take products off the market. As an example, in 1959, the FDA recalled the entire U.S. cranberry crop to test it for traces of a weed killer that had caused cancer in laboratory animals just three weeks before Thanksgiving. Recently, the FDA stated that it would be the agency to regulate human cloning in America, among other ethical issues.

The FDA has a great impact on medical practice, as it exercises considerable authority through the enforcement of the Federal Food, Drug, and Cosmetic Act and several other related laws, which include medical devices. FDA's most visible regulatory process by which it can force compliance is through recalling a product. With sufficient cause, the FDA can order the recall of any food, drug, medical device, biological product (like blood), or cosmetic sold for use by humans or animals. "Medical devices" can include anything from an X-ray machine to computer software used in practice of medical procedures. In addition, manufacturers themselves often recall products when they become aware that their production procedures were not in compliance with FDA regulations. Such "voluntary" recalls must be reported to the FDA and can trigger site inspections or even stronger enforcement measures. All recalls are reported on the FDA website. Every year, about 3,000 products are recalled and another 30,000 products being imported into America are held or seized due to non-compliance with FDA requirements. (For more information on this, see the FDA website http://www.fda.gov.)

FDA Enforcement Powers - Legal Sanctions

Under extreme conditions of non-compliance, FDA can go to court and obtain severe legal sanctions against manufacturers. A company can be forced to stop making a product and have existing stock seized and destroyed. In the worst cases, a business can be completely shut down and criminal penalties – including prison terms – can be sought.

State Departments With Overview of Medical Training Programs

While many federal programs mandate certain standards for safety and protection of the public, it is the domain of each individual state in most cases to set standards for educational programs and to certify graduates of the programs as being competent in his or her chosen field. These programs are established throughout the states to ensure economic growth by providing for educational needs. Georgia, for example, has established a Department of Technical and Adult Education that provides for training in most allied health fields. Other states have similar departments that also perform the vital role of ensuring a continued supply of health care workers to protect the health of its citizens. Curriculum is designed to ensure minimum competency as well as to provide for the safe and effective training of an adequate number of health care workers. Most states set curriculum standards and guidelines that are followed in the colleges and universities in their education and training of these professionals. In a number of states, this training and education begins during high school for those expressing an interest in the health care professions.

FIRST AID

OBJECTIVES

Upon completion of this unit of instruction, the student will be able to:

  a. Understand responses appropriate for basic emergency situation

  b. Demonstrate knowledge related to the need for prompt and effective action

  c. List types of consent for medical treatment and related conditions of understanding

  d. Describe victim assessment relative to condition of patient

  e. Understand proper communication with emergency services

  f. Describe major types of shock and the proper response

  g. Discuss types of bleeding and the appropriate response to each

  h. Relate significance of human and animal bites, with possible infection

  i. Demonstrate an understanding of skull and head injuries, and related symptoms

  j. Discuss assessment and treatment of injures to eyes and face

  k. Differentiate between levels of nosebleed, and proper treatment

  l. List basic dental and mouth injuries, and appropriate precautions and responses to each

  m. Indicate an understand of thoracic injuries and danger of interruption of effective breathing

  n. Provide the steps in performing assessment of abdominopelvic injuries

  o. Give precautions relative to treating blisters and boils of the skin

  p. Discuss poisoning by contact and ingestion, and symptoms of poisoning

  q. Compare symptoms of bites and stings by various insects and arachnids

  r. Identify poisonous species of snakes in the US, and emergency treatment

  s. Relate an understanding of fire-related injuries and the assessments for determining severity of a burn

  t. List degrees of, and signs and symptoms of, cold-related injuries

u. Identify levels of heat-related injuries, and rapid treatment required to lessen worsening conditions

v. Provide relief for various levels of musculoskeletal injuries

SECTION OUTLINE

Basic First Aid

Duty to Act

Refusal of Treatment

Victim Assessment

Contacting Medical Assistance

Communications Guidelines

Major Types of Emergencies

Miscellaneous Wounds With Bleeding

Types of Bleeding

Human and Animal Bites

Skull and Head Injuries

Injuries to Face and Eyes

Injuries to Teeth, Mount and Gums – Dental

Thoracic (Chest) Injuries

Abdominal (Abdominopelvic)

Blisters (Sometimes Called Boils)

Poisoning (May be Accidental or Intentional)

Insect Stings and Bites

Other Assorted Arachnids

Snake Bites

Fire-Related Injuries

Cold-Related Injuries

Bone and Musculoskeletal Injuries

Study Guide for First Aid

BASIC FIRST AID

Responses to Basic Emergencies

Emergency situations often arise rapidly and encompass a variety of problems to which the trained rescuer or layperson must respond. Treatment must be initiated rapidly and accurately, and time is of the utmost importance. Proper first aid, when rendered in a timely manner, will eliminate many of the long-term effects of the injury or illness. A small number of emergency situations comprise the most emergency room visits and need for first aid in this country. Many of these accidents or illnesses could have been prevented. A small amount of care and planning will avoid many accidents, while many illnesses are brought on by carelessness or lack of judgment. Emergency situations requiring treatment are most common in the following types of injuries or illnesses:

1. Automobile accidents

2. Heart attacks

3. Fainting

4. Strokes (cardiovascular)

5. Falls and playground injuries

6. Injuries with broken bones

7. Stings and bites (includes dogs)

8. Accidental poisonings

Proportions of Problems Related to Injury and Illness

Injuries are one of our most serious and challenging health problems. Injuries are the leading cause of death and disability in infants, children, and young adults. Older adults suffer from a different variety of problems, primarily heart attacks and strokes. These accidents and diseases destroy the health, lives, and livelihoods of many people annually.

Pertinent Facts

1. The Bureau of Labor Statistics, U.S. Department of Labor, reports on injuries and illnesses in private industry workplaces. These statistics are important as companies and government representatives seek ways to make the work place safer, and to eliminate the high cost of workers who are injured and unable to work. Another agency that focuses on unintentional injuries in the home, chiefly from falls, burns, poisoning, and a host of other incapacitating events that impact on the health of Americans, is the Home Safety Council. This office reports an estimated 20 million medical visits each year from accidental injuries and illness that occur in the home (http://www.homesafetycouncil.org)

2. Injury is the fourth leading cause of death among all Americans, superseded only by heart disease, cancer, and stroke.

3. Roughly 10 percent of hospital beds are occupied by an injured person.

4. Each year, more than 75,000 Americans suffer permanently disabling injuries of the central nervous system, which includes the brain and spinal cord.

5. Treatment of injuries is one of the leading expenditures in our health care system.

6. Possibly one-fourth of emergency room visits are for the treatment of injuries.

Who Needs First Aid Training?

Statistically, everyone must expect to eventually be present when injury or sudden illness strikes close by. The final outcome often depends not only on the severity of the injury or illness, but also on the quality of the first aid given by a responder. Every person should be trained in the basics of first aid in order to help with family members and friends as well as strangers.

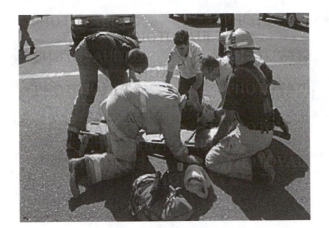

First Aid is the Immediate Care Given to the Injured or Ill Person

This immediate emergency treatment is not considered an alternative for proper medical treatment. Only temporary assistance is rendered until medical care as needed is received. Many injuries and illnesses require only first aid care with no further medical attention necessary. Properly administered first aid often ensures recovery of the patient. Sometimes complications requiring long hospitalization or disability and permanent injury are avoided through administration of proper first aid. Many of the lifesaving techniques performed today were nonexistent several decades ago, and many people died needlessly because quick first aid was not available.

Note: Emergency first aid requiring resuscitation will be covered in courses dedicated to cardiopulmonary resuscitation or basic life support. The American Heart Association and the American Red Cross furnish training programs and materials necessary for the proper teaching of these skills. An overview of the statistics and significance of coronary disease will be presented in this book, while certification is to be gained through a course designed by the American Heart Association or the American Red Cross. Please note that the Health Care Provider course by the American Heart Association is the most widely accepted program for basic life support in hospitals and clinics.

"Good Samaritan" Laws – Duty to Act

State laws vary, and many have laws providing immunity to prosecution for individuals attempting to help in emergency situations. Most of these laws give protection against liability when a person attempts to help in good faith, to the best of his abilities and training. Laws vary from state to state, and some may *require* that a layperson act prudently in coming to the aid of a victim of illness or accident. Moral obligations exist, but they may not be the same as a legal obligation to give aid. If you are a member of certain occupations in the health care field, you may be legally required to render aid if you come upon an accident or a suddenly ill person, as required by state or local law.

While first aid providers are covered by a "Good Samaritan" law in many states, the "Good Samaritan" laws protect only those acting in good faith and without gross negligence or willful misconduct. If first aid providers provide care within the scope of their training, lawsuits are rare. However, if the person providing first aid worsens a minor injury, litigation is possible.

WHEN DOES ONE HAVE A DUTY TO ACT?

1. **If One's Employment Requires it as Part of the Employee's Duties.** As part of the duties of your employment, you are trained to render first aid, and if you are called to an accident scene, you have a duty to act. Law enforcement officers, park rangers, lifeguards, and teachers who have a job description designating the duty of giving first aid would require that the person respond to an individual in need of medical attention.

2. **If a Person Had Previously Taken Responsibility as Follows.** If you have a preexisting relationship with another person who requires responsibility for him or her (e.g., parent-child, driver-passenger), even if it is not spelled out in your job description, you must give first aid as needed.

3. **If You Initiated First Aid.** Once first aid is initiated, you must continue until the condition is alleviated or until more highly skilled and competent aid arrives.

4. **State and Local Laws May Also Prevail.** In many states and locales, it is illegal to refuse to render aid to the best of one's ability upon either causing an injury or coming upon an accident or an ill patient needing aid.

Standards Related to Provision of First Aid

Standards of care ensure quality care and protection for injured or suddenly sick victims. The type of care rendered is dependent upon the training of the first aid provider, or equipment and supplies available.

1. **Type of Rescuer Happening upon the Scene.** A trained first aid provider should provide a level of care expected of a reasonable person with the same amount of training and in similar circumstances as the respondent, even a casual one.

2. **Emergency Procedures are Widely Published.** Emergency care-related organizations and societies publish recommended first aid procedures. For example, the American Heart Association and the American Red Cross publish procedures for giving CPR. The National Safety Council has a manual giving basic instructions for handling first aid procedures for a number of emergency situations. The council provides a route for certification in first aid if certification in first aid is needed for a chosen vocation.

Victim's Consent to Receive Treatment

If conscious and able, the victim should be asked to give consent to receive treatment or transportation. Consent may be given orally if necessary.

Types and Conditions of Consent

1. Actual Consent

When a victim gives verbal permission to a first aid responder to help, this is known as **actual consent**. Consent should be obtained from every conscious and mentally competent adult before treatment is initiated.

2. Implied Consent

This consent is automatic for giving care to an unconscious victim who is incapable of a rational response. A first aid provider should not hesitate to treat an unconscious victim for fear of being sued, as this situation is highly unlikely.

3. **Consent for Minor Patient**
   The parent or guardian of a child or of an adult that is mentally incompetent may give consent for treatment. If a parent or guardian is not available, first aid to maintain life may be given without consent. Do not withhold first aid from a minor due to lack of permission from a parent or guardian, as it would be only remotely possible that a parent or guardian would refuse aid.

4. **Substance Abuse Impaired/Psychological Impaired/Mentally Incompetent**
   In psychological emergencies, a police officer is the only person with the authority to restrain a person against his will. If the victim is not violent, treatment and restraint require parental or guardian consent if available.

REFUSAL OF TREATMENT

Right to Refuse Care

A rational, adult victim who is suffering from an actual or potential life-threatening injury or illness may refuse treatment. The rescuer should make a reasonable effort to convince the victim, or a friend or relative, to accept first aid and transportation, if indicated, to a medical facility. If a rational victim refuses treatment, **do not** give first aid or transportation. Inform the police, document the incident on paper, and procure witnesses if possible.

Drug-Altered, Intoxicated, or Belligerent victim

In the case of refusal of treatment by such a mind-altered victim, make every effort to persuade him or her of the need for treatment. This happens quite frequently following automobile accidents. If the person is incompetent to make a rational decision or if it is a young child, a relative may overrule the victim. If refusal continues, have witnesses sign documentation of your attempts to gain treatment for the victim. If the intoxicated person consents to first aid, bear in mind that drugs, including alcohol, often obscure symptoms of injury. It is easy to overlook serious injury, particularly if you are repulsed by the appearance of the victim. The responder who attempts to help a person who may be chemically altered must take care to protect himself and others before attempting to treat the victim. An irrational person who has been injured may be a dangerous individual and unable to perceive that the intent of the person attempting to assist him is not a threat to him. Every attempt should be made in an effort to provide emergency care even to those who may be unable to understand your efforts to help; however, we are not allowed to force a person to accept treatment, except in certain cases where the person has been legally declared incompetent to make rational and informed decisions for himself or herself.

Legal Issues

Abandonment

Abandonment occurs when a first aid provider begins care and then leaves the victim before another person arrives to take over. After starting first aid, you must remain with the victim until someone with equal or a higher level of training arrives, until the victim refuses further treatment, or until transportation to a medical facility has occurred as a result of the arrival of an emergency vehicle or emergency personnel. Upon arrival of trained first aid providers, continue to give treatment to the victim until the professionals are able to assess the site, make observations of the condition of the victim(s), and select and assemble equipment necessary to provide definitive treatment.

Crime Scenes

A person injured as an apparent victim of a crime should be treated to the best of one's ability and training. However, do not alter the scene in any way. Do not remove items, clean up, or disturb the environment around the victim. Many crimes have remained unsolved due to contamination of the crime scene or moving of some pieces of evidence. Crime scene investigators are trained to recognize certain patterns, and before disturbing the scene, everything is catalogued and pictured before any physical activity takes place, such as removing any physical objects, including the body if any death has occurred.

VICTIM ASSESSMENT

Assessment is a systematic examination of the victim and its surroundings. Do not move the injured or ill person until you have done a complete assessment of the injury or illness and have applied first aid. Even though the first appearance of the victim gives some evidence of the extent and breadth of the injuries, hidden or internal injuries may be present that may be worsened if certain movements of the victim's body occurs. The exception is when the victim is exposed to further danger at the accident scene. In this case, move the victim from harm's way. An example would be a victim of an automobile accident who is lying in the roadway, exposed to oncoming traffic. If the injury is serious and the victim is in a safe place, and if emergency medical service (EMS) attention is readily available, it may be a good idea to avoid moving the victim. The first aid provider would give only reasonable first aid at the injury scene until the EMS arrives. Most communities within the United States have emergency response teams no more than minutes away, even in isolated, rural areas.

Note: The victim assessment could be affected by either a preexisting medical condition or injury, or by the victim's mental status. The presence of life-threatening conditions may also affect the initial assessment. First, conduct a primary survey and correct any problems uncovered before going on to the secondary survey. Obvious life-threatening conditions will require treatment and will preempt completion of the initial assessment in some cases. If, for example, a person is hemorrhaging uncontrollably, direct pressure on the wound and as a last resort the placement of a tourniquet would be advisable before performing a head-to-toe assessment, as the first aid provider might be assessing a deceased person if treatment is delayed.

Making a Victim Assessment

1. If injuries are due to an accident, ask witnesses to describe the events of the accident. Do not delay treatment to do a lengthy analysis of the reasons and issues surrounding the accident. The police will most often do this after the victim has been stabilized and/or transported to a medical facility.

2. What is observable initially about the victim may yield clues as to the nature of the injuries, such as the position in which the victim is lying, bent or crooked limbs, visible cuts, or bleeding.

3. If responsive, ask the victim to relate his knowledge of how the injury occurred and any injuries of which he may be aware. This may yield some valuable insight.

4. Realize that less noticeable but more serious injuries may have occurred. Performing certain procedures may exacerbate damage to the central nervous system. Therefore, if for any reason a neck or back injury is suspected, DO NOT move the victim until trained help is available, unless the victim is in immediate danger from vehicles, animals, or the environment, such as submerged in water.

5. Determine the causes of injury, which may provide a clue as to the extent of physical damage. It is often easy to determine what has happened and this can enable the astute first aid provider to suspect certain injuries.

6. During the initial survey, do not move the victim any more than necessary to support life and to protect the victim. At any rate, keep the victim warm and as comfortable as possible if you are unable to provide any definitive treatment. If the victim is on a busy highway, treatment must be performed in a safe area for both first aid provider and victim.

Medical Alert Tags

These tags are worn as a necklace or as a bracelet to draw attention in a preexisting medical condition. This tag may also provide clues to the condition of an unconscious or confused person while an assessment is being made. These tags often contain information about the wearer's medical problem as well as a telephone number to call in case of an emergency. Do not remove this tag from an injured or sick person, as it may become important when the victim is moved to a medical facility. A prospective first aid responder should be able to

identify a victim's injury or sudden illness and determine its seriousness in order to provide proper first aid. The provider of first aid should follow a systematic assessment of the victim prior to initiating treatment.

Purpose of a Victim Assessment:

1. Procure the victim's consent using the conditions given previously in this section.

2. Earn the victim's confidence, assuring the victim you are going to help.

3. Identify the victim's problems. Prioritize multiple injuries in order to treat more serious and life-threatening conditions first. For example, heavy bleeding should be attended before a small cut or other minor medical problem.

4. Obtain information about the victim that may prove useful to EMS responders or other advanced medical personnel. This will often save time when the advanced medical personnel, such as EMTs and paramedics, arrive. Anything done to stabilize the patient prior to advanced medical treatment personnel's arrival will be to the advantage of the victim and may give him a chance to survive or avoid further serious damage by delayed treatment. It has been determined, partly by experiences by combat medics during the Vietnam War, that early and effective treatment often means recovery rather than death.

Victim Assessment of Injured Victim or Medically Ill Victim

1. Initial or Primary Survey

2. Advanced or Secondary Survey

In order to determine extent of injury or basis of illness, the first aid provider must use his own senses in order to perform an adequate assessment that would allow him or her to make informed decisions regarding first aid procedures. These determinations are based on signs and symptoms

Automobile Accident (used by permission)

exhibited by the victim upon initial assessment. In the case of severe, bleeding wounds, the injury is immediately obvious. Often, the position of the victim, the types of machinery or equipment around the victim, and verbal reports of eyewitnesses provide direct evidence of the type of injury incurred. However, be aware that some people may insist they are all right, and then later collapse. Victims should be observed for a period of time in this situation. Sometimes injuries are not obvious, as in the case of internal bleeding, and victims may not show evidence of injury for several hours, particularly in head injuries.

Definitions

1. **Signs**   Can be seen, felt, or heard by first aid provider. These are **objective** (they have nothing to do with how victim feels) and are more reliable. In a traumatic accident, many of the injuries are readily evident. Some are not, like closed head injuries, closed fractures, and internal bleeding.

2. **Symptoms**   A conscious victim may claim pain, weakness, and/or lack of feeling out of proportion to the injury. Therefore, the emotions of the patient are involved in his or her description; this information is called **subjective**.

Initial Survey

The primary survey is the immediate assessment of a victim. Its purpose is to find life-threatening problems and to treat them quickly, accurately, and effectively, if the first aid responder is trained to handle this type of emergency. This initial survey includes:

1. Is the airway open? If the victim is talking or is conscious, the airway is open. Gasping sounds may indicate that the victim has an inadequately open airway.

2. Is the victim breathing? If conscious, the victim will be breathing. Breathing difficulties including unusual sounds may indicate a medical emergency and require quick action. If the victim is unconscious, keep the airway open and look for the chest to rise and fall, listen for and feel for air coming out of the victim's nose and mouth. The first aider may feel the breath of the victim with his ear, as the ear is quite sensitive to air currents.

3. Does the victim have circulation? This is usually determined by feeling the carotid pulse at the side of the neck just in front of a line descending down from the ears and under the mandible. On an infant or very young child, one would feel for the brachial pulse, on the inside of the arm just above the elbow.

4. Is severe bleeding visible? Internal bleeding may not be readily apparent upon initial assessment, but it is as life threatening as external wounds with bleeding. A bruise or rigid abdomen may indicate internal bleeding, as well as the presentation of early signs of shock, including sweating and paleness.

Advanced Survey

After completing the initial survey and attending to any life-threatening problems, look at the victim more carefully, making a systematic assessment. Look for overt signs and symptoms of injury. The injuries discovered during the initial survey, particularly if life threatening, should be treated before progressing to the advanced survey. The advanced or secondary survey is to discover problems not uncovered in the initial survey but that may become serious if unattended. This assessment may reveal less easily noticed injuries. Internal bleeding will often be discovered at this time, as will spinal damage, which may lead to permanent paralysis if the victim is moved improperly. Closed fractures, or those with no outward signs of injury, may become open fractures if not immobilized. This advanced survey is a head-to-toe examination, usually starting with the victim's head, then neck, chest, abdomen, and extremities, looking for abnormalities such as swelling, discoloration, and tenderness, which might indicate a hidden injury. It must be remembered that moving a victim with neck or head injuries, or injuries of the back, if done improperly and without supporting the patient with the proper devices, may result in permanent paralysis from trauma to the central nervous system.

CONTACTING MEDICAL ASSISTANCE

Available Resources in Most Communities

1. **Rescue squad/fire department.** In some locations, medical assistance is available as EMT/paramedics based at the local fire department. These specially trained paramedics are trained for both rescue and emergency medical treatment. They are likely to respond swiftly and competently.

2. **Ambulance service.** Some services have trained paramedics, while others do not. However, all ambulance services are now required to have adequately trained first aid

Air Ambulance Landing

responders. These are often services provided by the county government. For rapid transport in cases of critical injury, helicopters specially adapted and equipped to transport patients to hospitals, particularly those for specialized procedures, are often used. Teams of paramedics and trauma nurses accompany these flights to provide in-flight treatment, as quick treatment prevents death or serious changes from occurring. Often, radio communication with the emergency center to where the patient is being transported is done to better prepare for treatment of the victim before he or she arrives for emergency treatment. This quick method of transport now saves many lives and is becoming more and more common. Air ambulances were pioneered to a great extent in the Vietnam War and helped save the lives of many soldiers that would not have survived if treatment had been delayed. Most hospitals now have a landing pad for helicopters and specially trained crews that may deliver definitive and lifesaving care even while in flight.

3. **Police.** They may not be able to respond with medically trained personnel; but in most communities, police can get a victim to the hospital quickly. The police also know the quickest way to summon medical personnel to the scene and the nearest medical facility for advanced procedures.

4. **Physician.** Your own doctor may not be available but should be alerted if an emergency has occurred. Usually, emergency room physicians will do initial treatment and provide information to your personal physician, particularly if you are away from home.

5. **Poison Control Center**. This is information available to physicians only in some areas. Local medical centers may have access to pertinent information online and will give instructions to callers from a readily available database. Often, victims of accidental poisoning require no drastic treatment and may be cared for at home with the proper information. A professional at a hospital, in coordination with the Poison Control Center, may enable effective treatment at home without bringing the patient to the emergency room.

Give the Following Information Over the Phone:
1. **The victim's location.** Give the city or town, street name, and street number, with obvious landmarks if possible. Much time may be lost if the emergency service is searching for the location with incomplete directions. Do not hang up until you have finished answering the questions of the telephone attendant.

2. **Your phone number.** This information is required to aid in preventing prank calls, but it can also be helpful if additional information is needed by rescue service. The ambulance service personnel should be able to call you if they are unable to locate you and the victim(s).

3. **What type of accident or illness has occurred.** Give information related to injury or illness. Also, victims may be in a relatively inaccessible location, and rescue equipment may be necessary. This enables the responders to have proper equipment and supplies as well as to help in alerting additional personnel who might be needed.

4. **How many victims, and special problems encountered in reaching victims**. Give the number of victims and information such as flights of stairs, dogs, hostile neighbors, criminals, unusual environmental factors, or other people, and so on.

5. **Condition of the victim(s).** Alert rescuers to known specific injuries, whether the victim or victims is/are conscious or unconscious, and if there is evidence indicating the type or severity of illness or injury.

6. **Efforts being used for aiding the victim(s).** Relate information as to current treatment, such as resuscitation efforts, if bleeding is present or is successfully being controlled, and if tourniquets, splints, or pressure bandages have been applied, as appropriate. What have you and other rescuers or first aid responders done to stabilize and treat the victim or victims?

COMMUNICATIONS GUIDELINES

Never hang up the phone before the EMS dispatcher does. Always be the last to hang up the phone. The EMS dispatcher may need to ask more specific questions as to location after consulting maps and other personnel for directions. The emergency personnel on the phone may be able to provide information to the first aid responder for more definitive treatment until help arrives.

Speak slowly and clearly. It is difficult to understand loud and excited voices. Time is of the essence, but certain pieces of information must be obtained by the emergency service in order for them to operate most effectively. The EMS is often communicating with physicians at the nearest medical facility prior to reaching the victim. Again, do not end the call before the EMT or paramedic indicates he has completed the conversation with you.

MAJOR TYPES OF EMERGENCIES

Shock – Discussion

Shock is the most likely and potentially most serious occurrence in an injury, so it is discussed first. Many injuries involve some level of shock, and shock is to be expected in extreme emergencies, where injuries are severe. Shock is sometimes called "hypoperfusion" and ocurs when the oxygenated blood is not delivered effectively to all the organs of the body, particularly the brain and the heart, which are vital to life. If not treated effectively and quickly, the victim may die of shock, even if he or she may have survived the injuries leading to shock.

Shock may occur due to a number of medical problems or injuries. Some of these are: hemorrhage; intense pain; infection with certain types of organisms; heart attack; cardiovascular accidents (stroke); poisoning; psychological events; and dehydration for any number of reasons. There are eight main types of shock, all of which diminish circulation to prevent effective oxygenation of the vital organs of the body.

In some cases, the body attempts to increase the blood flow to certain parts of the body, while other parts have a deficit. Shock is a medical emergency, and it is mandatory that shock be prevented by effective treatment from the start of delivering first aid. Even when signs and symptoms have not appeared in an injured victim, always treat for shock. **First aid providers can prevent shock, but they cannot reverse it.** Advanced medical treatment is necessary for reversal of shock. Remember, an ounce of prevention is worth a pound of cure, particularly in dealing with the prevention of shock! If shock can be prevented prior to the arrival of advanced medical treatment and transport to a hospital, the patient has a much greater chance of survival, even of the most grievous injuries.

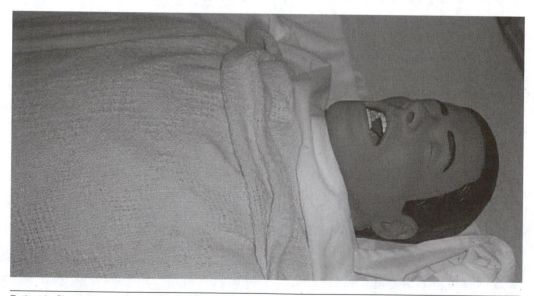

Patient in Shock, Covered and Comfortable

Basic First Aid to Prevent Shock

The victim should be kept lying flat on the back (supine) as this improves circulation to all organs of the body, since no part of the body is elevated. To increase flow to the vital organs, the brain and heart, the legs may be raised twelve inches by placing an object under the heels. However, if the person is vomiting or has head or mouth injuries or bleeding of the upper body, raising the legs is not advisable. The head may be raised to improve respirations for a victim who is having difficulty breathing, if no neck injury has occurred.

Cover the victim with blankets or any clothing or other cover available, even vegetation, to prevent chilling and cold exposure. This should be done even in fairly warm weather but not in hot weather, as the person may experience a heat injury if the body temperature is increased to a great extent. If the victim's body is warm to the touch and dry, you should reevaluate any decision to cover the patient. DO NOT give water to or feed the victim, even if he expresses hunger or thirst. A wet cloth may be used to wet the lips and tongue of the victim. Advanced medical help should be sought immediately for those exhibiting signs and symptoms of shock.

Eight Major Categories of Shock

While there are eight major categories of shock, three categories are most often seen in trauma and illness. The three categories most often seen by the layperson who is providing first aid will be discussed, along with major symptoms and treatment to alleviate or prevent shock. Remember, a first aid provider cannot reverse shock. It is a complex process that is best handled by advanced emergency care.

Anaphylactic – hypersensitivity or allergic reaction to bites, stings, food or medications

Cardiogenic – heart muscle is damaged so pumping of blood is diminished

Hypovolemic – usually due to hemorrhage, with severe bleeding causing loss of blood pressure

Metabolic – underlying diseases may contribute to fluid loss through vomiting, diarrhea, heat injury; pH changes of blood

Neurogenic – damage to central nervous system (brain, spinal cord)

Psychogenic – intense emotions such as anger, grief, fear, anxiety

Respiratory – injury to respiratory system, or arrest due to disease or choking

Septic – acute infection with certain bacteria that induce shock, for example, toxic shock syndrome

Three Major Categories Most Often Encountered in Shock

1. **Psychogenic – Syncope or Fainting**

   The brain is deprived of partial blood flow, and unconsciousness occurs in this common type of shock. Fainting involves a sudden, temporary loss of consciousness, occurring when the brain's blood flow is interrupted. This is a common type of medical emergency and rarely needs medical care extending beyond first aid. However, repeated cases of fainting often are due to a medical condition requiring diagnosis and treatment by a physician. Causes abound for this interrupted blood flow, and sometimes it is a psychological response to a situation.

   Signs and Symptoms

   Fainting may occur suddenly without warning. While the least severe form of shock, patients often act irrationally and injure themselves or others by uncoordinated and unexpected movements. Most who have fainted describe one or more of the following:

   A. Dizziness, often expressed before unconsciousness occurs

   B. "Seeing spots" as a subjective symptom

C. Nauseated feelings expressed before unconsciousness occurs

D. Pale appearance; skin may be bluish or gray in color with pale mucus membranes and nail beds

E. Noticeable sweating (diaphoresis)

F. Complaints of face feeling warm prior to unconsciousness

Treatment

A. Prevent falls with possible injury by helping patient to a comfortable position

B. Help patient avoid injury if the patient suffers seizures. Seizures often occur while patient is unconscious, and patient may harm himself, herself, or others.

C. Assure victim as he regains consciousness, making him aware of his surroundings

D. Elevate legs to increase flow of blood to brain

E. Prevent loss of body heat by covering with blankets, outer garments, or any other type of available cover

F. Insure other problems are not present by monitoring vital signs

G. Encourage the victim to relax for ten minutes before attempting to walk

2. Hypovolemic

This type of shock occurs when blood and body fluids become depleted and blood pressure falls, preventing flow of blood to vital organs.

Hypovolemic (hypoperfusion) shock results from blood or fluid loss and may be called "hemorrhagic shock" if a large amount of blood has been lost.

Signs and Symptoms

A. Most often observed first, the skin becomes pale and sometimes bluish, particularly around the mouth and nails

B. Cool, wet (clammy) skin; heavy sweating

C. Rapid breathing and pulse

D. Dilated pupils altered mental status

E. Slow capillary filling time in nail beds

F. Dull, sunken look to the eyes

G. Excessive thirst

H. Possible nausea and vomiting

I. Eventual loss of consciousness if untreated and progressive

Treatment

A. Maintain open airway and assess respirations. Perform CPR if necessary.

B. Control bleeding from wounds by pressure or elevation, or both

C. If there are no serious fractures of extremities, elevate legs –ten to twelve inches only

D. Splint any suspected fractures to immobilize breaks and/or damaged joints

E. Prevent loss of body heat by covering with blankets, outer garments, or any available cover. This will often be most important in helping to prevent shock.

F. Transport victim to nearest medical facility. Remember, the first aid provider is not able to reverse shock, but may prevent the onset of the condition.

3. **Severe Allergic Reaction (Anaphylactic Shock)**

Often known as a severe allergic reaction, this type of shock may be characterized by rashes and itching as well as respiratory difficulties. **This is a life-threatening situation!** Most anaphylactic deaths are caused by inability to breathe due to swollen airway passages obstructing airflow to the lungs. A powerful agent, called an allergen is recognized by the body as a foreign agent, which may occur after one or more exposures. The allergen, may come in physical contact with the person or may be injected, breathed, or taken orally. This elicits a powerful reaction entailing the production of antibodies to the allergen, which is interpreted as an enemy to the body. It is a more powerful reaction than the relatively mild condition in which the body produces a rash or itching in response to the foreign body. This reaction must be treated immediately, as death can occur within minutes and sometimes seconds. When subjected to the offending materials, the tissues of the body release a chemical called histamine, which attacks lungs, vascular system, intestinal system, and skin. Death occurs because of a decrease or cessation of blood circulation throughout the body following the histamine release.

Signs and Symptoms

Any or all of these signs and symptoms may appear:

A. Respiratory signs, such as coughing, rattling, wheezing, sneezing

B. Complaints of feeling pain or tightness in the chest

C. Difficulty in breathing, appearance of labored breathing

D. Tightness and swelling in the throat, with possible accompanying breath sounds

E. Swollen face, tongue, mouth

F. Extreme itching, rash, burning, or hives

G. Nausea and/or vomiting

H. Expressing feelings of dizziness

I. Abdominal pain or severe cramps

J. Blueness (cyanosis) around the lips and mouth

K. Stupor or complete unconsciousness

Treatment

A. Ensure the patient's airway and breathing are adequate

B. Immediately apply oxygen, if available, for help in tissue perfusion

C. Victims with known allergic reactions may carry injectable epinephrine. If able, victim may direct first aid provider to administer epinephrine, or do a self-injection

D. Provide CPR if patient is unable to breathe adequately

E. Transport victim to medical emergency facility immediately

MISCELLANEOUS WOUNDS WITH BLEEDING

An average-sized adult has about six quarts of blood and can safely lose a "unit" of approximately one pint during a blood donation. Rapid blood loss of one quart or more may lead to shock and possibly death. A loss of one pint for a child is extremely serious. While blood and airborne infections have been discussed extensively in previous sections, general statements will be reiterated to emphasize the importance of avoiding the contraction of these organisms while providing treatment.

Blood can be lost from arteries, veins, or capillaries. Often, bleeding involves all three types of vessels. Blood from arteries is bright red and spurts. Bleeding from arteries constitutes the fastest blood loss, is difficult to control, and is the most dangerous. Venous blood flows steadily and appears to be a darker red, as it is deoxygenated. Blood oozes slowly from capillaries. Various blood vessels exhibit differing shades of red, but an inexperienced person may have difficulty detecting the difference. Regardless of the source of the blood loss, there are two basic types of bleeding: external and internal.

Precautions When Handling Injuries and Diseases With Blood or Body Fluid Involvement

Precautions for Bloodborne Pathogens: HIV and HBV

Bloodborne pathogens are microorganisms that may be introduced into the blood supply of the body. These organisms cause disease and are numerous and of a wide variety. Many attack specific organs in the body, while others cause a systemic disease by being carried in the bloodstream. Most often, these organisms are transmitted by exposure to blood. The two most significant bloodborne pathogens are Hepatitis B virus (HBV) and human immunodeficiency virus (HIV). A number of bloodborne diseases other than HIV and HBV exist, such as hepatitis C, hepatitis D, and syphilis. Body fluids other than blood are frequently implicated in the transmission of bloodborne pathogens. Any time there is an exchange of body fluids, particularly blood, semen, and vaginal fluids, there is a risk of contracting a bloodborne pathogen. While these organisms may be found in sweat, tears, and saliva, they are not known to be readily spread through these media.

Organ Damage by Hepatitis B

HBV attacks the liver. HBV is extremely infectious and may cause the following symptoms and clinical signs:

1. Active hepatitis B-a flu-like illness that can last for months

2. A chronic carrier state-the person may have no symptoms but can pass HBV to others

3. Cirrhosis, liver cancer, and death

Prevention of AIDS and HBV

Only in the past two decades have vaccines become available to actually prevent HBV infection. Even if you are vaccinated against HBV, you must continue to treat all blood and certain human body fluids as if you know they are infected with bloodborne pathogens. This practice is known as Universal Precautions. There is another term called Standard Precautions. The difference between the two is that in Universal Precautions, only blood and body fluids containing blood are considered, while in standard precautions, ALL body fluids are considered potential sources for infection by bloodborne organisms.

HIV causes AIDS (Acquired Immune Deficiency Syndrome). HIV attacks the immune system, making the body less able to fight off infections. In most cases, these infections, called opportunistic infections, eventually prove fatal rather than the patient dying from the HIV infection. At present, there is no vaccine to prevent infection and no known cure for AIDS, although many AIDS patients live for years on large doses of medication.

Personal Protection Equipment

Use personal protective equipment (PPE) when possible while giving first aid

1. Keep open wounds covered with dressings to prevent contact with blood.

2. All first aid kits should have several pairs of latex gloves. Use these gloves in every situation involving blood or other body fluids.

3. If latex gloves are not available, use the most waterproof material available, such as plastic sandwich bags or extra gauze dressings to form a barrier.

4. Whenever possible, use a mouth-to-barrier device for protection when doing rescue breathing. Every first aid worker should have one in his kit, which should be with him in his vehicle or on his person. While saliva is not considered a high risk, there may be blood in the mouth.

A person exposed to blood or other body fluids should:

1. Wash the exposed area immediately with soap and running water. Scrub vigorously with lots of lather.

2. Report the incident promptly to the appropriate office according to your workplace policy. If it is deemed that you have been exposed to a potentially infectious agent, you should be immediately evaluated by a health care professional.

3. Get medical help, treatment, and counseling in order to protect yourself against unwarranted worry and danger of a serious infection. If your workplace is covered by OSHA's bloodborne standards, ask about confidential medical evaluation, testing, counseling, and treatment. Almost all categories of health care facilities fall under OSHA's standards, with the exception of some government facilities that may have similar or more stringent regulations.

4. Ask about HBV globulin (HBIG) if you haven't had the HBV vaccine. It can provide short-term protection. HBIG is followed by vaccination against HBV.

TYPES OF BLEEDING

External Bleeding

This type of bleeding involves seeing blood coming from a wound. It is most often discovered during the initial assessment of an injury victim. In most cases, bleeding stops after five to ten minutes with proper first aid.

Internal Bleeding

This type of bleeding occurs when the skin is unbroken, and it is not usually visible. It is often discovered on the secondary, or advanced, assessment. A victim of an accident may have both internal and external bleeding. Sometimes there will be no obvious bruising or bleeding, and in a short time, the victim may go into shock. It is more advantageous for the first aid provider and the victim of trauma to prevent shock rather than to treat it after it occurs. Many if not most cases of shock can be prevented with rapid and effective preventive measures.

Signs and Symptoms, Internal Bleeding

1. Blood from mouth, rectum, or blood in the urine

2. Bleeding from the vagina other than menstrual

3. Readily visible bruise or contusion on the surface of the body

4. Rapid, sometimes thready pulse

5. Cold, clammy skin

6. Dilated pupils

7. Nausea, vomiting

8. Pain, particularly in chest cavity or abdomen

9. Tender, rigid, bruised abdomen

10. Fractured ribs or bruises on chest

Treatment

1. Identify the body site that is bleeding. Sometimes copious bleeding will make it difficult to identify the location of the wound.

2. Apply continuous and direct pressure over wound, elevating the area if possible.

3. If bleeding continues, DO NOT remove the pressure bandage. Increase the padding and pressure to control the bleeding. Removal of the pressure bandage may damage any clot that may have started forming, increasing the bleeding.

4. In the absence of pain with movement, or with broken bones, elevate the wounded area above the level of the heart.

5. Keep the victim quiet and warm. Victims who have lost blood will often shiver uncontrollably and complain of feeling cold, even on a warm day.

6. For heavy bleeding, called hemorrhaging, apply pressure over any appropriate pulse points to reduce bleeding.

7. Transport the victim to an emergency medical center as soon as possible, while avoiding further injury by moving the victim carefully and correctly.

HUMAN AND OTHER ANIMAL BITES

While animal bites rarely cause an extreme degree of bleeding, they can produce various types of tissue damage, including muscle and nerve tissue. Most of the animal bites in the United States come from dogs, with possibly more than a million per year by conservative estimates. Generally, the larger the species of dog, the greater the tissue damage from the animal's teeth.

Animal bites of all kinds account for about 1 percent of all hospital emergency department visits. Only a small number of these bites needs stitches, but they do require conscientious cleaning, which may be impossible for a first aid provider. An animal's mouth carries a large number of different species of bacteria, some of which may be lethal to humans, such as untreated rabies. Human, cat, and other animal bites are also contaminated from bacteria found in the mouths of these animals and are extremely dangerous. Human bites may cause serious injury to tissue as well as provide a seriously contaminated wound. The human mouth contains a wide range of bacteria, and the likelihood of infection is greater from a human bite than from other warm-blooded animals. Sometimes, tendon and ligament damage, muscle and nerve damage, and heavy bleeding occur. In these cases, the victim should be transported to a medical facility for advanced and definitive treatment. In cases of mild bites, the following treatment is often adequate. If the wound begins to swell and turn red, an infection may be present, and medical treatment requiring antibiotics may be warranted.

First Aid Treatment

1. Wash the wound gently with soap and water.

2. Apply pressure with a clean towel to the injured part to stop the bleeding.

3. Apply a sterile bandage to the wound.

4. Keep the injury elevated above the level of the heart to slow swelling.

5. Report the incident to the proper authority in your community (for example, police or animal control).

6. Apply antibiotic ointment to the area twice every day until it heals. If signs of infection occur, seek medical treatment immediately.

SKULL AND HEAD INJURIES

Scalp wounds normally bleed profusely because of the scalp's rich blood supply. Look in the wound for skull bone or brain exposure and indentation of the skull. Since the bony case of the skull covers and protects the largest organ of the central nervous system, the brain, any break in this covering causing pressure or a portal to environmental pathogens is a serious emergency.

Important! Consider the following when evaluating a head injury:

A head injury, even if seemingly minor or inconsequential, should be evaluated as to need for medical attention. The following guidelines should be observed. Remember: When in doubt, consult with medical professionals. Complications and untreated conditions do not often give a second chance to the victim and may prove to be fatal if ignored!

Symptoms of Head Injury

1. **Headache.** The victim will almost always have a headache, even for a minor concussion. If it lasts more than two days or increases in severity, seek medical advice.

2. **Nausea, vomiting.** Nausea and vomiting may be for only a brief period of time following any type of brain trauma. If nausea lasts more than two hours, seek medical advice. Vomiting once or twice, especially in children, may be expected. Vomiting does not indicate the severity of the injury, but if it begins several hours following the injury or after the initial episode subsides, consult a physician.

3. **Drowsiness.** It is permissible to allow a victim to sleep, but wake the victim frequently (every hour) to check the state of consciousness. Evaluate the victim for sense of orientation by asking his or her name, address, telephone number, and whether information can be processed, as in counting fingers or adding numbers. In the event the answers are inaccurate or inappropriate, or if the victim appears confused or disoriented, call a physician.

4. **Vision problems.** If the victim complains of double vision, or if the eyes fail to both move in coordination or in the same direction, or if the pupils are unequal, seek medical advice.

5. **Mobility.** If the victim cannot move his or her arms or legs in a normal fashion or is unable to walk normally and in a balanced manner, seek medical care.

6. **Speech.** If the victim has slurred speech or is not able to speak intelligibly, a physician should be consulted.

7. **Seizures or convulsions.** If the victim's voluntary muscles (used in movement of the arms and legs, for example) start to contract involuntarily, seek medical assistance.

Grades of Concussion

Treatment is Accomplished Depending on Grades or Levels of Concussions

1. **Mild**   Manifested by a momentary or no loss of consciousness
   Treatment   Delay return to activity until medical evaluation has been made

2. **Moderate**   The victim is unconscious for less than five minutes
   Treatment   Avoid vigorous activity for a few days or longer. Resume activity only when symptoms of headache, and any visual disturbances, have been resolved

3. **Severe**   The period of unconsciousness lasts for more than five minutes
   Treatment   Avoid rigorous activity for one month or longer. Consultation with a neurosurgeon is advised.

Types of Head Injuries

1. **Skull Fracture**

   A skull fracture is a break or crack in the bony protective structure of the skull surrounding the brain. Skull fractures may be either open or closed, as is the same with bone fractures of other parts of the body. One of the major dangers is that of splintered bone of the skull intruding into the brain. DIRECT PRESSURE SHOULD NOT BE PERFORMED ON A HEAD WOUND WHERE BONE IS BROKEN! Use a doughnut device made from something like a sock by rolling the top and placing the open part over the broken bone and applying pressure to prevent or control bleeding.

   Signs and symptoms

   A. Pain in the location of the suspected injury

   B. Deformity or asymmetry (unevenness) of the skull

   C. Bleeding from either the nose or ears, or both

   D. Clear or pink thin watery fluid dripping from the nose or ear or both

   E. This watery fluid may be cerebrospinal fluid, or CSF. If CSF leakage is suspected, it can be detected by collecting the fluid on a white cloth. CSF will form a pink ring that is lighter in the center, and possibly bloody around the perimeter; this is called the "halo sign."

   F. Discoloration or darkening under the eyes

   G. Discoloration behind an ear (Battle's sign)

   H. Unequal or unreactive pupils of the eyes

   I. Profuse scalp bleeding if skin is broken, possibly exposing skull or brain tissue

2. Concussion

A concussion is the result of a blow to the head or other trauma, such as shaking, that results in a violent banging of the brain against the inside of the skull. There is often a change in brain function, including loss of consciousness in many cases. Any or all of the following signs and symptoms may occur. This is one type of concussion that is occurring more often today or is being recognized more readily. Cases of the shaken baby syndrome, which often has fatal results, are increasingly being reported in emergency rooms.

Signs and Symptoms

A. Severe generalized headache

B. Stupor or actual loss of consciousness

C. Visual disturbances sometimes called "seeing stars"

D. Memory loss called amnesia

E. Dizziness

F. Weakness (may be generalized or in one or more particular areas of the body)

G. Double vision, called diplopia

H. Paralysis in part(s) of body

3. Contusion

Contusions should be treated as more serious than concussions. Blows to the head produce both. Contusions include bruising and swelling of the brain, and blood *vessels* in the brain have been ruptured and are bleeding. Trapped inside the skull, there is no way for the blood to escape and no room for it to accumulate. Swelling of the brain also contributes to this medical emergency, and the swelling must be alleviated by draining and/or treatment with steroids on an emergency basis.

Signs and Symptoms

A. Same as those for a concussion but more severe

B. Unconsciousness for more than a brief period of time

C. Paralysis or weakness

D. Unequal pupil size

E. Vomiting and feelings of nausea

F. Blurred and/or double vision

G. Amnesia or lapses of memory

H. Severe headache

INJURIES TO AREAS IN AND AROUND THE EYE

Correct treatment of an eye injury and the bony socket around the eye, called the orbit, immediately following an accident can prevent loss of sight. However, because it is difficult to determine the extent of damage to the eye, seek medical help as soon as possible. Flushing the eye for chemical burns is always acceptable. Call an ophthalmologist or a family physician, or go to a nearby hospital emergency department immediately.

Treatment – General Instructions

It is advisable when bandaging the eyes to cover both eyes, even if only one has an injury. This is because it is impossible to move only one eye at a time for most people. The eye has a large number of nerve endings in the body of the eye, and extreme pain often results form any type of injury. Often the injury, when a puncture wound, will have an object remaining in the eye. Do not place a bandage that compresses or places pressure on the eye in such a case. Paper cups taped over the eye will protect the eye from pressure or possibly further damage until the victim is transported to a medical facility. Do not pull the foreign object from the eye.

1. **Small, Nonpenetrating Foreign Object in Eye**
   Eversion of the Eyelid

   a. If tears or gentle flushing do not remove object, gently pull lower lid down. Remove an object by gently flushing with lukewarm water or by using wet sterile gauze.

   b. If no object is seen inside the lower lid, check the upper lid. Often, when a person has rubbed their eye, or when the pain is generalized, it is difficult to determine where the foreign object is.

   c. Tell the person to look downward, and then pull gently downward on the upper eyelashes. Laying a swab or matchstick across the top of the lid is helpful in this procedure.

   d. Fold the lid over the swab or matchstick. Remove an object by gently flushing with lukewarm water or by gently dabbing the object with the corner of a twisted, wet sterile gauze.

2. **Corneal abrasion, cut, or burn**
   The cornea is the transparent covering over the front of the eye, through which our vision is projected onto the retina. Corneal abrasion may result from a sharp foreign object, such as a piece of metal, wood or glass being projected into the eye from an industrial accident or children at play, for example. Even a hot piece of ash from a cigarette can burn the cornea.

3. **Bony socket around the eye**
   Eye injuries can also involve the bony structure around the eye designed to protect the eye from blows. Injuries to this bone may cause swelling and splintering of bone, possibly injuring

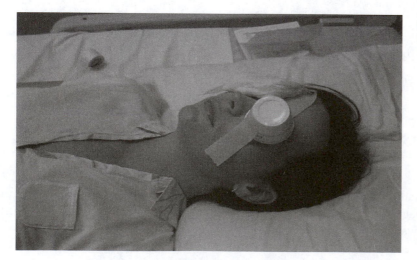

Eye Injury Requiring Bandaging of Both Eyes

the eye even if the eye did not receive a direct blow. Evaluation of this possibility should not be overlooked.

Treatment

Except for flushing the eye with water or eyewash to remove small particles, an injury to the eye requires expert medical treatment and is beyond the scope of the first aid provider except for protecting the injured eye and transporting the victim to the nearest medical facility. Prompt treatment is necessary in severe injuries to the eye in order to preserve vision. Abrasions to the cornea are treated by putting anesthetizing agents on the eye to diminish the pain and treating for infection. The cornea will largely heal within a few days, but sometimes surgery is needed to repair tears in the eye. In badly scarred corneas, transplants are often indicated.

Nosebleeds

A severe nosebleed will most likely frighten a victim and is sometimes difficult for the first aid provider to handle with basic skills. While most nosebleeds are self-limited and seldom require medical attention, it must be determined if emergency medical treatment by a professional is necessary. Nosebleeds may at first appear serious, but the amount of blood lost, which is usually diluted with mucus, may be minimal. However, in some cases a nosebleed may accompany head or neck injuries, so the first aid provider should stabilize the head and neck for protection. In rare cases, enough blood could be lost that the victim could go into shock. Exacerbating conditions involving nosebleeds may include broken cartilage and facial bones associated with the bony structures of the face. These additional injuries, along with head or neck injuries, may complicate treatment for the condition. If both the nose and mouth, and possibly teeth and tongue, are injured, special skills are needed to enable the patient/victim to be able to breathe adequately. If injuries other than a simple nosebleed are present, advanced medical care is often required as quickly as possible. The patient must be reassured in order to avoid shock and the head stabilized as quickly as possible. Keep the victim calm through reassurances. Excitement increases the blood pressure, and sometimes causes more pain and swelling as well as continued bleeding.

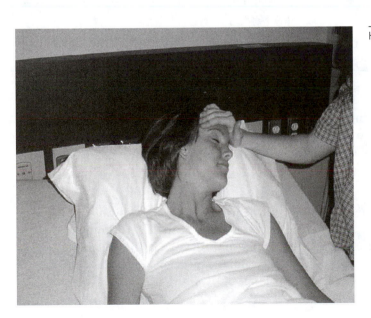

Head Elevated by Pillows, Raised Head of Bed

A. Types of Nosebleeds

1. **Anterior (front of nose).** The most common (90 percent); bleeding occurs from one nostril and usually involves a capillary rupture.

2. **Posterior (back of nose).** Massive bleeding backward into the mouth or down the back of the throat with bleeding starting on one side and then coming out of both sides of the nose and down the throat. This is serious and requires quick medical attention. Swallowing blood passing down the back of the throat can cause nausea and vomiting and may in some cases be aspirated into the trachea and the lungs.

B. Treatment

After a nosebleed has stopped:

1. Ask the victim to sneeze through an open mouth if he cannot avoid sneezing.

2. Ask the victim not to bend over or exert himself or herself physically, as this increased the circulation and can lead to increased bleeding.

3. Ask the victim to elevate his head and maintain pressure under the nose with a folded cloth or paper, which usually suffices to stop the bleeding. However, the first aid provider must be aware of any accompanying problems of a more serious nature.

4. Elevate the head with two pillows when lying down.

5. Keep the nostrils moist by applying a little petroleum jelly just inside the nostril for a week and increase the humidity in the bedroom during the winter months with a cold-mist humidifier.

6. Avoid picking or rubbing the nose vigorously, as bleeding may start again.

7. Avoid hot drinks and alcoholic beverages for at least a week.

8. Avoid smoking or taking aspirin for a week, as both of these activities may increase the bleeding time and slow the clotting process.

INJURIES TO TEETH, MOUTH, AND GUMS – DENTAL

1. Treatment

A number of injuries dealing with the structures found in the mouth, including the cheeks, may require specialized treatment. First aid treatment is based on type of injury and is categorized in the following sections.

A. Toothache

Rinse the mouth vigorously with warm water to clean it out. Use dental floss to remove any food that might be trapped between the teeth. (Do not place aspirin on the aching tooth or gum tissues as the tissues may be damaged.) See the dentist as soon as possible to avoid unnecessary pain and possibly further damage.

B. Problems with braces

If a wire is causing irritation, cover the end with a small cotton ball, beeswax, or a piece of gauze until you can get to the dentist. If a wire gets stuck in the cheek, tongue, or gum tissue, do not attempt to remove it. Go to the dentist immediately. If an appliance becomes loose or a piece of it breaks off, take the appliance and the piece and go to the dentist. Pain may be somewhat alleviated by placing a cold pack over the affected area to reduce inflammation and swelling.

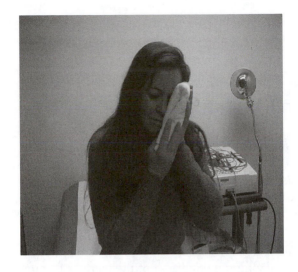

C. Knocked-out tooth

If the tooth is dirty, rinse it gently in running water. Do not scrub it or remove any attached tissue fragments. Gently insert and hold the tooth in its socket. If this is not possible, place the tooth in a cup of milk or a special tooth-preserving solution available at your local drugstore. If you can get to the dentist within thirty minutes, there is a good chance the tooth can be saved. Do not forget to bring the tooth with the victim!

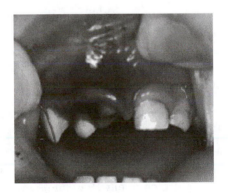

D. Broken tooth

Gently clean dirt from the injured area with warm water. Place cold compresses on the face, in the area of the injured tooth, to decrease swelling. Go to the dentist immediately.

E. Bitten tongue or lip

Apply direct pressure to the bleeding area with a clean cloth. If swelling is present, apply cold compresses. If bleeding does not stop, **go to a hospital emergency room**.

F. Objects wedged between teeth

Try to remove the object with floss; guide the floss carefully to avoid cutting the gums. If you're not successful in removing the object, go to the dentist. Do not try to remove the object with a sharp or pointed instrument, such as a pocketknife or sharp toothpick.

G. Possible broken jaw

Do not move the jaw. Secure the jaw in place by tying a handkerchief, necktie, or towel around the jaw and over the top of the head. If swelling is present, apply cold compresses.

Go immediately to a hospital or emergency room, or call your dentist. Carry the patient smoothly and gently or have him walk slowly and smoothly to avoid aggravating any broken bones.

THORACIC (CHEST) INJURIES

Closed chest wounds result from blunt blows. Many vital organs are enclosed within the bony cage of the ribs, sternum, and vertebrae and are easily damaged, burst, or badly bruised. Open chest wounds compromise the vacuum needed for breathing by movement of the diaphragm and prevent proper breathing. An open chest wound must be closed immediately, or the patient may suffer a collapsed lung or lungs. Injuries to the esophagus, trachea, heart, lungs, and diaphragm may occur, providing signs of internal injury. Opening of the airway is complicated by injuries to the mouth, nose, throat, lungs, and ribs. Establishment of an open (patent) airway is the first step toward stabilizing the condition of the victim of trauma, so address this problem immediately.

1. **Signs and Symptoms**

   Important signs of chest injuries include:

   A. Pain at the injury site for a week without improvement

   B. Breathing difficulty (may include pain, or just general difficulty in getting air)

   C. Blueness of the lips and/or fingernail beds, indicating oxygen deficiency (cyanosis)

   D. Coughing or spitting up blood with no visible mouth or throat trauma to produce blood

   E. Bruising of the chest or a visible open chest wound

   F. Failure of one or both sides of the chest to expand normally when inhaling (called bilateral symmetry when condition is visible)

2. **Treatment**

   A. Maintain airway and provide CPR as needed.

   B. Open wounds must be sealed as soon as possible. An open wound may be closed by pressure from a gloved hand or a piece of pliable plastic or rubber. This material may even be sealed by application of petroleum jelly (Vaseline) and then a pressure placed over it.

   C. If available, administer oxygen.

   D. Treat for shock even if no symptoms are apparent, as the onset may be sudden.

   E. Transport to a medical facility as soon as possible.

   F. Patient may be placed on uninjured side to enable uninjured side to expand normally.

   G. Other life-threatening injuries may also be treated as appropriate when the victim has had his respirations restored.

ABDOMINAL (ABDOMINOPELVIC) INJURIES

Abdominal injuries may be open or closed, and may include the stomach region or the lower region, called the pelvic area. Open injuries occur when a foreign object enters the abdomen, resulting in external bleeding. Evisceration, or protrusion of abdominal organs, may occur in open injuries. Closed injuries result from severe blows that show no open wound or bleeding on the outside of the body. Internal injuries must always be considered in an accident where trauma has occurred. Sometimes a bruise is present in the abdominal area, but often there is no bruise evident on the exterior tissue of the abdomen. Hollow organ (e.g., stomach, intestines) ruptures spill their contents into the abdominal cavity, causing inflammation. This inflammation can quickly kill if it is not immediately treated by proper surgery. Solid organ (e.g., liver, pancreas, spleen) ruptures result in severe bleeding.

Internal Abdominal and Chest Organs

As can be seen from this model of the human body, there are a number of vital organs that have little protection if blows or force from the front of the body is exerted upon it. The only protection afforded the body from the front (anterior) are the ribs encasing the upper part of the body, where the heart and lungs are located.

Below the ribs, only layers of muscles are present to provide protection to the vital organs of the abdominopelvic region. These muscles are in layers with the fibers crossed with the underlying layers to provide more strength.

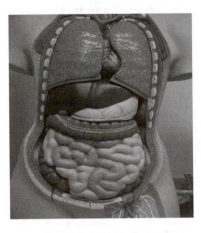

Signs and Symptoms

1. Pain in the abdomen, which may involve cramping

2. Legs drawn up to the chest, sometimes clutching of the legs by the arms

3. Visible skin wounds and penetrations

4. Nausea and/or vomiting

5. Organs visibly protruding to the exterior of the body

6. Urine or stool showing visible blood

7. Guarding of the abdomen

8. Tachycardia (rapid pulse)

9. Clammy (moist and cool) skin

Treatment

1. Maintaining the airway is of primary importance.

2. Observe victim for nausea and vomiting, preventing aspiration of vomitus into lungs.

3. If other injuries permit, flex victim's legs (raise by bending the knees) to relieve the stretching and pulling upon abdominal muscles.

4. DO NOT attempt to force organs protruding from a wound into the abdominal cavity. Cover the organs with sterile dressing moistened with **sterile** saline if available.

5. Treat to prevent shock even if no symptoms are apparent, as the onset may be sudden.

6. Administer oxygen if available.

7. DO NOT allow the victim to eat or drink. Victim may complain of thirst.

8. Monitor vital signs and observe for other life-threatening injuries that necessitate first aid.

9. Transport the victim to an emergency medical facility as soon as possible.

BLISTERS (SOMETIMES CALLED BOILS, ETC.)

A blister may result from various traumas to the skin and is a collection of fluid in a "bubble" under the outer skin. Burns, scrapes, and rubbing against the skin often cause an accumulation of watery fluid under the skin to protect the deeper tissues from damage. These blisters may become infected if not properly treated and may develop into open sores or lesions. Usually, very little treatment is required for simple blisters.

Signs and Symptoms

1. Fluid collection under the skin's outer layer

2. Pain resulting from touch or pressure

3. Swelling and redness around the blister

4. If not infected, blisters usually heal in three to seven days.

Treatment

1. Area should be cleansed with soap and placement of a protective dressing or Band-Aid applied to avoid unnecessary infection

2. If absolutely necessary, when a blister is painful or interferes with movement, blisters may be lanced using a **sterile** needle

Blister in Palm of Hand

3. After puncture, the skin should be left intact, with a sterile bandage over the area

4. Dead skin should be debrided (cut or scraped away) after two days if necessary. Most blisters are self-healing with no treatment, if they do not become infected.

POISONING (MAY BE ACCIDENTAL OR INTENTIONAL)

A poison is a relatively small amount of any substance (solid, liquid, or gas) that when swallowed, inhaled, absorbed, or injected can by its chemical action damage tissue or adversely change organ function and thus can affect health or cause death. Most poisonings occur by accident, where a product is consumed or comes in contact with the victim. Often the poison product is a common, familiar household product. Deaths by swallowing poisoning have dramatically decreased in recent years, particularly in children under the age of five, possibly due to childproof caps on medicine bottles. Despite this reduced number of cases, nonfatal poisoning remains one of the most common reasons for emergency room care and of hospital admissions, particularly among children. It has been estimated that there are more than 1 million accidental poisonings in the United States annually. For each poisoning death among children under the age of five, there are probably nearly one hundred thousand nonfatal cases seen in emergency rooms and clinics, with about 20,000 children hospitalized each year for this problem. The focus here is on ingested poisons, as this is the category that comprises the majority of poisoning emergencies. As mentioned before, most poisonings are accidental and involve common household products.

Signs and Symptoms

1. Most often, initial symptoms will be abdominal pain, cramping, or both

2. Nausea and/or vomiting

3. Diarrhea or feeling of urgency

4. Burns, odor, stains, and other discolorizations around and in mouth

5. Drowsiness, stupor (slow functioning), or unconsciousness

6. Containers that may have held poisonous products or leaves from household plants that may be poisonous found nearby

7. If conscious, victim may state that he has taken some product that may in excess be poisonous (even aspirin and acetaminophen (Tylenol) may be poisonous in high levels)

Critical Information for Poison Control Center Related to Accidental Poisoning

1. Victim – name, age, and size of victim

2. What – the type of poison swallowed if known (type of container or plant)

3. How much, if possible to determine – taste, spoonful, several leaves, half a bottle, etc.

4. How – circumstances surrounding exposure or ingestion

5. How long ago – approximate time elapsed since taken

Important

Contact the Poison Control Center, hospital emergency department, or a physician immediately, before departing for the emergency treatment facility. Some poisons produce little damage until later, while others do damage immediately. More than 70 percent of poisonings can be treated through instructions taken over the telephone. Otherwise, victims should be transported to a medical facility.

If information is available on the container, look to see if vomiting should or should not be induced. Some suggest that milk be drunk immediately, while others do not. Flushing of eyes and skin for contact poisons is never wrong.

Treatment

1. Remove any unswallowed materials, such as pills, capsules, powder, or bits and pieces of the material from the victim's mouth or skin as quickly as possible. This will stop the cycle of absorbing more material from the poisonous product.

2. Treat life-threatening problems discovered in your initial assessment. Prevent shock, and keep the patient comfortable for transport to a medical facility.

3. Perform vital signs and determine if CPR is needed. Be observant for signs of poor breathing, circulation, and skin color.

4. Transport victim along with any containers, labels, or other products found near the victim to an emergency medical treatment facility.

5. Monitor patient's condition on the way to a treatment facility. Be observant of the patient's vital signs, and perform life support if necessary to insure the patient's condition does not deteriorate. The treatment provided before the victim arrives for emergency treatment may make the difference of a good or poor outcome.

INSECT STINGS AND BITES (SPIDERS)

Stings

Bees and wasps are the primary insects that sting as a means of protection. Scorpions are not insects but are the major contributor of stings from animals other than bees and wasps, except for some sea-dwelling creatures, such as jellyfish. The stinger is a modified ovipositor that most insects also use for laying eggs. For a severely allergic person, a single sting may be fatal within fifteen minutes. Although accounts exist of individuals who have survived some 2,000 stings, generally 500 or more stings will kill even people who are not allergic to stinging insects. Some experts report that 1 percent of all children and 4 percent of adults have an allergy to the bites and stings of insects and related creatures (for example, scorpions, spiders). An estimated 50-100 sting-related deaths occur yearly. The number of cases may actually be higher but not reported as involving insect stings because they are mistaken for hearts attacks or they are reported as death due to natural causes. People working alone in woods and fields, in agricultural and logging activities are at risk for being stung and have nobody nearby to observe a severe reaction to the sting. Those who know themselves to be allergic often carry a prepared adrenaline (epinephrine) syringe for self-inoculation if stung by a bee or wasp. If this medication is injected immediately, a victim may avoid going into what is called anaphylactic shock, which may be rapidly fatal.

Bumblebee

Signs and Symptoms

Usual reactions are:

1. Momentary pain near the site of the sting

2. Redness and inflammation at the area of the sting

3. Itching and redness, producing heat in the area where the sting was focused

Worrisome reactions are:

1. Skin flush (redness), and a rash or hives

2. Localized swelling of lips or tongue and in no other area of the body

3. "Tickle" or scratchiness in the throat

4. Audible (can be heard) wheezing of the throat and lungs

5. Abdominal pain and cramps

6. Diarrhea within a short time following the sting

Life-threatening reactions are:

1. Bluish or grayish skin color (cyanosis)

2. Seizures and perhaps reduced awareness of surroundings

3. Unconsciousness, with possibly sudden collapse

4. Inability to breathe due to swelling of vocal cords, making it difficult or impossible to speak

5. Severe swelling of the lips, mouth; more marked than the localized swelling called "worrisome"

6. Some of these signs of "worrisome" and "life-threatening" are similar; exercise caution

History of Sting Reactions

Those who previously have had a reaction to an insect sting should be instructed in self-treatment so they can protect themselves from severe reactions by carrying an antihistamine or other drug. These people should also be advised to purchase a medical alert bracelet or necklace identifying them as insect-allergic.

Treatment

1. Alkaline solutions such as ammonia or baking soda paste made with water will relieve the symptoms of pain; some types of toxin from stinging insects have both an alkaline and an acid component.

2. Observe for signs of shock.

3. Symptoms are self-limiting in most cases, but if respiratory problems arise, transport victim to emergency treatment facility immediately.

4. People with history of adverse reactions to insect bites and stings should carry an emergency ID tag or bracelet warning of hypersensitivity to not only insect stings but to food allergies also.

Spider Bites

In the United States, two spiders, the black widow and the brown recluse, can be deadly. It is possible to be bitten by one of these spiders and be unaware that one has been bitten. Symptoms may occur later, and it would be difficult to determine what caused the symptoms.

Black Widow Spider

The black widow spider is found throughout the world. A red spot (often in the shape of an hourglass) on the abdomen identifies the female: she is the one that bites. Females have a glossy black body. The red hourglass figure is on the abdomen of the female spider, so it is difficult from first glance to identify the spider as a black widow. By volume, black widow spider venom is more deadly than the rattlesnake's, but it is injected in much smaller amounts. Most black widow spiders characteristically live around man-made objects such as wooden steps, posts, and metal objects that come in contact with the ground. This spider is so-called due to her propensity to eat her mate following mating.

Signs and Symptoms

Determining whether a black widow spider has bitten a person is difficult. A sharp pinprick of the spider's bite may be felt, although some victims are not even aware of the bite. Bites by other insects and harmless species of spiders would provide the same sensation as a black widow bite. But in no more than fifteen minutes, a dull, numbing pain usually develops in the bitten extremity. Faint red bite marks appear. Muscle stiffness and cramps occur fairly rapidly, usually in the abdomen when the bite is in the lower part of the body or legs, and affecting the shoulders, back, or chest when the bite is on the upper body or arms. This is followed by:

1. Generalized headache

2. Chills, often accompanied by fever

3. Extreme sweating (diaphoresis)

4. Dizziness sufficient to make walking difficult

5. Nausea and/or vomiting, along with severe abdominal pain

Treatment

1. Treat for shock, even if no symptoms are present. Shock almost invariably ensues, and the emotional trauma associated with having been bitten does little to alleviate the problems.

2. Transport the victim to emergency medical facility as soon as possible, as the patient's condition may rapidly deteriorate. First aid is extremely important, but do not neglect to take the patient for treatment, even if he insists that he is feeling "better."

Brown Recluse Spider

The brown recluse spider has a brown and sometimes purplish violin-shaped figure on its back. Usually bites are not fatal, except for people with a hypersensitivity to this type of spider, or for small children, the elderly, and people with chronic diseases. These spiders are widely distributed throughout the United States. They are often found hiding in attics and unused rooms of the house. They shy away from people and other animals, hence their name, recluse.

Identification of the Brown Recluse Spider

There is a violin or fiddle configuration on the back of the brown recluse. Most often, an ulcer will form within a week following the bite. Tissue often becomes necrotic (dead), and gangrene may develop in some cases. Gangrene is caused by the *Clostridium perfringens* bacterium and may be lethal if untreated. Brown recluse spiders are quite private; one must take care when cleaning or searching in storage areas, where boxes and materials have been traditionally placed for long-term storage.

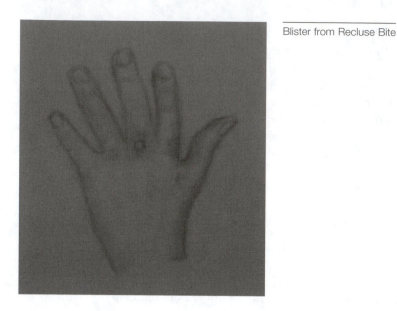

Blister from Recluse Bite

Signs and Symptoms

1. Initial pain felt may be slight, and overlooked

2. A blister at the bite site, along with redness and swelling, appears after several hours

3. Pain, which may remain mild but can become severe, develops within two to eight hours at the bite site

4. Fever, weakness, joint pain

5. Vomiting/nausea

6. Occasionally, a rash may occur

Treatment

1. May require debridement (surgical removal) of necrotic (dead or non-vital) tissue.

2. Treatment with antibiotics to combat the contraction of gangrene or other serious infections must be given due to the prevalence of post-bite gangrene.

3. Always be aware of potential side effects for those that may be hypersensitive to some aspect of the brown recluse. A person may have a bad side effect even with no history of being allergic to these bites.

OTHER ASSORTED ARACHNIDS (HARD OUTER SHELL-LIKE BODY COVERINGS)

If the species of organism that has bitten or stung the victim is unknown, or if you think you can identify it, capture the organism if possible and take it in a glass container to the medical treatment facility for identification. Treatment is often based on a definite identification of these animals. Exotic pets from other countries now frequently are found in the country, and those unfamiliar with their traits and characteristics may become victims of their desire for an unusual pet.

Tarantula Spider

The tarantula has a bite that rarely produces symptoms other than mild to moderate pain, but they are larger and more vicious looking than black widow and brown recluse spiders. Tarantulas have been portrayed on TV and in movies as villainous and dangerous, but they rarely cause more than minor discomfort when they bite. There are numerous species of tarantulas, many of which are quite beautiful and colorful. Many keep them as pets in their households, and there are websites dedicated to the care of this exotic pet. They vary greatly in size, but fortunately their bites offer only about as much pain and discomfort as that of a bee or wasp sting.

Scorpion Stings

Death from scorpion stings in the United States is rare, with children being at the greatest risk. Scorpions are most numerous in the American West, but they are distributed around the United States. They are more numerous in the southern portion of the country, and particularly in the arid Southwest. A scorpion's sting causes immediate pain and burning around the sting site, followed by numbness or tingling. Severe cases may include paralysis, spasms, or respiratory problems requiring

treatment. Scorpion bites are often seen when a person is camping, and a scorpion seeks refuge in the tent, clothing, or boots and shoes of the victim.

Tick Bites

Most tick bites are harmless, although ticks can carry serious diseases including Lyme disease, Rocky Mountain Spotted Fever, and Colorado tick fever, among others. Some diseases from other parts of the world are finding their way into the United States and are creating challenges in control of diseases. Ticks should be removed as soon as possible, as the rickettsial organisms that are similar to a bacterium are transmitted to a human over a period of a

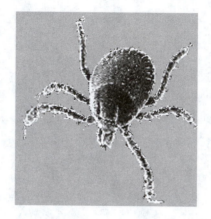

number of hours in most cases. Rapid removal may not afford the organisms time to gain access to the human. It takes 8-24 hours in most cases for the organisms to be transmitted from the tick to the human. The organisms live in the tick's throat, and sometimes the actual reservoir is not in the tick but in a mammal, such as the Lyme disease organism, *Borrelia burgdorferi,* which lives as seed ticks on the skin of deer of North America. The disease is named after the town in which it originated, in Lyme, Connecticut. The sequalae of the disease if untreated results in a type of arthritis and is often discovered when a bull's-eye rash, along with flu-like symptoms and headache, appears. Common antibiotics are used to treat long-term illnesses resulting from Lyme disease and Ehrlichiosis, eliminating many symptoms accompanying the infection. Remember that ticks must remain implanted in the skin of a human for 8-24 hours before the rickettsial organisms are transmitted from the ticks to the human.

Treatment

1. In the case of a bee sting, venom sac is sometimes visible. It may be scraped from the puncture site with the edge of a stiff card, such as a credit card. Other species will not leave a stinger or venom that can be expressed from the sting or bite site.

2. Do not grasp the venom sac with the fingers, as pressure will inject more venom.

3. If symptoms of shock present, transport victim **immediately** for medical aid.

4. Remove jewelry from affected limbs or digits, in case swelling occurs and injury results from tightening of the jewelry near the affected site.

5. Keep the patient's limb immobilized to avoid spreading of toxin.

6. For minor symptoms, signs from sting or bite, cold compresses may relieve the discomfort.

SNAKE BITES

Throughout the world, about 50,000 people die each year from snakebite. In the United States, of the 40,000 to 50,000 annually bitten, over 7,000 are bitten by poisonous snakes. Fortunately, most snakebites occur within a few hours travel of a medical facility where antivenin is available. Just a dozen or so Americans die each year from snakebites. Of the many different snake species, only four in the United States are poisonous: rattlesnake, copperhead, water moccasin, and coral snake. The first three are known as pit vipers, so named after the shallow depression between their eyes. Rattlesnakes are often found in open spaces, even very dry, desert-like areas. They rarely bite unless threatened or their territory is encroached upon. The rattlesnake must coil before it can strike. Rattlesnakes have actually become quite scarce in many areas of the country due to a misunderstanding of their role in nature. Organized hunts are held in many areas, where the rattlesnake population has been decimated.

Rattle Snake

Pit Vipers

The three types of pit vipers are rattlesnakes, copperheads, and the water moccasin, sometimes called a cottonmouth. Common characteristics include:

1. Triangular, flat head wider than its neck

2. Elliptical pupils that are slitted, as in a cat's eye

3. Heat-sensitive "pit" located between each eye and nostril

Signs and Symptom

Severe burning and stinging pain at the bite site

1. Two small puncture wounds about ½ inch apart (some cases may have only one puncture wound)

2. Swelling (happens within five minutes and can involve an entire extremity)

3. Discoloration and blood-filled blisters

4. In severe cases: nausea, vomiting, sweating, weakness

5. No venom injected into the victim in about 25 percent of all poisonous snakebite cases, only fang and tooth wounds

Treatment

1. Bites showing no sign of venom injection require a tetanus shot if indicated (history of immunization within the past five to ten years depending on physician's decision)

2. Cleaning and care of the bite wounds if no complicating factors, such as pain or swelling, are present

3. Controversy exists about proper first aid procedures for snakebite, related to aspiration of the poison. Years ago, snakebite kits included a surgical blade for making an X-marked cut over the puncture site, along with a rubber bulb to be used in aspirating the venom. This is no longer recommended, as the results were not found to be effective.

Coral Snake

The coral snake is usually very small, but some grow to several feet. They are very colorful, with a series of bright red, yellow, and black bands around their bodies. Every other band is yellow, so if red and yellow stripes occur next to each other, the snake is probably a coral snake. A black snout also marks the coral snake. Coral snakebites, while the venom is deadly, are rarely a problem; the mouths of the coral snakes are small, and they actually have to chew on their victims in order to inject the venom.

Antivenin is stored in a number of locations about the country, particularly in Florida, where most coral snakes live. Few people who are bitten get a significant dose of venom, due to the small size of the coral snake, and the amount of time it takes for the snake to inject venom.

Poisonous Plants

In general, poisonous plants are usually merely an annoyance, causing a rash if a person comes into contact with them. Although mushrooms are not plants, many think of them as such. Certain varieties of toadstools form a nerve toxin and are rapidly fatal if eaten. Leave collection of mushrooms to the professionals who either collect them from the wild or most commonly grow them in controlled environments.

Poison Ivy, Oak, and Sumac

Signs and Symptoms

Poison ivy, oak, and sumac plants cause contact dermatitis or an allergic reaction in about 90 percent of all adults. Most people cannot recognize these plants, as they are difficult to identify, especially those in a vine form. A good rule of thumb is to avoid plants that have a pattern of leaves where three leaves stem from a single location on the trunk of the plant. An old saying, "If leaves of three, beware thee!" applies in almost all cases. Also, to test a plant for poison, use the "black spot test" if necessary. Perform this test by crushing the suspected plant's leaf. The sap of poison ivy or oak turns dark **brown** in ten minutes and black in one day. Actually, more than sixty plants can cause an allergic reaction, but the three named previously are by far the most common offenders. Allergic people may come in contact with the juice of these plants from their clothes or shoes, from pet fur, or even from smoke of burning plants. No one can develop the dermatitis by touching the fluid from blisters, as the blister does not contain the olcorcsin that comes from the juice of these poisonous plants. Often, the rash seems to grow worse after several days following the contracting of the dermatitis until the sap's toxins reach the tissue under the top skin layer, the epidermis.

Sometimes within a few short hours, plants with resins that cause dermatitis will cause skin damage, and the levels are categorized as follows:

1. Mild: Some itching

2. Mild to moderate: Itching and redness of the skin's surface

3. Moderate: Itching, redness, and swelling, reaching into the inner layer of skin

4. Severe: Itching, redness, swelling, and blisters that may become infected

Severity is important but so is the amount of skin affected. The greater the skin involvement, the greater the need for medical attention. Although symptoms may appear within a few hours of exposure, most often a day or two elapses between contact and the onset of the above signs and symptoms (http://www.outdoorplaces.com/Features/Hiking/poisonivy/). Most symptoms will subside within a few days without treatment.

Treatment

1. A variety of topical preparations are available over-the-counter to relieve symptoms.

2. For severe cases, steroidal medications including injectable steroids are available.

3. If the toxins are inhaled, severe symptoms of the lungs are possible. In the case of pulmonary involvement, rapid and definitive treatment by a physician is required.

4. Severe cases where large areas of skin are involved may require placing sterile dressings with topical ointment on the affected areas.

Household Plants/Outdoors Plants

Also remember that many household plants are poisonous to both humans and pets. Other than those plants that cause extreme dermatitis, as in poison oak and poison ivy, some plants cause serious poisoning if chewed or swallowed. Children and pets may handle or eat the leaves from houseplants and some may make the child or animal quite ill. You may obtain information regarding common household plants that may have been ingested from the Poison Control Center and from the Internet. It is desirable to have some knowledge about plants you may have in your home and the effect they may have on humans and animals. Many of the familiar plants we commonly use in our homes may be poisonous, particularly to small children and to pets.

Carbon Monoxide

Victims of carbon monoxide (CO) poisoning are often unaware of its presence. The gas is invisible, tasteless, odorless, and nonirritating. Carbon monoxide produces its toxicity due to several factors. CO becomes tightly bound to hemoglobin (red blood cells) that normally carries oxygen to the organs and tissues of the body. With conscious victims, it takes four to five hours with ordinary air (21 percent oxygen) or thirty to forty minutes with 100 percent oxygen to reverse CO's effects. When CO levels in the air are high, the level of oxygen is probably low. Even if a probable victim of CO poisoning insists he will be all right, seek medical assistance.

People who heat with gas should have a CO detector in the home to alert the residents to increased levels of CO. Faulty heating and use of kerosene heaters, as well as improperly vented or designed heaters, place the inhabitants of the dwelling in danger. Fireplaces may also be capable of producing carbon monoxide, and charcoal grills should never be operated indoors. CO is also a popular method of suicide, with the victim most often using a hose attached to the exhaust and running the gases back into the car. There is also a danger in starting a car in a garage and allowing it to idle for more that a short time, EVEN WITH THE GARAGE DOOR OPEN!

Signs and Symptoms

It is difficult to tell if a person is a victim of carbon monoxide poisoning. Carbon monoxide gas is colorless, odorless, and tasteless. Carbon monoxide is cumulative, and a small leak in a heating device may eventually build up a level within its victims sufficient to induce unconsciousness. CO replaces the oxygen our bodies need to perform our bodily functions, such as cellular metabolism, so it is extremely dangerous. Sometimes, a complaint of having the flu is really a symptom of carbon monoxide poisoning. This occurs when a victim is gradually exposed to low levels of carbon monoxide and eventually becomes quite ill. Some entire families are exposed to carbon monoxide for long periods of time and suffer only vague symptoms. Carbon monoxide alarms are becoming more numerous and are found in many homes today. Some symptoms include:

1. Headache

2. "Ringing" in the ears (tinnitus)

3. Chest pain and tightness

4. Breathing difficulties with possible cyanosis

5. Cardiac failure

6. Weakness and feelings of fatigue

7. Nausea, vomiting

8. Dizziness and altered mental state

9. Visual changes

10. Unconsciousness

Treatment

It is false that victims of carbon monoxide poisoning always have cherry red lips! This may occur, but it is not the usual sign that would alert someone to the possibility of CO poisoning.

1. Remove victim from carbon monoxide-saturated area

2. Administer oxygen if available. Continue to administer oxygen even after the victim reports that he is feeling fine.

3. Serious consequences may occur from this type of poisoning, so get the patient medical care as soon as possible, while continuing administering oxygen.

4. Symptoms and signs of a progressive poisoning by carbon monoxide by improperly vented heating appliances may be easily missed or dismissed as merely a respiratory ailment that

will soon pass. The best protection is to have regular maintenance inspections on furnaces, and to have a carbon monoxide detector in the home.

FIRE-RELATED INJURIES

Smoke Inhalation

Smoke inhalation may occur in conjunction with fires as well as chemical burns. This smoke may contain a number of poisonous toxins that may injure or be lethal to the victim. A victim of smoke inhalation is at risk if immediate treatment is not started. Even if no lung damage from heat or fire has occurred, a person who breathed smoke may be unable to have good

oxygen and carbon dioxide exchange, even after being removed from the source of the smoke. Specialized treatment must be commenced immediately in order to save the lives of these victims. Firefighters are also at risk for smoke inhalation, although respirators are employed during fire-fighting activities. Some people, instead of fleeing a house fire, have a mistaken idea that water will protect them from smoke's toxins. The best protection is to crawl toward the nearest exit as quickly as possible, avoiding raising the head and taking great breaths of air. The synthetic fabrics and other materials used in building materials, paints, and even kitchen appliances and utensils release toxic fumes when burning and may rapidly cause the victim to go to an unconscious state. Most experienced people, when staying in hotels and motels or in unfamiliar houses, will mentally mark the nearest exits, and will in an emergency be prepared to escape. Smoke alarms are now found in almost all homes and by law are found in businesses. Still, an unnecessarily large number of people are killed by smoke inhalation each year. Smoking in bed usually starts the fires; the smoker falls asleep, dropping the cigarette into the bed, a chair, or even the carpet with often disastrous results. Many local governments provide alarms free of charge. Firefighters are prepared by training and by possession of specialized equipment to fight and survive in fiery conditions. Respirators with tanks of air are provided along with fireproof suits and lights for use in movement in heavy smoke. They often provide training to schools and to groups desiring to become knowledgeable about surviving a fire if trapped, either indoors or outdoors.

Signs and Symptoms
1. Problems with breathing

2. Coughing, choking, or coughing up dark-colored sputum

3. Breath may smell of smoke or chemical odor

4. Patient's nose and mouth may be blackened or gray

5. Singed hair on head, in nose

6. The entire body may be blackened by smoke residue, even if no skin burns have occurred

Treatment

1. Remove patient to safe area immediately, a great distance away from the fire.

2. Administer oxygen if available, and as quickly as possible.

3. Always transport the patient for more advanced care – don't risk the person's life by delaying treatment.

4. The rescuer should remember to protect himself or herself from smoke inhalation when attempting rescue of someone from a burning building. The best protection is use of a properly designed respirator. A would-be rescuer overcome by smoke would be of little help to himself or herself, or to the person needing help.

Heat Burns

It is estimated that there are several million burn injuries each year that require medical attention or restrict the mobility and activity of the burn victims. Of these, perhaps one-third is treated at hospital emergency departments. Several thousand people die annually from injuries caused by burns. The skin is sensitive to heat. Skin damage usually does not occur below 111 degrees Fahrenheit. Temperatures between 111 degrees and 123 degrees cause significant tissue damage. Temperatures above 123 degrees destroy skin within a brief moment. Few first aid providers will be called upon to perform assessments of burns. However, it is important that one know some general precautions about and the severity of burns. Treatments for the various burns are based on the severity and type of burn. Most victims of severe burns require immediate, definitive, and specialized treatment in order to survive. Consult the following information to provide guidance for proper first aid.

Assessing a Burn

Assess a burn after breathing, bleeding, or more life-threatening problems have been treated. There is an argument about whether or not first aid providers should perform burn assessments. On the one hand, some first aid educators agree that it is almost impossible to determine accurately the percentage and depth of a burn during the initial stages of assessment, and it would be a waste of time, as the first aid steps would be the same. It is thought that estimates of depth and area affected will not be accurate until several days after being burned. On the other hand, a quick assessment of area and depth of burn is helpful in communicating to an emergency facility the approximate extent of damage to the skin and tissues involved. So most would recommend a rapid and as complete as possible assessment.

How large is the burn?

The extent of a burn is expressed as a percentage of the total body surface. The familiar "Rule of Nines" defines a hand and arm as 9 percent of the body surface. Each leg, since it is much larger than the arm, is considered as 18 percent of the body's surface. The front and back torso (chest, belly, back) are each counted as 18 percent with the genital area at only 1 percent. The victim's head comprises about 9 percent. Using these estimates, it is possible to calculate most burns. The Rule of Nines is accurate only for adults, as it does not make allowances for the differing proportions of a child. In small children, the head is larger than the body size, and accounts for 18 percent, with each leg considered as 14 percent. Accordingly, the Rule of Nines is modified when assessing a child who has suffered burns. The higher the amount of body surface that is burned, the greater the mortality rate, and if more than one-third of the body is burned, the prognosis is poor unless specialized care is received as soon as possible. Use of synthetic materials as well as skin from cadavers are common at burn centers located around the country. These specialty facilities now save the lives of many who would have died years ago.

Depth of Burn Indicates Severity of Burn

First-degree burns (superficial). These burns affect the skin's outer layer. Characteristics include redness, mild swelling, tenderness, and pain. Healing occurs without scarring within a week.

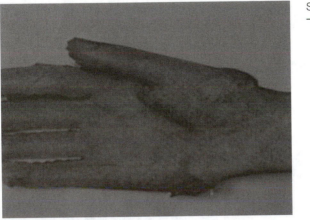

Second-degree Burn

Second-degree burns (partial-thickness). These burns extend through the entire outer skin layer and into the inner skin layer. Blister formation, swelling, weeping of fluids, and severe pain characterize second-degree burns. Intact blisters maintain a sterile covering, whereas a broken blister results in a weeping wound.

Third-degree burns (full-thickness). These severe burns extend through all skin layers and into the underlying fat, muscle, and bone. Discoloration (charred, white, or cherry red) and a leathery, parchment-like, dry appearance indicate this degree of burn. Pain is absent because the nerve endings have been destroyed. Accompanying burns of lesser degrees (first- and second-degree) cause any pain found with this burn. Proper healing requires a skin graft, which is a long-term treatment involving repeated removal of dead skin and grafting of bits of normal skin tissue from an unburned part of the body to the affected areas. The greatest causes of death from severe burns are loss of fluids and entry of infection through the broken skin barrier.

What parts of the body are burned?

Areas of most importance are the face (especially the eyelids), the hands, the feet, and the genitals. Respiratory tract burns are especially serious if associated with inhalation of fumes or heat. The loss of tissue or damaged tissue in the lungs greatly affects oxygen and carbon dioxide exchange, exacerbating the other associated problems of burn injuries. If the limbs are badly damaged by heat, mobility will be affected immediately following the injury, and of course scar tissue that later develops may handicap the victim for the rest of his life. Efforts to avoid injury from fires are of the utmost importance in our schools and communities, as most fires can be avoided.

How old is the burned victim?

A burn is considered more serious in an infant and in an elderly person (over 65) than in other victims. Small children are usually burned in kitchen or bathroom accidents where they come in contact with hot water, so prevention of burns to children can largely be accomplished by using care when cooking and by not leaving small children unattended in the bathtub. Elderly people are most often burned in house fires, where fires start from lack of attention to excessive heat applied to cooking vessels in the kitchen, and in the winter when loose clothing catches fire from heaters and fireplaces.

Does the victim have any injuries other than burns or medical problems?

Burns can aggravate diabetes, heart disease, and lung disease, as well as other medical problems. Presence of chronic disease greatly diminishes the chances of survival, as these people may already be in a weakened or debilitated state; treatment of their chronic conditions may be difficult or neglected while treating the burns.

Chemical Burns

At least 25,000 products found in industry, agriculture, and the home can burn and cause tissue damage. A chemical continues to cause damage until it is inactivated by the tissue, is neutralized, or is diluted with water. The "burning" process may continue for long periods of time after initial contact. Alkali burns are more serious than acid burns because they penetrate deeper and remain active longer. Advanced chemical or toxicological education is not needed to treat most common chemical burns, because first aid is the same for all except a few special burns that require something added to neutralize the chemical. Breathing of fumes from volatile chemicals, or those that form vapors in the

Industrial site with Drums of stored chemicals

air, may damage the lungs after only a short period of exposure. It should be noted that some chemicals, particularly pure sodium, will burn in the absence of oxygen, so stopping the damaging actions of fire is sometimes quite difficult. People who work in environments that require the use of volatile chemicals require a great deal of training and understanding in order to avoid injuries. Material Safety Data Sheets (MSDS) must be posted or available where potentially dangerous chemicals are stored or used. The manufacturer of the chemicals provides them. Training in the use of reading and understanding prevention and first aid when exposed is derived from these MSDS.

Cleanup of toxic spills and areas where industrial sites have become contaminated is a specialized activity that is best left to the experts. In past generations, knowledge of these spills and of contamination of large areas of the earth was not well understood. As we now know, disposal of batteries, tires, computers and their parts, as well as chemicals no longer needed or viable consumes a large part of our governmental efforts. In the past two decades, a superfund has been formulated by the federal government to protect unborn children who may be damaged by residual chemicals in the earth, as well as land and water animals. Even disposal of residential wastes from our homes may be hazardous to our environment and our population if not done properly. Laws regarding the creation of landfills and proper management to prevent leakage of toxic materials have become increasingly rigid over the past few years. Specialized types of contamination, such as that of radioactive materials from nuclear plants and medical procedures, are also strictly regulated. Specialized teams called Haz-Mat (Hazardous Materials) teams are formed about the country for rapid response to spills and leaks of dangerous materials. These teams are trained in eliminating the risk to the general population, and their training is updated periodically. Various governmental entities from local, state, and federal agencies sponsor these teams. Some larger industries may even have their own teams to respond to spills and leaks within the confines of their own work areas.

TABLE OF RAPID TREATMENT FOR BURNS AND PRECAUTIONS IN TREATING

Burn	Do	Don't
First-degree Redness, mild swelling, pain	Apply cold water and/or dry sterile dressing	Apply butter, margarine, oils
Second-degree Deeper; blisters develop	Immerse in cold water; blot dry with sterile cloth for protection Treat for shock. Obtain medical attention if severe	Break blisters or remove shreds of tissue. Use antiseptic preparation, ointment spray, or home remedy on severe burn
Third-degree	Cover with sterile cloth to protect Treat for shock Watch for breathing difficulty Obtain medical attention quickly	Remove charred clothing that is stuck to burn. Apply ice. Use home remedy.
Chemical Burn	Remove by flushing with large quantities of water for at least fifteen minutes. Remove surrounding clothing. Obtain medical attention.	

Electrical Burns

Electrical injuries are devastating to the body, but they sometimes produce no visible damage initially. Even with just a mild shock, a victim can suffer extremely serious internal injuries. A current of 1,000 volts or more is considered high voltage, but even the 110 volts of household current can be deadly. High-voltage electrical currents passing through the body may disrupt the normal heart rhythm, cause cardiac arrest, burns, and other injuries. Often, a person who has experienced a serious shock does not feel he has been injured or even realize the extent of tissue damage until days later.

Downed Electrical Lines

When someone is electrocuted, electricity enters the body at the point of contact and travels along the path of least resistance, which is usually along nerves and blood vessels. A patient with implanted metal devices may suffer from currents passing through these devices. The current travels rapidly, generating heat and causing destruction. Usually, the electricity exits where the body is touching a surface or is in contact with a ground (e.g., a metal object). Sometimes, a victim may have more than one exit site.

Precautions: Contact with Power Line (Outside Situations)

1. Observe caution following traffic accidents and storms, when power lines are often forced to the ground. If electrocution comes from contact with a downed power line, the power must be turned off before a rescuer can approach anyone in contact with the wire.

2. If the victim is in a car with a power line fallen across it, tell him or her to stay in the car until the power can be shut off. The only exception to this rule is when fire threatens the car. In this case, tell the victim to jump out of the car without making contact with the car's frame or any wire on the ground or over the car. Caution must be exercised as to which door to use as an exit.

3. If you approach a victim and you feel a tingling sensation in your legs and lower body, **stop immediately!** This sensation signals you are on energized ground and that an electrical current is entering through one foot, passing through your lower body, and leaving through the other foot. If this happens, raise a foot off the ground, turn around, and hop to a safe place.

4. If you can safely reach the victim, do not attempt to move any wires with wood poles, tools with wooden handles, or objects with high moisture content. Even dry, dead wood may have moisture content sufficient to carry a current. Do not attempt to move downed wires at all unless you are trained and equipped with tools able to handle the high voltage.

5. Wait until the power company can cut the wires or disconnect them. Prevent bystanders from entering the danger area by guarding the perimeter, being on the lookout for approaching people.

6. People caught in a storm and in an open area may experience electrical shocks from high-voltage discharges of lightning. One should never go to high ground or stand under a tree during an electrical storm. Seek shelter in a building or an automobile until the storm has passed.

Precautions: Contact inside Buildings

Most electrical burns inside occur from faulty electrical equipment or careless use of electrical appliances. Turn off the electricity at the circuit breaker, fuse box, outside switch box, or unplug the appliance if the plug is undamaged. Do not touch the appliance or the victim until the current is off. Electrical outlets in areas where water is often used, such as in restrooms and kitchens in homes, and restaurants, to name a few, are often required to have special provisions for outlets that will automatically "trip" or turn themselves off in the event they contact water. Many small appliances, such as hair dryers and radios, also have this safety feature built into them.

COLD-RELATED EMERGENCIES

Cold injuries, just as with heat injuries, are graded in degrees of severity. There are four degrees of cold injury. Low outside temperatures, when present along with wind, may cause cold-related injuries within minutes.

1. Hypothermia

Hypothermia occurs when the body's core temperature decreases to less than an average temperature of 37°C. Hypothermia can occur at temperatures above freezing as well as below it.

A. Protecting Oneself against Hypothermia

The victim may also suffer frostbite if the body continues to lose more heat than it produces. A person lost in a wilderness area may suffer from exposure quite rapidly. Before nightfall, if a person finds himself or herself in an area with no protection, a cave, a windfall built of brush, and piles of dry leaves are helpful. Gathering firewood before darkness falls and starting a fire would be prudent. The fire might also guide would-be rescuers.

If the body temperature falls to 80°F, most people die. Hypothermia is not caused by outdoor exposure alone, and the elderly with inadequate home heating may fall victim. Cool indoor temperatures may bring the body to a hypothermic state, or exposure to cold water may do so even more quickly than cold air. A victim's core body temperature determines the type of hypothermia. To take the temperature, you need a specialized low-reading thermometer, not the standard rectal thermometer, which is calibrated from 94 to 108°F. The recommended type is a rectal thermometer capable of reading temperatures between 84 to 108°F. These thermometers are only available in specialized treatment facilities. The first aid provider is not normally equipped to provide the level of care a person with hypothermia needs, except for specialized rescue teams found in some remote areas. Trauma centers located in cold climates are able to handle these cases adequately.

B. Levels of Hypothermia

a. **Mild** (above 90°F). Shivering, slurred speech, memory lapses, and fumbling hands. Victims frequently stumble and stagger. They are usually conscious and can talk. While many people suffer cold hands and feet, victims of mild hypothermia experience cold abdomens and backs, too.

b. **Profound** (below 90°F). Shivering has stopped. Muscles may become stiff and rigid, similar to rigor mortis. The victim's skin has a blue appearance and doesn't respond to pain; pulse and respirations slow down, and pupils dilate. The victim appears to be dead. More than half of profoundly hypothermic victims die.

2. Frostnip

This occurs after long exposure to cold but is not a serious problem. The condition is not usually painful. The skin becomes white or pale. First aid for frostnip consists of gently warming the affected area. This can be done with bare hands or by blowing warm air on the area.

Signs and Symptoms
A. First Degree is Superficial (only skin surface is affected)

a. Skin color is white or grayish-yellow.

b. Pain may occur early and later subside.

c. Affected part may feel only very cold and numb. There may be a tingling, stinging, or aching sensation.

d. Skin surface will feel hard or crusty and underlying tissue soft when depressed gently and firmly.

3. Frostbite

Frostbite occurs when temperatures drop below freezing. Tissue is damaged in two ways. There is an actual freezing of the tissue fluids, resulting in the formation of ice crystals

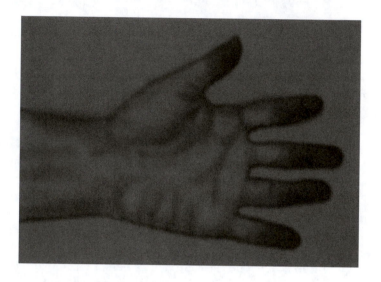

between the tissue cells. The ice crystals enlarge as they extract water from the cells. The blood supply to the tissues is also obstructed as the blood becomes similar to sludge and forms blood clots, which prevent blood from flowing to tissues. Obstruction of the blood flow does more severe damage than the actual freezing does. Frostbite mainly affects the feet, hands, ears, and nose where blood flow is minimal. These areas do not contain large heat-producing muscles; they contain mostly small vessels, such as capillaries near the surface, and are some distance from the heat-generating sources of the body. In addition, when the body conserves heat, the blood supply diminishes first in these areas farthest from the core of the body.

The most severe injury possibilities of frostbite include both the contraction of gangrene and amputation. Each year, small children wander into the cold from their houses and are usually discovered only after they have suffered frostbite or hypothermia. Some people are more prone to frostbite than others. Frostbite victims may also suffer from hypothermia. DO NOT rub the area with snow as this is erroneous information. The very young, the elderly, and people with alcohol and drug addictions are more likely to find themselves in situations where frostbite is probable. They often lack the capacity to determine that they are in danger from exposure to extreme cold.

Signs and Symptoms of Frostbite
A. Deep (Deeper tissues are affected)

a. Affected part feels hard, solid, and cannot be depressed when pressure is placed on the affected areas.

b. Blisters appear in 12 to 36 hours.

c. Affected part is cold with pale, waxy skin. No natural warmth from the body will be felt in these parts as blood circulation has largely ceased.

d. A painfully cold area suddenly stops hurting due to nerve damage and nerve destruction at the site.

B. Degrees (Based on the Stage Following Thawing)

After an area has thawed, frostbite can be categorized into degrees similar to the classification of burns, with the addition of a fourth category. First-degree frostbite is superficial, while the other three are determined by depth of tissue injury and destruction.

a. **First-degree frostbite.** Affected part is warm, swollen, and tender.

b. **Second-degree frostbite.** Blisters form within minutes to hours after thawing and enlarge over a several day period.

c. **Third-degree frostbite.** Blisters are small, and contain reddish-blue or purplish fluid. Surrounding skin may have a red or blue color and may not blanch when pressure is applied.

d. **Fourth-degree frostbite.** No blisters or swelling occurs. The area remains numb, cold, and white-to-dark purple in color. This is the most severe of cold injury and the tissue is completely destroyed.

C. Treatment

All frostbite injuries follow the same first aid treatment.

a. Seek medical attention immediately.

b. Rewarming of frostbitten parts seldom takes place outside of a medical facility, as special equipment is used. The body must be warmed from the inside by administration of warm fluids intravenously.

c. **Never** use the old-fashioned remedy, which recommended rubbing the frozen area with snow! This will only make the situation worse, wetting the area with cold moisture and allowing evaporation to cool the area further. Remember, this is a true emergency, and rapid and proper treatment should be left to the experts.

Heat-Related Emergencies

There are major and minor levels of heat injury. Each of these levels has two categories of injury. If a lesser-degree injury is not treated quickly, the injury may rapidly progress to a more serious level. When working outside in hot weather, people must observe each other for signs of heat injury. It is advisable to consume adequate water and to take frequent breaks in the shade. Sometimes the heat injury comes on insidiously, and a person develops a heat injury without being aware that they are in any danger. Prevention is much better than treatment after an injury has occurred. A person whose injury has progressed to heat stroke status has a very poor prognosis for survival. As in other risks, the elderly who may be somewhat insensitive to temperature are at great risk. Also, heat injuries can occur inside the home if fans or air conditioning are not available.

Person Sweating, Flushed From Exertion

Minor Category	Major Category
Heat cramps and heat syncope	Heat Stroke and Heat Exhaustion

Heat Cramps

Heat cramps are painful muscle spasms in the arms or legs. They may occur when an excessive amount of body fluid is lost through sweating. Controversy exists regarding what type of liquid to drink: plain water, a commercial sports drink, or a saltwater solution. The body loses more water than electrolytes (sodium, potassium, etc.) during exercise. Experts generally agree that the primary need for those sweating in hot environments is to replace the water lost from heavy sweating, rather than the electrolytes. No proof exists that muscle cramping results from a shortage of electrolytes. Routine use of salt tablets to prevent heat cramps is no longer recommended since they can induce high blood pressure and hinder adjustment to heat. The ingestion of adequate amounts of fluids to replace those lost through sweating is effective. Alcoholic beverages are not indicated and may actually contribute to the development of heat cramps, as they dehydrate the tissues of the body. The best prevention for heat cramps is providing for a well-hydrated body. Drinks such as those with electrolytes in them are extremely popular for athletes as an aid in preventing heat cramps.

Signs and Symptoms

1. Severe cramping, usually affecting arms or legs

2. Abdominal cramping

Treatment

1. Replace the water lost from heavy sweating

2. Remove the victim to a cool area

Heat Syncope

The term *syncope* refers to fainting, and heat syncope is characterized by dizziness or fainting while standing still in the heat for periods of time. Agricultural workers and soldiers are most vulnerable to the disorder, but anyone is subject to this condition if remaining relatively motionless in a hot environment for more than a few minutes. The blood tends to pool in the skin and lower part of the body when remaining relatively motionless, causing decreased blood flow to the brain. Heat syncope is the least serious of heat-induced disorders, but it may cause the victim to become injured when falling, or to be exposed to dangerous moving parts of machinery. Effective treatment simply requires resting in a cooler environment until recovery before resuming duties in the heat. However prevention is best, and it can be accomplished by acclimating oneself to the heat and not standing still in the heat for protracted periods of time.

Heat Exhaustion

Heat exhaustion results from either excessive perspiration or the inadequate replacement of water lost through sweating. It is less critical than heat stroke, but it requires prompt attention because it can progress to heat stroke if left untreated. Immediate treatment should be initiated at the earliest signs of being affected by heat. A person may not recognize that he is suffering from the heat and will not often ask for help. Prompt treatment will avoid the more serious aspects of heat-related injuries. A person who appears to be suffering from heat, probably is, and the condition should be addressed quickly. The elderly, who may be somewhat insensitive to heat, are often the first to suffer from heat-related conditions, and lack of fans and air conditioning for the elderly contributes greatly to the onset of heat injury.

Signs and Symptoms

1. Heavy sweating

2. Muscle weakness

3. Fast pulse

4. Normal body temperature

5. Headache and dizziness

6. Nausea and vomiting

Heat Stroke (Sunstroke)

Heat stroke is the most dangerous heat-related emergency. The death rate from this condition approaches 50 percent, even with appropriate medical care. Untreated victims always die. Heat stroke occurs when the body is subjected to more heat than it can handle, losing its normal capacity to rid the body of heat, which is accomplished through perspiring and drying of the perspiration.

Types

Classic   This type affects the elderly, chronically ill, obese, alcoholic, diabetic, and those with circulatory problems. It results from a combined hot environment and loss of body-cooling mechanisms.

Exertional   This type affects a healthy individual who is working or playing strenuously in a warm environment.

Signs and Symptoms

1. Loss of consciousness

2. Skin that is hot to the touch; victims do not sweat because the sweating mechanism is overwhelmed in victims with heat stroke

3. High body temperature

4. Rapid pulse (tachycardia) and breathing (tachypnea)

5. Weakness, dizziness, headache

BONE AND MUSCULOSKELETAL INJURIES

Fractures

The terms fracture and broken bone have the same meaning: a break or crack in a bone. Fractures are classified as being **open** (when the skin is broken and bleeds externally) or **closed** (when the skin has not been broken). Fractures, particularly open ones, may do a large amount of tissue damage if untreated or inadequately treated. Bleeding may be to the extent that the victim may become anemic and need transfusion to improve the blood volume. The danger of infection is great when there is an open wound, particularly one that is jagged and torn, leaving a large amount of surface area exposed to an unclean environment. Since the bones and muscles are major systems of the body, with more functions than just movement for the muscles and support for the skeletal system, there are many side effects of injuries to these systems.

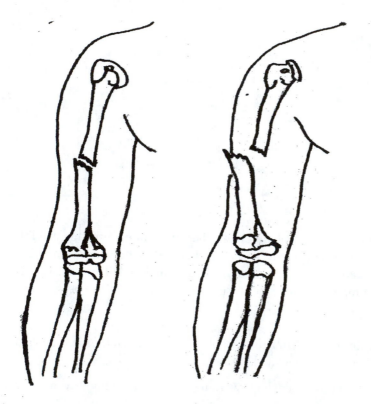

Drawings of Broken Humerus. Drawing on left is of closed fracture Drawing on right is of open fracture – note bone protruding through skin and other tissue

Fracture Classification

1. Open or compound fracture.
   The overlaying skin has been damaged or broken. The wound can be produced either by the bone protruding through the skin or by a direct blow cutting the skin at the time of the fracture. The bone may not always be seen in the wound. Any broken bone that is covered by damaged skin is classified as an open fracture. Open fractures are more serious than

closed fractures because of greater potential for blood loss and greater chance of infection through breaks in the skin and underlying tissue.

2. Closed or simple fracture. The skin has not been broken and there is no visible wound near the fracture site.

Signs and Symptoms

1. Swelling: Caused by bleeding if present; occurs rapidly following a fracture.

2. Deformity: This is not always obvious with initial assessment. Compare the injured with the uninjured opposite part when checking for deformity.

3. Pain and tenderness: Commonly found only at the injury site. The victim will usually be able to point to the site of the pain. A useful procedure for detecting fractures is to feel along the bones gently; complaints about pain or tenderness serve as a reliable sign of a fracture.

4. Loss of use: There is an actual inability to use the injured part, which is called "guarding."

5. Grating or grinding: Do not move a limb in an attempt to see if a grating sound or sensation (called **crepitus**) can be felt and sometimes heard when the splintered bone ends scrub against each other.

6. History of the injury: One should consider a fracture when severe accidents occur. The victim may relate that he heard or felt a snapping sound during the accident.

Bandaging and Splinting

Bandaging and splinting dislocations and broken bones, as well as severe sprains, is important in minimizing further damage and discomfort to the victim. It is important to stabilize the victim before he or she can be moved to a trauma facility to perform advanced procedures to stabilize the patient and set them on the road to recovery. Immediate and adequate treatment is extremely vital to the well-being of a victim of a traumatic injury. The methodology for stabilizing and protecting joints and broken bones is essentially the same. A rigid piece of board may be padded to avoid chafing of the tissue, and the limb is aligned with the board or boards and tied securely to maintain a stable position. Fingers may be taped together if no splint is available, and one leg may be strapped to the other in the absence of long splints. Sprained joints, torn muscles, dislocated joints, or broken bones should not be allowed to move about, as pain or injury to the surrounding tissues will result. Delay in treatment also makes it more difficult to have a positive outcome following medical treatment.

Procedure

If you as a first responder suspect that a bone is broken or a joint is dislocated, the affected limb should be splinted or immobilized, or both. If done adequately, a splint will prevent further injury and sometimes provide a great deal of relief from pain. If manufactured splints are not available, pad materials such as tree branches, boards, heavy cardboard, or stiff foam. Wrapping materials, such as handkerchiefs, torn clothing, or possibly tent fabric, may be used to wrap the splint and for tying the limb to the splints.

Unless the patient is in a dangerous setting (middle of a road, at the foot of a gully exposed to frequent ice or rock fall), all injuries should be splinted before the victim is moved to minimize further injury. If sensations and/or pulses are diminished, deformed fractures should be straightened before beginning the process of splinting (take care not to worsen the injury). A basic rule of splinting is that the joint above and below the affected limb should be immobilized to adequately protect the fracture site. For example, if the lower leg is broken, both the ankle and knee should be immobilized by the splint.

Check for pulses and sensation below the splint at least once per hour, or if the patient complains of tightness, tingling, or numbness, as circulation may be decreased due to pressure. If there is a possibility of decreased circulation or pressure on a nerve, release the wrapping material completely and rewrap the splint slightly looser. A sling fashioned from a cravat bandage or any cloth available is effective in immobilizing collarbone, shoulder, and upper arm injuries extending down to the elbow. The immobilized limb should be tied slightly higher than the waist, and should not be allowed to dangle. Wrap the arm sling to the person's body with a large bandage encircling the person's chest. Injury to the forearm and wrist requires a straight supportive splint that secures and aligns both the wrist and the elbow. Almost any stiff material is useful in fashioning a supportive mechanism for the arm or leg, temporarily, until the victim can be transported for emergency care.

Finger injuries are usually fairly simple and can be buddy-taped to the adjacent, unaffected fingers or splinted with small pieces of wood or cardboard until more sturdy splints can be applied. Pelvis, hip, and femur (upper leg) fractures often completely immobilize the person. Because broken bones of the pelvis and upper leg can cause massive, life-threatening internal bleeding, victims should be evacuated unless splinting and carriage is absolutely necessary. In these cases, the splint should extend to the low back and down past the knee of the affected side. Don't forget to stabilize the foot, as it might move and cause excruciating pain to the victim.

Knee injuries require splints that extend to the hip and down to the ankle. These are applied to the back of the leg and buttock to minimize movement of broken splintered bone or dislocated joints. Ankle and foot injuries can be wrapped alone. Use a figure-eight pattern: under the foot, over the top of the foot, around the back of the ankle, back over the top of the foot, under the foot, until all of the material has been used. A stretchable Ace bandage is useful, but exercise caution to avoid compressing circulation with this material. Alternately, splinting supports can be used along the back and sides of the ankle to prevent excessive movement. The ankle should be kept at the right angle in the splint. Toe injuries can be buddy-taped to the adjacent, unaffected toe until evaluated in an advanced care medical clinic or other facility.

Finger, Buddy-Taped

Two fingers may be buddy-taped together in the absence of any splinting material to afford some minimal protection. This provides for some decrease of motion as the joints are at differing points on adjacent fingers and this anatomical feature provides for some rigidity.

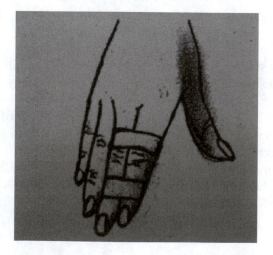

Finger taped to tongue blade for support

A tongue depressor may be used if available, or a popsicle stick or any suitable flat rigid material to avoid movement of the injured finger or fingers. Fingers usually heal and the bone repairs itself without surgery or considerable treatment. However, the finger must be aligned or deformities causing crooked growth may occur.

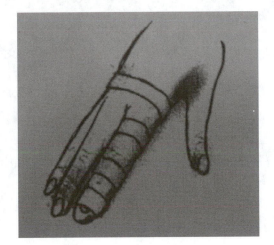

Broken Long Bone of Leg

A broken long bone must be supported to prevent movement, which would further aggravate an already serious condition. Upper leg injuries may require a short splint on the inside of the thigh to the groin, and a longer splint for the lateral side of the leg, extending to the pelvic girdle or above. When an injury occurs in an isolated area, the first aid provider or the injured person must be creative in order to find materials that will protect the injured limb until the person is rescued or finds a way to get to an area where he may have a possibility of being rescued.

Forearm, Wrist, or Hand Injury

The splint should extend from the fingertips to the elbow. This is because there are two joints to immobilize to prevent injury to the broken bone that is located between the joints. Use a sling or a cravat bandage to cover the area, elevating the extremity for comfort and support. This will help to prevent swelling somewhat.

Dislocated or Injured Knee

Knee may be immobilized between two boards. Boards must be padded to avoid chafing. Elevation on a pillow may be necessary for comfort and to help reduce swelling and further damage.

Bleeding (Often Accompanies Musculoskeletal Injuries)

Treatment

Elevations of the area of bleeding, along with placing pressure bandages, are often necessary to stop the bleeding from a cut or tear in the skin and perhaps the muscles. If the bleeding continues after placing a pressure bandage, place another bandage over the original one. NEVER remove the original bandage, as it may tear loose a forming clot and worsen the bleeding. A tourniquet should never be used except in the most extreme emergency, such as in the traumatic amputation of a leg or arm. Tissue is always permanently damaged by applying a tourniquet, so this is a last-ditch effort.

Pressure points are arteries that pass close to the surface of the skin and lie directly over a bony area. This procedure should only be employed after direct pressure or direct pressure with elevation of the area has failed to alleviate the bleeding. There are twenty-two major pressure points of the body, twelve on each side of the body. However, the only sites normally used by first responders would be brachial artery pressure point on the inside of the upper arm, running along the humerus. You should be able to place two or three fingers against the inside of the humerus, midway between the shoulder and the elbow, and feel the pulsations there. The other major site is the upper femur, where the leg joins the body. Direct hard pressure against this area with the heel of the hand should help to control bleeding. A wad of cloth or other pliable material applied directly over the bleeding site, then wrapped by strips of cloth or rolls of gauze, affords the best protection. Materials that may break up and place debris into the wound or that is dirty should be avoided. The hand may be an effective stanch against the hemorrhage if nothing else is available.

Back or Spinal Injuries

The spine is a complex column of vertebrae stacked one on the next from the skull's base to the tailbone. It encloses the spinal cord, which consists of long tracts of nerves that join the brain with all body organs and parts. It also contains cerebrospinal fluid and protects the spinal nerves. This is potentially the most dangerous for the victim, since if a broken spinal column pinches spinal nerves from the actual trauma or by improper movement by rescuers or the victim, paralysis can result. All unconscious victims should be treated as though they had spinal injuries. All conscious victims sustaining injuries from falls, diving accidents, auto accidents, or cave-ins should be carefully checked for spine injuries before moving. A mistake in handling a victim with a spinal injury could mean a lifetime in a wheelchair or bed for the victim. Assessment consists of a series of questions to determine if a spinal injury is present.

Ask the conscious victim the following questions:

1. **Are you feeling pain? Where?** Neck injuries (cervical) radiate pain to the arms; upper back injuries (thoracic) radiate pain around the ribs and into the chest; lower back injuries (lumbar) usually radiate pain down the legs. Often, the victim describes the pain as "electric."

2. **Can you move your legs and/or feet?** Ask the victim to move the feet against your hand. If the victim is unable to produce any motion or only a weak motion, the spinal cord of the victim may have been injured.

3. **Can you move your arms and fingers?** Moving the fingers is a sign that nerve tracts for the upper extremities are intact (located high on the spinal column).

Perform an assessment of the unconscious victim as follows:

1. Look for cuts, bruises, misshapen limbs, head, or other deformities.

2. Test responses to pain stimulus such as a pinprick to hands and feet of injured person. Failure to react to a stimulus might indicate spinal cord damage.

3. Ask onlookers to describe the accident in order to determine if the injury might have been severe enough to cause spinal cord damage.

Note: Anyone with a head injury must also be assessed for damage to the spine. Moving this type of patient is unwise unless specially trained to do so, and a backboard is a must!

ASSUME THAT THE VICTIM HAS A SPINAL CORD INJURY IF YOU ARE UNABLE TO DETERMINE THAT NO SPINAL INJURY HAS OCCURRED AND IF HEAD INJURY IS PRESENT.

Signs and Symptoms

1. Consider a spinal injury in all severe accidents, as abrupt movement may cause a spinal injury and permanent damage to the central nervous system

2. Head injuries are often accompanied by a spinal injury, since the connection between the head and the central nervous system extends into the spinal cord

3. Numbness, tingling, burning, and/or painful movement of arms and/or legs

4. Paralysis (inability to move) arms and/or legs

5. Incontinence due to loss of bowel or bladder control

6. Abnormal, crooked, and asymmetric appearance in the angle of the victim's head and neck

Muscle Injuries

Muscle injuries are numerous during exercising and in a trauma to the victim. Some are minor and will resolve themselves, while recovery time in others will be shortened by use of anti-inflammatory drugs and other treatments. The following types of muscle injuries are indicated by the accompanying symptoms and signs:

1. Strains: When a muscle is pulled beyond its normal range of motion

2. Sprain: Muscle is torn

3. Contusion: Bruise

4. Cramps: Spasm and contraction with fluid loss or possibly an improper diet

Signs and Symptoms of Strain or Sprain

Sharp pain usually follows the injury

Tenderness at injury site

Deformation or disfigurement, usually of a joint

Severe weakness, inability to move the affected area

Snapping sound when tissue is injured

Treatment

1. Muscle tears may require suturing to facilitate regrowth and healing.

2. Rest and immobilization usually suffices to enable muscle to repair itself.

3. Antiinflammatory medication is often prescribed for patient's comfort.

4. Ligament and tendon damage often require surgery.

5. Sometimes called sports injuries, specialized clinics are able to provide effective treatment, avoiding costly and painful surgery in many cases.

6. During athletic events, a muscle tear or sprain is treated by cold packs or ice to minimize swelling and reduce the risk of further damage.

STUDY GUIDE FOR FIRST AID

Review the following situations requiring first aid. Try to relate clinical facts about the conditions or injuries, the symptoms, and treatment for each.

I. Shock

    1. Circulatory system failure

    2. Types of shock (describe)

       a. Fainting

       b. Hypovolemic

       c. Anaphylactic

    3. First aid personnel can prevent shock, but not reverse it

II. Bleeding

    1. Precautions

    2. Types of bleeding

       a. External (give symptoms and signs)

       b. Internal (give symptoms and signs)

    3. Types of vessels involved

III. Animal and Human Bites

    1. Infection risk from mouth flora

    2. Types of animals most often implicated

    3. Treatment

IV. Head Injuries

    1. Symptoms

    2. Types of head injuries (open, closed)

    3. Skull fracture

    4. Concussion
       A. Three grades of concussion related to period of unconsciousness

V. Eye Injuries

    1. Chemical injuries - flushing

    2. Non-penetrating foreign body or object

    3. Corneal abrasion, cut, burn

VI. Nosebleeds

    1. Site of bleeding

    2. Causes

    3. Treatment

VII. Dental injuries

    1. Toothache
      A. Treatment

    2. Knocked-out tooth
      A. Treatment

    3. Broken tooth
      A. Treatment

    4. Bitten tongue or lip
      A. Treatment

    5. Objects between teeth
      A. Treatment

    6. Broken jaw
      A. Treatment

VIII. Chest Injuries

    1. Signs and symptoms

    2. Treatment

IX. Abdominal Injuries

    1. Signs and symptoms

    2. Treatment

    3. Precautions

X. Blisters

    1. Signs and symptoms

    2. Treatment

XI. Accidental Poisoning

    1. Signs and symptoms

    2. Precautions during treatment

    3. Necessary information to be provided to Poison Control Center

XII. Insect Stings

    1. Signs and symptoms

    2. Dangerous signs and symptoms

    3. Treatment

VITAL SIGNS

OBJECTIVES

Upon completion of this unit of instruction, the student will be able to:

a. Identify the components of vital signs

b. Describe procedure for counting pulse rates and respiration rates

c. Identify abnormal patterns of breathing

d. Differentiate between a weak, strong, and regular pulse

e. Identify methods and types of temperature measurement

f. Describe the methods for determining blood pressure

g. List reasons for low or high blood pressure

h. State the importance of accurate determinations of base-line vital signs

i. Explain significance of changes in vital signs

j. Demonstrate ability to accurately determine pulse and respiration rates, blood pressure, and temperature

SECTION OUTLINE

Vital signs – components of

Temperature measurement – various methods

Determining pulse and respiration

Blood pressure discussion

Measuring the blood pressure

Review of blood pressure determinations

Study Questions

VITAL SIGNS

Introduction

Vital signs are the "signs of life." The presence of these signs indicates that a person is indeed alive and gives some information as to the health of the individual. Homeostasis is the balance that is needed by an organism in order to function as a living organism, and to do all of the things necessary to maintain life. Normal values for the vital signs of an individual indicate that all of the major systems of the body are functioning adequately. An abnormality in one vital sign often affects the values obtained from the measurement of another of the four vital signs.

What is a sign? A sign, from a medical sense, is something that can be seen, felt, measured, or heard. This is an objective manifestation or evidence of normal functioning of the body, or a disease state in the patient. To the contrary, a symptom relates to the diagnostician or other medical worker. It is subjective in that the patient might state that he has a headache, but the medical worker is unable to ascertain if the patient indeed does have a headache. Since the medical worker is unable to measure the intensity, feel the intensity, see the intensity, or even know for certain that a headache is present, this is a symptom and not a sign. Therefore, "vital signs" are an objective measure of a patient's well-being, and they must be done accurately in order to yield any useful medical information for diagnosis or treatment.

Components of Vital Signs

1. Temperature

2. Blood Pressure

3. Pulse

4. Respiration

Note: Sometimes height and weight are measured as part of this assessment of vital signs. The correct measurements of these signs are an important function of any level of medical worker. Vital signs are normally performed several times per day for the ill patient, and changes in or maintenance of certain levels of readings give an indication as to whether the patient is progressing toward health, has become chronic, or is getting sicker. Usually, the temperature, pulse, and respiration are grouped together as the TPR, and the blood pressure follows the TPR.

Conditions that Affect Vital Signs

1. Age of the patient

2. Sex of the patient

3. Level of physical conditioning

4. Environment and type of lifestyle

5. Amount and time of food and fluid intake

6. Mental status (anxiety, depression, anger, psychosis, etc.)

7. Underlying and exacerbating pathological (disease) conditions

8. Medications being taken, and time since administration

Age

Age affects the expected range for all of the components of the vital signs. At birth, an infant's temperature is not stable until the brain develops, and the entire body matures. The pulse and respirations are faster than an older child. Generally, the rate of respirations and pulse decreases as a person matures. By adolescence, the values for vital signs approximate the average for adults. With aging, vital signs often change in certain people. Blood pressure is usually elevated with athero- and arteriosclerosis. Frequently, the temperature of the elderly decreases slightly from that of the very young and the young adult.

Sex

Sex affects certain components of the vital signs to a small extent. A male has a slightly lower pulse rate than the average for females. The body temperature of an ovulating female is approximately one-half to one degree warmer.

Physical Conditioning

Respiratory rates increase with an increased demand for oxygen. Those who engage in regular exercise programs have a much lower pulse rate while resting than those who live a more sedentary life. The hearts and lungs work more efficiently in an individual who is physically active and in good physical shape. After exercise, the respiratory and pulse rate return to normal within a short period of time. While engaging in vigorous exercise, the temperature, pulse rate, and respirations increase to keep up with the demands of the body, therefore taking these measures immediately following exercise will give falsely elevated readings.

Environment and Lifestyle

In cold climates, the body must expend a great deal of energy in order to maintain a constant and normal temperature. In hot weather, the body's temperature may rise simply because it is exposed to high temperatures. In warmer climates, the heart works harder to circulate the blood so the blood pressure and pulse rates may be somewhat higher. In mountainous regions, where the level of oxygen is lower than at sea level, the rate of respirations will increase in order to compensate for the reduced oxygen level in the air available for breathing.

Food and Fluid Intake

Very hot and very cold food and drink may affect the temperature of the body for a period of time following ingestion. The temperature of the mouth may be altered for up to fifteen minutes or more after hot or cold food and drink are taken. Never measure body temperature with an oral thermometer for twenty minutes following eating and drinking. Cigarette smoking will also affect the temperature of the mouth for a short period of time.

Mental Status

Some mental disorders will affect the vital signs of the body. Vital signs may change rapidly and even return to normal over only a short span of time. Additionally, fear and anxiety will cause the heart to race and the respirations to increase. Blood pressure also increases when undue stress is placed on the body. When the causes for fear and anxiety are removed, vital signs usually return to normal unless other factors are involved.

Pathological (Disease) Conditions

Disease processes in the body may alter the values obtained when measuring vital signs. If an infection is present, the temperature is usually increased, and sometimes the pulse rate and respirations increase due to the increased demand for oxygen in response to the high temperature. Cardiovascular diseases, such as arteriosclerosis (hardening of the arteries) and atherosclerosis (hardening of the entire vascular system), will increase the blood pressure due to the lack of elasticity of the blood vessels. Narrowing of arteries and veins for any reason will increase the blood pressure. Certain metabolic problems, such as those affecting the thyroid glands or the kidneys, may speed up or slow down the rate at which the body functions.

Medications Taken

Some medications affect the vital signs, particularly those taken for chronic conditions, or those taken only a short time beforehand. The measurement of vital signs is often performed to assess the effects of a drug on the body. Medications such as aspirin (salicylic acid) or acetaminophen (Tylenol) will affect the body temperature. Some medications are given to increase or slow the patient's heart rate. These measurements are vital to the well-being of the patient and must be performed with great accuracy, as even a slight change may indicate a need to increase or decrease the dosage. Medications should never be taken in combination with those prescribed by another physician or practitioner. Reactions between two or more medications may actually do severe harm to the patient.

Never Combine Medications Without a Physician's Knowledge

Old medications should be discarded when they expire, after completing the course of therapy, or after the physician recommends discontinuation of use. People should never self-medicate.

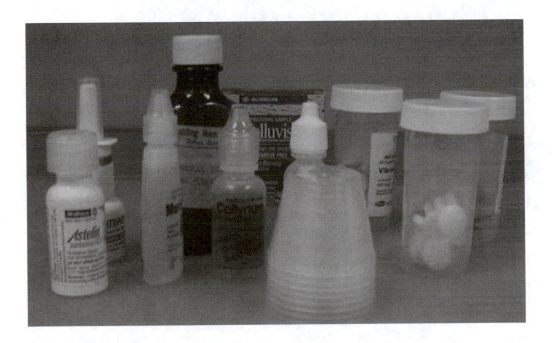

Unscheduled Measuring of Vital Signs

The medical worker should always be alert to changes in the patient's condition. While vital signs are often scheduled at regular intervals, the medical caregiver must measure vital signs if certain signs or symptoms are present. Some of these conditions or changes are:

1. Shortness of breath

2. Increased heart rate

3. Patient feels hot or complains of feeling hot

4. The patient complains of other unusual or different feelings

When in doubt, measure the vital signs! **Always document your findings on the correct form.**

TEMPERATURE MEASUREMENT

An instrument called a thermometer is used to measure the heat within a body. There are several types, and these will be discussed in this section. Break down the word "thermometer": "therm" means heat, while "meter" means to measure. Therefore, the word thermometer indicates an instrument to measure heat.

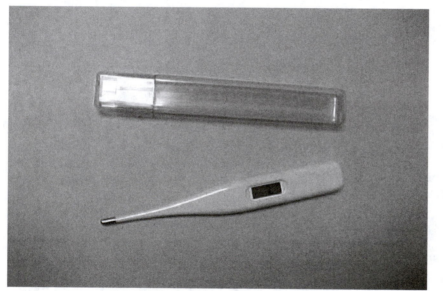

Digital Thermometer

How Heat is Produced

The hypothalamus portion of the brain functions as the body's thermostat. The hypothalamus monitors the body temperature, allowing a variation of as little as 1° during a 24-hour period. The circadian rhythm of all animals, including humans, is characterized by a slight swing in the temperature range during a 24-hour period. The body temperature is usually lowest during the early morning, and highest in the late afternoon and early evening.

Heat is produced mainly by contractions of the muscles of the body. As an example, a person who shivers when in a cold environment is rapidly flexing the muscles in order to produce heat for the body. Thickening of the skin also acts to preserve loss of heat from the body when "chill bumps" occur. Breakdown of food is another process by which the body produces heat. Certain hormones act to increase the heat by affecting the metabolism of the body as an internal factor. External factors, such as heat produced by the sun and absorbed by the body, will increase bodily functions and therefore heat production within the body.

How heat is lost

The young and elderly are particularly vulnerable to heat loss in cold environments. The very young have immature systems unable to cope with temperature extremes, while the elderly are inefficient due to a variety of factors, including a lack of physical activity in many cases. Routes by which there is heat loss are:

Types of Loss of Heat

1. **Convection** – wind is certainly effective in causing heat loss, as we know from hearing the "wind chill factor" during weather reports. The wind speed and humidity are taken into account when calculating the true temperature. Remember that when a part of the body is wet and exposed to wind, one begins to feel cool. To test this theory, get out of a shower and stand before a large fan.

2. **Radiation** – heat is given off in energy rays from the body. This process works in a similar fashion to steam radiators used for heating. One can observe the effects of radiation by looking closely at a blacktop highway during a hot day. Visual distortions just above the surface of the highway are evidence of radiation of heat from the surface.

3. **Evaporation** – when a person perspires, the body is attempting to rid the body of heat. Evaporation removes heat away from the surface of a body. For example, if you have on wet clothing and wind blows across your clothing, you feel much colder than if your clothing were dry. The evaporation of the water from the body cools the body quite rapidly and efficiently.

4. **Conduction** – body heat is carried away from one's body and serves to warm the object that it touches if the object is cooler than the body. The reverse is also true.

Scales of Measurement for Body Temperature

Two scales are used for measurement of temperature, and you should be familiar with both. Only one of these scales is normally used in a facility. The two scales are Fahrenheit and Celsius, and an "F" or a "C" will be used to indicate the preferred scale. If it is necessary to convert recording in one scale to the other, simple calculations are as follows:

Fahrenheit to Centigrade $\quad °F = (°C \times 1.8) + 32$ or $\{°C \times 9/5\} + 32$

Centigrade to Fahrenheit $\quad °C = (°F - 32) \times 0.556$ or $\{°F - 32\} + 5/9$

Sites Where Temperatures May be Taken

1. **Oral** (By mouth)

   An oral temperature is the most common method due to convenience and comfort for the patient. However, patients having difficulty breathing through their noses most often will have their temperatures measured rectally.

2. **Rectal** (In rectum)

   The rectal method is the most accurate method for measurement. Children under the age of 6 usually have their temperatures measured rectally. Other situations also call for rectal measurement. Often a facility has a policy regarding when rectal temperatures will be used. A rectal temperature will be approximately 1 degree higher than an oral measurement.

3. **Axillary** (Under the arm/armpit)

   This is the least accurate method for measurement. This method may be used when oral methods are not feasible, as in patients with mouth injuries, or are confused or combative. The measured temperature will be approximately 1 degree lower than that of an oral measurement on the same patient.

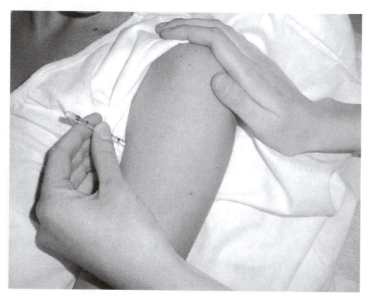

Axillary Temperature Measurement

4. **Tympanic** (In the ear)

   This method is quick and fairly accurate. The temperature is measured from the temperature of the eardrum and is completed within seconds. Often infants and young children are good candidates for this method for measurement of body temperature.

5. **Chemical strips** (Affixed to the skin's surface)

   Temperature-sensitive strips react to body heat but do not give an exact temperature measurement. The color of the strip changes only when the body temperature is normal or above normal. This method takes about fifteen seconds.

Temperature Variations by Site

Generally, a rectal temperature is **one degree higher** than an oral temperature, and an axillary temperature is **one degree lower** than that of an oral measurement. The type of temperature measurement taken is usually indicated in the recording of the reading, such as 99 R for rectal, 99 A for axillary, 99 T for tympanic, and so forth.

AVERAGE BODY TEMPERATURE

Method	Average	Range
Orally	98.6°F or 37.0°C	97.6°F — 99.6°F, or 36.5°C to 37.5°C
Rectally	99.6°F	98.6 —100.6°F, or 36°C to 37°C
Axillary	97.6°F	96.6°F — 98.6°F, or 36°C to 37°C

Activities Affecting Temperature

Chewing gum, drinking cold or warm beverages, smoking, eating, or vigorous exercising will either lower or raise an oral temperature measurement. A person who has just had a cold or a warm beverage should wait at least fifteen minutes before having his or her temperature measured.

Types of Thermometers

There are several basic types of thermometers. They are identified by the materials from which they are made and the manner in which the reading is derived. Each type will be discussed as will the procedures for using each type.

Glass thermometers have been the most convenient to use for a number of years and will be discuss widely in this section. Glass thermometers may be used to determine oral, rectal, and axillary temperatures. A rectal thermometer usually has a rounded stubby bulb and differs from the oral thermometer as it has a red top. Even though electronic thermometers are used most often today, glass thermometers are still in fairly wide usage.

Standard Glass Thermometer (Oral)

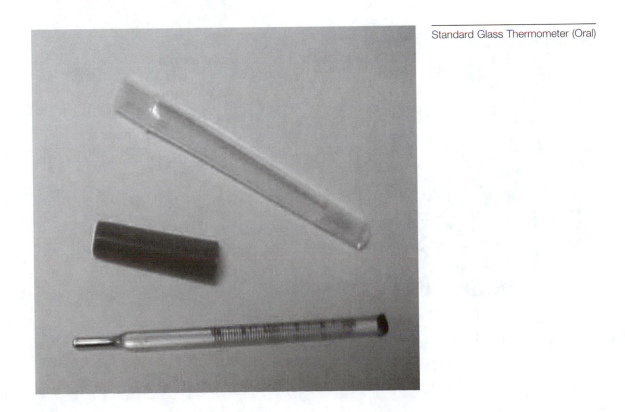

Measuring Body Temperature Orally With Glass Thermometer

Contraindicating Factors

Do not take an oral temperature under the following conditions

1. Patient is 12 years of age or under, so level of understanding may be inadequate

2. Patient has had nasal surgery with packing, causing mouth breathing

3. Patient is unconscious and may suffer a seizure

4. Oxygen cannula or mask in use, drying the tissues of the mouth

5. Patient has a nasogastric tube

6. Patient is mentally confused and may bite the thermometer

7. Patient is a mouth breather

8. Patient has had stroke and has swallowing difficulties

9. Patient has had surgery of mouth, neck, or head

10. Patient is under the influence of drugs or alcohol

11. Patient has history of seizures

12. Patient has deformities of the mouth or lips

13. Patient has mouth injuries

When reading a glass thermometer, hold the thermometer horizontally at eye level. This makes it easier to locate the end of the mercury or alcohol column and to read the number where the expanded column of mercury or alcohol ends. The number corresponding with the end of the column of expandable material is the temperature of the individual patient.

Determining Temperature Using Glass Thermometer

Care of Standard Glass Thermometers

Proper care of glass thermometers includes cleaning after use. Microorganisms from the mouth must be removed to avoid spread of infection. The thermometer should be cleaned before and after each use. Hot water may damage a thermometer, sometimes causing it to break. The thermometer must be cleaned in disinfectant after use and wiped with a tissue or alcohol swab before using. All chipped thermometers should be discarded in a sharps container, as they are glass and may break, causing injury to anyone coming in contact with them. In some facilities, plastic sheaths are used by being placed over the bulb and most of the thermometer. These sheaths are discarded following use, but the thermometer must still be cleaned before reuse.

Storage and Handling of Glass Thermometers

Some health care institutions use a system in which a thermometer is kept in each patient's room and is used for that patient only. This is effective in avoiding the spread of microorganisms from patient to patient, but the same precautions must be used to protect the health care worker, and proper maintenance of equipment and supplies must be exercised.

Procedure for Obtaining Oral Temperature by Glass Thermometer

The glass thermometer must be cleansed in a special solution to disinfect it. The oral thermometer is used for older children (>11) and for adults. In the previous section is a list of conditions that would preclude the use of an oral thermometer.

Procedure

1. Wash hands.

2. Explain procedure to patient.

3. Rinse thermometer in cold water to remove disinfectant.

4. Dry thermometer with dry tissue.

5. Check thermometer for damage and ensure that mercury or alcohol column is well below the normal temperature range (at least two degrees). If it exceeds the normal range, shake it down with a quick flick of the wrist while holding the top of the thermometer firmly between the thumb and fingers.

6. Use sheath if applicable in your institution.

7. Ask patient to wet his lips by rubbing his tongue over them.

8. Insert the bulb end of the thermometer under the patient's tongue near the frenulum.

9. Ask the patient to close his mouth and leave the thermometer in place for several minutes. The time varies according to institutional policy.

10. Remove the thermometer and hold at eye level to read. Slowly rotate the thermometer until the colored column inside the shaft of the thermometer is visible.

11. Record the reading, then wipe the thermometer with an alcohol swab.

12. Shake down the thermometer and place the thermometer into disinfectant as prescribed by institutional policy.

Electronic Thermometers

The electronic thermometer provides a quick and accurate method for measuring body temperature. The digital display shows the correct temperature reading when the probe senses

Electronic Thermometer

the temperature has reached the highest peak. The electronic thermometer is portable, and a charger or holding area is provided for when the thermometer is not in use. Two detachable probes are available with the electronic thermometer: an oral (blue-tipped) and a rectal probe are provided.

A rigid plastic sheath protector covers the probe when the temperature is taken. The sheath protectors are disposable. A supply of sheath protectors is carried on the electronic unit. The electronic thermometer determines the temperature more quickly than the glass-mercury type and beeps when the temperature is ready to be read and recorded. A digital display is accurate and easy to read, and this type of thermometer greatly reduces the risks associated with the spreading of microorganisms. This thermometer is expensive for routine use, and there is a schedule for routine cleaning and care of the electronic thermometer.

Procedure (Oral Electronic Measurement)

1. Wash hands.

2. Explain procedure to patient.

3. Ensure that the oral probe is connected securely to the **charged** unit (usually located in or near the nursing station).

4. Insert the probe into the probe covers provided.

5. Place thermometer in patient's mouth, under tongue, and have patient close his mouth.

6. Hold the probe in place in order to ensure an accurate reading, as the probe is somewhat heavier than the glass-mercury type.

7. Listen for beeping tone or flashing indicator, signifying completion of procedure.

8. Remove the probe, read digital results, and record as required.

9. Get rid of probe cover, ejecting it into a waste container, and return the probe to the proper holder used for storage of the probe.

Temperature-Sensitive Stick-On Devices

A temperature-sensitive tape reacts to body heat. It is not an exact temperature measurement but is only an estimate. The change is read as a color or intensity of a color, and indicates only whether the temperature is normal or above normal. The body temperature is read according to methodology and time indicated on the package containing the tapes and varies with brand.

Taking a Rectal Temperature With Glass Thermometer

A rectal temperature is the most accurate method for measuring the body's temperature. A glass or an electronic thermometer is used to take a rectal temperature in children under the age of 6, and in adolescents (older children) and adults when an oral measurement of temperature is not possible due to the mental and physical condition of the patient. Remember, the letter (R) must annotate a reading of a rectal temperature so appropriate determinations may be made, as a rectal temperature is usually one degree higher than that of an oral measurement.

Explain to the patient that you will measure his body temperature by inserting the thermometer into the rectum. Ensure that the glass thermometer is not broken or chipped, in order to avoid injury. Care must be taken to insert the thermometer only as far as is indicated by the procedure. The distance a rectal thermometer may be inserted is dependent on the age and size of the patient. For instance, a rectal thermometer should be inserted only one-half inch or less for an infant.

Procedure for Rectal Temperature by Glass Thermometer

1. Wash hands.

2. Don gloves.

3. Identify yourself to the patient.

4. Provide privacy.

5. Use cold water to rinse the thermometer.

6. Lubricate the bulb tip of the thermometer with KY Jelly or other water-soluble lubricant.

7. Raise the buttocks and spread the gluteal folds to reveal the anus.

8. Insert bulb of the thermometer one inch into the rectum (one-half inch for infants).

9. Hold the thermometer in place for three to five minutes.

10. Remove thermometer carefully and wipe the bulb portion with tissue paper. Wipe the thermometer with the toilet tissue from the flat end toward the bulb end. If you used a plastic sheath, remove and discard it. This paper is potentially infectious and should be placed into a biohazard bag or the commode.

11. Hold the thermometer at eye level and determine the temperature and record properly, according to institutional policies, indicatingscale of measurement (C for Celsius, F for Fahrenheit). An "R" to indicate that the temperature was taken rectally, should be noted after the scale of measurement, e.g., 99.6°C – R.

12. Place used thermometer into receptacle containing disinfectant for proper cleaning according to protocol in your facility.

13. Clean any work surfaces and remove any clothing or bed linen that may have become soiled with body wastes.

14. Remove and discard gloves; wash hands thoroughly using soap, water, and friction covering the entire hands, including between the fingers.

15. Properly record results of temperature, identifying site where temperature was obtained.

Definitions

A. ANUS – is the posterior opening of the body through which waste materials are expelled

B. WATER-SOLUBLE LUBRICANT – is a substance that reduces friction and dissolves in water

C. ABSORBENT MATERIAL – wipes of paper or cloth to remove lubricant from anus

Taking a Rectal Temperature With an Electronic Thermometer

Explain to patient that you are preparing to measure his body temperature using an electronic thermometer. Explain that the thermometer will be inserted into the rectum for less than a minute. The medical worker will need a **charged** electronic thermometer, water-soluble lubricant, red-tipped rectal probe, disposable gloves, probe covers, and toilet tissue.

Procedure for Taking Rectal Temperature by Electronic Thermometer

1. Wash hands to prevent spread of microorganisms.

2. Explain the procedure you are performing in order to reassure the patient.

3. Check that the rectal probe is connected securely to the charged unit.

4. Remove the metal probe from the charged unit. Insert it into a probe charged unit and insert it into a probe cover, to be discarded after use.

5. If raised, lower the head of the bed and position the patient on his left side.

6. Apply lubricant to the probe cover tip.

7. Don disposable gloves to avoid potential exposure to harmful organisms.

8. Raise the buttocks to expose the anus. Sometimes it is necessary to spread the gluteal folds.

9. Insert the lubricated end one inch into the rectum.

10. Hold the probe in place until a beeping tone or a flashing light indicates the measurement is complete.

11. Remove the probe from patient's rectum.

12. Read the digital results displayed.

13. Eject the probe cover into the waste container and return the probe to the receptacle on the electronic unit.

14. Record the results on the correct document and indicate that the measurement was performed rectally, e.g. 99.6°F – R.

15. Wipe the anal area with tissue and discard used tissue into the commode.

16. Cover and reposition patient to provide for comfort.

17. Remove any soiled linen or clothing.

18. Remove disposable gloves and discard in the container provided.

19. Wash hands and report significant changes or extreme results for medical intervention if appropriate.

20. Safely and properly dispose of necessary materials used in the procedure.

Taking An Axillary Temperature

The axillary temperature is less accurate than any other method of measurement for body temperature. This method is used when the oral and rectal routes are not indicated due to medical conditions or surgical procedures involving the mouth and rectum. The axillary area must be dry, and the thermometer (glass or electronic) must be held in place until the temperature recording completes its change. Often, the arm must be held close to the side in order to create a warm reservoir of air. Less heat is available in the axilla compared with other body sites, and you will need to hold the glass thermometer in place for – ten to twelve minutes. An extremely hairy axillary area will not yield an accurate axillary measurement, as air trapped in the mass of hair will alter the temperature obtained.

Procedure for Taking an Axillary Temperature with a Glass Thermometer

Explain to the patient that you are going to measure their body temperature by placing the thermometer under the armpit. The patient must be informed that the thermometer will be placed next to the skin for a period of time.

Ensure that you have the equipment and supplies needed for this procedure. The following will be needed: disposable gloves, a glass thermometer (usually clear or blue-tipped), tissue paper, plastic thermometer cover if applicable, and the storage container. NOTE: No lubricant is needed for measuring an axillary temperature.

1. Wash hands thoroughly.

2. Explain the procedure thoroughly.

3. Use cold water to rinse the thermometer if it is soaked in disinfectant solution and dry thermometer with tissues.

4. Ensure the thermometer has no damage to the glass, such as cracks and chips.

5. Shake down the thermometer if the temperature is above 96°F or 35°C.

6. If applicable in your institution, cover the thermometer with the thin plastic cover provided.

7. Remove an arm from the sleeve of the shirt or gown as applicable.

8. Place the bulb end containing the mercury under the arm.

9. Have the patient place his arm close to his body to hold the thermometer under the axilla for eleven to twelve minutes.

10. After a minimum of eleven minutes, remove the thermometer from under the arm.

11. Restore patient's clothing to its former condition.

12. If used, discard the plastic sheath. Wipe the thermometer toward the bulb end with tissue, discarding the used tissue.

13. Holding the thermometer at eye level and rotating it until the column of mercury is visible, read the thermometer.

14. Record the results as specified in the policies of your institution, with an "A" for axillary after the number and the scale (F or C) used for measurement, e.g. 37°C – A

15. Shake down the thermometer.

16. Rinse and dry the thermometer.

17. Replace thermometer in the original storage container.

18. Place patient in a comfortable position.

19. Raise the side rails of the bed if they were in that position when you came to the room to measure the patient's temperature.

20. Wash hands and report results if significantly high or low.

Procedure for Taking an Axillary Temperature With an Electronic Thermometer

Explain to the patient that you are preparing to measure his body temperature with an electronic thermometer. Explain that the thermometer will be inserted under the armpit for less than a minute. The medical worker will need a charged electronic thermometer, blue-tipped or clear probe, disposable gloves, probe covers, and toilet tissue. Ensure that the person performing the procedure may easily reach all supplies and equipment.

1. Wash hands to prevent spread of microorganisms.

2. Explain the procedure you are performing in order to reassure the patient.

3. Check that the probe is connected securely to the charged unit.

4. Remove the metal probe from the charged unit. Insert it into a probe charged unit, then insert it into a probe cover, to be discarded after use.

5. If raised, lower the head of the bed and position the patient on his left side.

6. Don disposable gloves to avoid potential exposure to harmful organisms.

7. Wipe axillary area dry with tissue.

8. Place the probe under the patient's armpit.

9. Hold the probe in place. A beeping tone or flashing light indicates reading is complete.

10. Withdraw probe. Eject the probe cover into the waste container and return the probe to the receptacle on the electronic unit

11. Read the digital results displayed

12. Record the results on the correct document and indicate how the measurement was performed, e.g. 99.6°F – A (axillary)

13. Cover and reposition patient to provide for comfort.

14. Remove disposable gloves and discard in the container provided.

15. Wash hands and report significant changes or extreme results for medical intervention if appropriate.

16. Insure patient is safe with side rails up, if needed, before leaving the patient.

Taking a Tympanic Temperature With a Tympanic Thermometer

Explain to the patient that you are going to measure his body temperature with a thermometer that is placed in the ear canal. Equipment and supplies include a charged electronic tympanic thermometer and disposable probe covers.

Procedure for Using Tympanic Electronic Thermometer

1. Wash hands.

2. Explain the procedure to the patient. If the patient is a very young child, it is advisable to have a parent present, or someone to distract the patient, to avoid anxiety for the patient.

3. Check that the tympanic probe is connected to the charged unit.

4. Insert the cone-shaped end of the tympanic thermometer into a probe cover.

5. Ask patient to turn his head so that the patient's ear is in front of you, the medical worker. If the patient is unable to move his head, the worker should position himself or herself to the side of

the patient. (It is sometimes easier to sit in a chair with the bed as a working platform in this case).

6. Don gloves.

7. For adults, grasp the external ear (pinna) and pull up and back. In the case of infants, pull the pinna straight back without an upward lift.

8. Place a clean probe cover on the probe in order to have the device ready for the following patient.

9. Ensure the thermometer is set on correct mode.

10. Place the covered probe into the ear canal until it seals the ear canal, but do not apply heavy pressure.

11. Press the activation or start button and leave the probe for the manufacturer's suggested time period.

12. Listen for a tone or look for a flashing light that indicates the measurement is complete. If a tone or flashing light is not provided, the digital display itself may signify the measurement is complete by stopping or flashing. Remove the probe from the patient's ear.

13. Dispose of plastic probe cover.

14. Record the results on the correct document and indicate how the measurement was performed, e.g. 99.6°F – T (tympanic).

15. Remove disposable gloves and discard in the container provided.

16. Wash hands and report significant changes or extreme results for medical intervention if appropriate.

Cleaning Glass Thermometers

Glass thermometers must be cleaned, even if probe covers are used. The proper procedure for cleaning glass thermometers in order to avoid contaminating yourself and other patients is as follows. If both rectal and oral glass thermometers are used, they should be separated following use and not mixed together. The cleaning procedure is the same for both types.

Equipment and supplies needed are: soiled thermometers in tray of soapy water; containers for clean thermometers, liquid soap, and disinfectant (alcohol is used in most institutional policies), along with towels and labels for the various types. Note that reusable glass thermometers are not used in many offices and medical facilities today. The readily available disposable thermometers and those requiring disposable probe covers are most often seen.

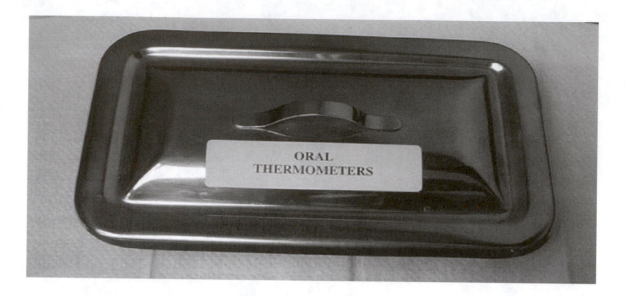

Procedure for Cleaning Glass Mercury Thermometers

1. Find room for cleaning thermometers. A sink and running water should be available.

2. Don gloves and place towel near sink.

3. Wash and dry container and cover where clean thermometers will be stored.

4. 4 × 4 gauze sponges should be placed in bottom of storage container to avoid breakage and chipping.

5. Use a large plastic basin or the sink. Both should be cleaned prior to use with cleanser.

6. Place a towel or washcloth in the bottom of the basin or sink to avoid breaking the thermometers if they are dropped.

7. Turn on the cold water faucet and wet the sponge with soapy water.

8. Clean the thermometers, one at a time, from the stem toward the bulb.

9. Rinse the thermometers, and dry each with a towel or washcloth.

10. Shake down thermometers until the top of mercury column is at 96°F or 35°C or below.

11. Fill **clean** thermometer tray with sufficient alcohol or other disinfectant approved by the clinical facility to cover the number of thermometers to be stored for later use.

12. Allow thermometers to soak for time specified for disinfecting of the thermometers. This time length is usually approved by the Infection Control/Exposure Control Committee.

PULSE, RESPIRATION

Introduction

The pulse and respiration of the patient are usually counted during the same procedure. Because breathing is partly under voluntary control, a person is able to stop or alter breathing temporarily for a short period. For example, when a patient realizes that his breathing is being watched and

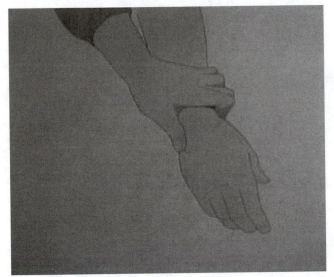

Taking a Radial Pulse

counted, he may alter his breathing pattern without meaning to do so. To avoid this, the respirations are counted immediately following the pulse count without telling the patient. The patient's hand is kept in the same position, and your fingers remain on the pulse so that you seem to be taking the pulse still.

The **pulse** is pressure of the blood felt against the wall of an artery as the heart alternately contracts (beats) and relaxes (rests). The most common area for measuring the pulse is in the radial artery, on the inside of the wrist, in a line extending from the thumb.

1. The pulse is more easily felt in arteries that lie somewhat close to the surface of the skin and can be pressed against a hard structure, such as bone or cartilage.

2. In most patients (with no obstructions or occlusions) this measurement should be the same in all arteries throughout the body.

3. The pulse signals how well the cardiovascular system is meeting the body's needs for blood flow, and therefore exchange of oxygen and carbon dioxide.

Common Terms Associated With Pulse Assessment

1. Thready   A pulse that is fine and difficult to feel

2. Bounding   Pulse of higher intensity than normal

3. Sinus rhythm   Normal heart rhythm

4. Systole   Contraction of the chambers of the heart

Radial Pulse

The **radial pulse**, located in the wrist on the thumb side, is the most commonly used site for measuring a person's pulse. The radial artery is located near the radial bone of the lower arm, and it is easily felt in the wrist. There are a number of sites in the body where large blood vessels come near enough to the surface for an artery to be used for counting the pulse. Conscious patients are normally checked at the radial artery, unless injuries or absence of a limb or limbs prevent its use. Unconscious patients should be checked at the carotid artery, located under the jawbone and along the front of the neck, just in front of a line descending from the eye. Unconscious patients may also have their pulses measured apically (over the heart).

Pulse Measurement Includes Determining the:

1. Rate or speed

   A. Bradycardia – an unusually slow pulse

   B. Tachycardia – an unusually fast pulse

2. Character

   A. Rhythm – regularity

   B. Volume of blood in circulatory system

Note: Certain values outside the normal range must be reported to the proper authority for medical intervention if necessary. Some of these measurements are:

1. Tachycardia   Pulse rates over 100 strokes per minute

2. Bradycardia   Pulse rates under 60 strokes per minute

3. Irregularities in character   Rhythm and volume

Pulse Rates May be Altered by:

1. Current illness

2. Emotion state

3. Age of patient

4. Recent exercise

5. Elevated temperature due to underlying illness

6. Sex or gender of the patient

7. Position of the patient: lying, sitting, standing, legs crossed, and so on.

8. Level of physical training

9. Lowered temperature

10. Drug and alcohol ingestion

Note: Not all people have the same baseline values for pulse rates. In addition to the conditions listed above that affect the pulse rate, some people fall outside of the normal average ranges. Therefore, the pulse rates for some may exceed or be lower than the published averages, but they will be normal for those particular people. It is also important to remember that people who exercise regularly and vigorously, such as jogging for several miles daily, will have a pulse rate that is as low as one-half the rate of a person who is not a runner or jogger. This may also be true of other vital signs findings, and it can also affect other clinical test values.

AVERAGE PULSE RATES BY AGE GROUPING

PATIENT	BEATS/MINUTE
Adult woman	65 – 80
Adult man	60 – 70
Adolescents	75 – 100
Preschool children	80 – 110
Infants	120 – 160

Note: Average and normal are two different things. A person may be normal for his individual count but not fall within the average for everyone.

Apical Pulse

The **apical pulse** is measured by counting the contractions of the heart. The stethoscope is placed over the apex (pointed extremity or bottom) of the heart, just below the nipple of men, and in women it is located under the left breast. To take this measurement, place the stethoscope over the fifth left intercostal (between the ribs) space. You should hear the heart sounds as the valves of the heart close. These sounds occur as blood is pumped from the heart and into the arteries. The radial artery (at the wrist) should occur at the same rhythm as the beating of the heart. In certain vascular conditions, however, this is not the case. Administration of certain medications that affect the heart require an apical measurement of the pulse rate prior to giving the medication, as the rate of heartbeats heard apically may differ from the pulse rate felt in the extremities (arms and legs).

The medical worker should hear two sounds described as a "lub dub" sound. The "lub" sound corresponds to the closing of the valves to prevent the backflow of blood during the contraction of the ventricles, as the blood is pushed through the arteries. This "lub" sound is the one to be counted. The softer sound, "dub," corresponds with the relaxation of the ventricles as they fill with blood before the next contraction and the closing of the semilunar valves to prevent backflow from the arteries. There are many medications available for accentuating and smoothing the action of the heart to compensate for diminished cardiac function. You will also find that some people with extremely low pulse rates must have artificial stimulation by internal pacemakers.

Remember, it is vitally important that people on cardiac drugs or that may suffer from occlusion (blockage) of blood vessels be evaluated for a pulse rate apically.

Comparison of the Apical-Radial Rate

1. The apical and radial pulse rate is a comparison of the apical rate and the radial rate, and should be the same.

2. When the contractions of the heart are weak, insufficient blood is forced into the arteries to expand them. In this case, no pulse will be felt. Insufficient blood being pumped into the arteries because of weak contractions will give a disparity between the number of pulses in the radial artery and that of the apical pulse rate.

3. Two people measure the heart rate and the radial pulse simultaneously. One medical worker measures the apical pulse while the second counts the radial pulse for one full minute.

4. The rates are then compared. If there is a difference, it is called a **pulse deficit**, which is the difference between the apical and radial pulse. Pulse deficits are found in a variety of heart

diseases. Extreme differences may indicate blockage of an artery in the extremity, or an occlusion delaying the flow of blood through the vessel.

When and How are Apical Pulse Rates Checked?

1. When medical history indicates a pulse deficit exists, or if one is suspected

2. Before the nurse gives medications that may alter the heart rate and/or rhythm, the apical rate must be measured

3. In children whose rapid rates might be difficult to count at the radial site

4. Always for one full minute, since an irregularity would be compounded if measured for only thirty seconds

5. On any child 12 months of age or younger

6. Whenever you are uncertain of the accuracy of the radial pulse or it is irregular

7. Obstructions of the vascular system may cause a difference in the rate of the heartbeats and the pulse felt in a limb (peripheral vascular system)

Counting the Radial Pulse

1. Place patient in a comfortable position. Remember, radial pulse is taken on conscious patients.

2. Have the patient rest his hand on a flat surface with the palm of the hand down.

3. Locate the pulse on thumb side of the wrist using just the tips of your first three fingers.

4. Do **not** use your thumb as it also contains a strong pulse that may be confused with the patient's pulse.

5. When the pulse is felt, exert **slight** pressure. Hard pressure may occlude the blood flow. Use the sweep (second) hand of a watch and count for one minute, unless institutional policy allows the medical worker to count for one-half minute and multiply by two, effectively correcting the rate to a one-minute period. A one-minute count is preferred and **must be done if the pulse is irregular.**

6. Complete the procedure by properly recording the results. Breathing difficulties and rates greater than 22 breaths per minute or fewer than 12 per minute, should be reported for possible medical intervention.

Counting the Apical Pulse

1. Ensure that you have a watch with a sweep hand and that the proper document for recording the pulse is available.
   Note: If it is necessary to examine for a pulse deficit, two people will be needed to make the simultaneous measurements.

2. Clean stethoscope earpieces and bell with an alcohol swab or other disinfectant.

3. Place stethoscope earpieces in your ears, with the earpieces angled slightly forward.

4. Place the stethoscope diaphragm or bell over the apex. The apex is located between the fifth and sixth intercostal spaces, and left of the sternal portion of the patient's heart. If the stethoscope bell is cold, warm the diaphragm with your hands before placing it on the patient's chest.

5. Listen carefully for the heartbeat.

6. Count the louder beats for one full minute.

7. Also check the radial pulse at the same time, for one full minute. The best way to obtain these numbers is for one medical worker to count the apical pulse while another takes the radial pulse.

8. Record results on a worksheet for comparison.

9. Clean earpieces and bell of stethoscope with alcohol swabs or other disinfectant.

10. Complete the procedure by calculating the pulse differences and record appropriately.

Calculation for Determining Pulse Deficit

Apical pulse = 97
Radial pulse = 84
Pulse deficit = 13
Pulse deficit calculation = (97 − 84 = 13)

Respiration

The main function of respiration is to supply oxygen to the cells in the body and to get rid of excess carbon dioxide, produced during cellular metabolism. When respirations are inefficient, there is less oxygen in the blood available for the body's vital functions, and carbon dioxide may build up, causing severe medical conditions. The skin of a person with poor oxygen and carbon dioxide exchange may turn bluish or dusky in color and the patient develops a condition known as **cyanosis.** Skin has a vast supply of capillary vessels where exchange between tissues of the body and oxygen takes place. Assessing skin color is an excellent way to assess oxygenation.

Respiration is also both internal and external, and both are important for proper metabolic functioning of the body. When the rate of respiration is measured, this is called external respiration, as the outside air comes into contact with the lungs and other organs of the pulmonary system. Internal respiration relates to the actual exchange of gases (oxygen and carbon dioxide) between the cells inside the body and the capillaries, which are the smallest elements of the vascular system.

The rate of respirations is the chief reason for performing this portion of the four vital signs, but other factors are also to be considered. The rate of respirations is determined by counting the rise or fall of the chest for one full minute, using a watch equipped with a second hand. As a health care professional, you should be alert to medical conditions as evidenced by signs the patient exhibits that are characteristic of various disease states. These types of information are invaluable to the medical practitioner (physician, physician's assistant, nurse practitioner, respiratory therapists, and other health care providers responsible for total patient care). In addition to the rate of respirations per minute, the following should be checked and abnormalities reported:

Assessment

1. Symmetry of the chest refers to whether both sides of the chest are expanding equally with an equal amount of air entering each lung

2. Volume and depth of respirations

3. Character – terms used to describe the characteristics describing a person's respirations include:

    A. Regular

    B. Irregular

    C. Deep

    D. Shallow

    E. Difficult or labored

There are Two Separate Functions Related to Each Respiration:

1. Inspiration   Inhaling, or bringing air into the body

2. Expiration   Exhalation, or ridding the body of excess carbon dioxide

What is a Respiration?

One respiration consists of inspiration (chest rising) and exhalation (chest falling). This counts as one respiration when measuring the respiratory rate. Both of these body processes equal one complete respiration.

Procedure for Counting Respirations

1. When the pulse rate has been counted, you should leave your fingers on the radial pulse while starting the count of the number of times the chest rises and falls for one full minute.

2. Be aware of the depth and regularity of the patient's breathing.

3. Appropriately record the rate of respirations. The medical worker should also assess the depth, time, and regularity of respirations.

Note: You may count respirations before, during, or after counting the radial pulse. Counting respirations while also counting the pulse requires experience. At the beginning of your health care career, you should concentrate on one measurement at a time. If you count the respirations following the pulse rate determination, continue pressing on the pulse area while counting respirations. This will prevent the patient from altering his breathing pattern subconsciously.

Some Factors Affecting Respiratory Rates Include:

1. Elevated or decreased temperature

2. Emotional state

3. Accompanying illnesses

4. Age

5. Sex

6. If measured immediately or following strenuous exercise

7. Medications or illicit drugs

8. Body positioning

9. Physical conditioning

Rates and Types of Respirations

Temperature, pulse, and respiration (TPR) rates and types of respirations (shallow, deep, etc.) are properly documented and then recorded appropriately on the patient's chart. Special terms describe different breathing patterns as indicated in the following list of terms.

Terms of Gradation Associated With Respirations

Apnea	Periods in which there are no respirations
Auscultation	Listening for sounds, particularly thoracic (chest) and abdominal
Bradypnea	Slow respirations
Cheyne-Stokes	Periods of dyspnea followed by periods of apnea
Crackles	Abnormal bubbling sounds from bronchial tubes
Depth	Shallow or deep and full breaths
Dyspnea	Poor or difficult breathing, poor and partial filling of the lungs
Friction	Rubbing together of membranes (irritation of pleural membranes lining chest cavity)
Normal-regular	16 to 20 breaths per minute
Rales	Gurgles-moist respirations caused by collection of fluid (mucus) in lungs
Stertorous	Snoring-like respirations
Stridor	High-pitched crowing or barking sounds during inspiration
Symmetry	Expansion of chest equally or unequally on both sides
Tachypnea	Rapid respirations
Wheezing	Sighing whistling sound due to narrowing of bronchioles, often found in asthma or with increased production of mucus

Always Report the Following Conditions

Fact: The average rate for adolescents and adults is 16 to 20 respirations per minute.

1. If the rate is more than 25 per minute, it is reported as accelerated.

2. If the rate is less than 12 per minute, it is too slow and may be a medical emergency.

3. Patients with certain metabolic illnesses may compensate for the condition by "blowing off" excess carbon dioxide through pursed lips, or may increase respirations (panting) in order to gain more oxygen from the air.

BLOOD PRESSURE

Introduction

Measurement of the blood pressure is usually taken following the first three of the four vital signs. Normally, temperature, pulse, and respiration are taken first and recorded under the acronym

TPR. In a medical facility, it is generally understood that the measurement of TPR will always be in that order and are often recorded as such, except when forms provide a separate area or box in which to record the three measurements.

Blood pressure, the fourth vital sign, is the measure of the force of the blood against the walls of the arteries. Some traits, characteristics, and temporary conditions may either increase or decrease the blood pressure. Some factors are beyond the control of the patient and cannot be changed. In addition to individual differences, which will be listed later, blood pressure depends on certain factors common to everyone.

Factors Affecting Blood Pressure

1. Volume of fluid and blood

2. Strength of the heart and the force of each beat

3. Arterial condition – Arteries with poor elasticity, or stretch, give more resistance within the arteries, therefore blood pressure is greater in arteries that have lost their elasticity due to arterial plaque, calcification, and so on.

4. Distance of the site where blood pressure is being measured from the heart affects the value. For example, blood pressure in the legs is lower than in the arms. The pressure varies with contraction of the heart's ventricles (systole) and relaxation of the heart's ventricles (diastole). This gives us a ratio between two measurements, with the systolic pressure, the higher of the two, being reported over the diastolic, which is the lower of the two measurements. A forward slash separates the upper number from the lower, and it is written in the form of a fraction, for example, 120/80.

5. Systolic blood pressure is the period when the pressure within the arteries is the greatest, during contraction of the ventricles, which gives a higher value than that of the diastolic.

6. Diastolic reading indicates the lowest point of pressure between ventricular contractions.

Blood Pressure May be Temporarily Elevated by:

1. Exercise

2. Eating

3. Stimulating substances such as caffeine and certain cold remedies that may speed up all body functions

4. Emotional stress, such as anger, fear, or sexual activity

Factors that Increase the Blood Pressure

As in the rate of the pulse, a number of factors or characteristics of the patient yield a value that is affected by certain conditions.

Conditions Affecting Blood Pressure Determinations

1. Sex of the patient (males slightly higher than females before menopause)

2. Pain

3. Obesity

4. Age

5. Condition of blood vessels

6. Some drugs

7. Disease conditions, such as arteriosclerosis (hardening of the arteries), elevated cholesterol, or diabetes mellitus

8. Emotional state

Factors That May Lower the Blood Pressure

1. Fasting (not eating)

2. Rest

3. Depressants (medications that tend to slow body functions)

4. Weight loss

5. Emotions (such as grief)

6. Abnormal conditions (loss of blood) or shock from reasons other than blood loss

7. Antihypertensives (drugs that are designed to lower blood pressure)

8. Medications that cause the body to lose fluids

Factors that Cannot be Changed by the Patient

1. Who your parents are

2. Your sex

3. Viscosity of blood

4. Condition of blood vessels

Equipment Required to Measure Blood Pressure

1. Sphygmomanometer – Blood pressure-measuring instrument

   A. **Cuff** (different sizes are available) that fits around the patient's arm.

   B. An **expandable rubber bladder** inside cuff – air pumped into it from rubber bulb.

   C. A **pressure control button** is attached to the connection between bulb pump and the tubing leading to the pressure cuff.

   D. The other tube leads from the inflatable rubber bladder in the cuff to the **pressure gauge.**

   E. Automatic blood pressure machines use a similar process to the manual variety. The pressure gauge may be a round aneroid gauge, dial, or a column of mercury. Either of these types will be marked with numbers. There are also a number of commercially available electronic blood pressure instruments for measuring blood pressures at home. These instruments are relatively inexpensive and easy to use, giving a printed result or a digital, easy-to-see reading, even if the person taking the blood pressure is alone. A number of these instruments also have large digital reading displays for those with difficulty seeing the anaeroid gauges with an indicator needle. Since many medications should not be taken if the blood pressure is either too high or too low, it is a wise investment for a person who is on a regular medication schedule.

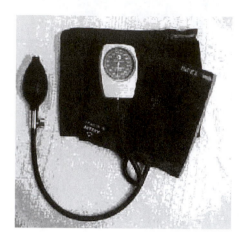

Blood Pressure Cuff (Sphygmomanometer)

2. The **stethoscope**

   A. Magnifies sounds

   B. Consists of a bell, a diaphragm, and earpieces

   C. Earpieces direct the sounds into the listener's ears. The earpieces and diaphragm must be cleaned with alcohol or other antiseptic before and after each use to prevent transmission of disease

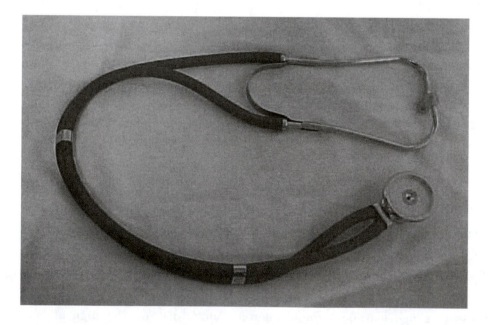

Errors May Occur Due To:

1. Cuffs that are too wide or too narrow will give inaccurate readings. The width of the cuff should measure roughly 80 percent of the diameter of the patient's arm.

2. Tubing from the sphygmomanometer is stretched when gauge is too far from the cuff (more than two feet)

3. Noise and movement from the patient and the environment may make it difficult to obtain an accurate measurement

4. An improperly wrapped cuff

5. Incorrect positioning of arm

6. Not using the same arm for all readings

7. Not having the gauge at eye level

8. Deflating the cuff too rapidly or too slowly

9. Be aware that there could be a phenomenon called an **auscultory gap** (a silent interval between the true systolic and diastolic pressures). An auscultatory gap is a diminishing or disappearance of sound for a short period of time. The true and reportable diastolic pressure is obtained when the pulse becomes audible again. This procedure may require more skills than the novice learning to take blood pressure readings possesses, and should be discussed further when the student enters into a medical program where routine blood pressure testing is performed.

10. Restrictive clothing, particularly where sleeves are tight or rolled up

Note: Electronic sphygmomanometers with attached cuffs are used in some facilities. These units do not require a stethoscope but automatically register the readings on a digital display. Some of these devices also measure the pulse rate and even print out the results.

MEASURING THE BLOOD PRESSURE

Blood pressure is usually measured in the upper arm over the brachial artery. Blood pressure readings from other sites may be necessary due to amputations or injury to limbs, but they must be approved by a physician and be noted as to the site where the blood pressure is measured. Also, people with emotional problems and those who are chemically altered present special problems in getting an accurate determination.

1. The blood pressure cuff is applied directly over the brachial artery on the arm (one inch above the antecubital area, or bend of the elbow). The medical worker should ensure that there are no wrinkles in the fabric of the cuff.

2. The stethoscope diaphragm is placed over the brachial artery, and a firm pressure is placed to the bell of the stethoscope.

3. Pressure is then increased by inflating the rubber bladder in the cuff to stop the flow of blood through the artery.

4. The pressure is slowly released and the sounds of heart valves closing can be heard. The sounds correspond to pressure changes in the blood.

5. The blood pressure is measured:

   A. At its highest point as the systolic pressure. This will be the first regular sound you will hear. This is the sound of the bicuspid and tricuspid valves closing.

   B. At its lowest point as the diastolic pressure. This will be the change or last sound you will hear. This is the sound of the semilunar valves closing.

   C. The difference between systolic and diastolic pressure is called pulse pressure. The pulse pressure gives important information about the health of the arteries. The average pulse pressure in a healthy adult is about 40 millimeters (mm) of

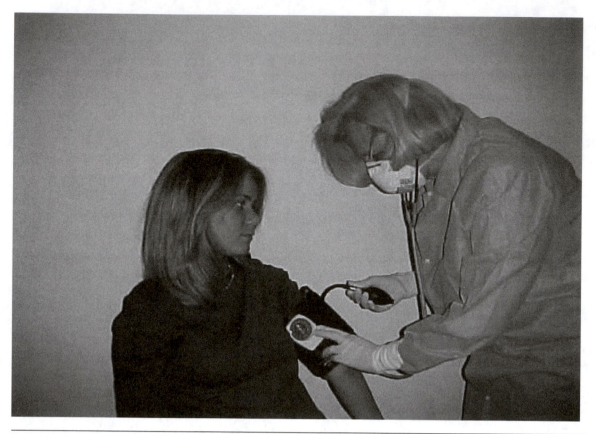

Performing a Blood Pressure Determination

mercury (Hg) (range 30–50 mm Hg). However, factors in both health and disease can alter the pulse pressure. An increase in blood volume or heart rate or a decrease in the ability of the arteries to expand may result in an increased pulse pressure.

6. Blood pressure readings are recorded as an improper fraction, for example, systolic/diastolic or 120/82. This means the systolic pressure is 120 and the diastolic pressure is 82. In this set of measurements, the pulse pressure would be 120 − 82 = 38.

Blood Pressure Average Values

Average resting adult brachial artery pressure is between 90 and 140 millimeters of mercury (mm Hg) systolic, while the diastolic pressure is between 60 and 90 millimeters of mercury (mm Hg). An average reading of 120/80 has for some time been considered an ideal blood pressure. More recently, this has been considered to be borderline elevation, and treatment to lower the pressure to a lower level has been initiated in many patients.

Before Using a Sphygmomanometer:

1. If using a mercury column style of manometer, observe the movement of the mercury column. If the mercury moves up the column very slowly or in jerky patterns, it may have oxidized. Use another instrument and ensure that the faulty device is reported for repair or replacement.

2. When using an aneroid manometer, ensure that the needle is at the zero level prior to inflating the cuff. If the pressure indicator is not on zero when no pressure has been introduced into the inflatable bladder within the cuff, use another sphygmomanometer and tag the faulty instrument for repair or replacement in order to avoid errors in measurement.

Influences and Distractions that May Produce Erroneous Results

1. Sounds from radios and television sets are often distracting and make it difficult to hear the sounds being addressed.

2. Ask the patient not to talk. Vibrations from talking may be transmitted through the stethoscope.

3. Do not take blood pressure on an arm that has been injured or has an intravenous device inserted in it. Injuries such as burns, broken bones in the arm, and sutured cuts or surgical procedures may result in damage to the extremity by inflating a pressure cuff around the limb.

Note: Remember that blood pressure determinations may be measured in other limbs, such as the legs, but this must be approved by a physician and be noted as to site used for measurement. Also, hypertension is not diagnosed with a single measurement. A sustained reading of values found in the following set of terms is necessary for a diagnosis of hypertension. An elevated reading may be a temporary phenomenon.

Terms Associated With Blood Pressure Determinations

1. Hypertension (high blood pressure)
   Values are greater than 140 mm Hg systolically and 90 mm Hg diastolically over a period of time.

2. Hypotension (low blood pressure)
   Values are less than 100 mm Hg systolically and 70 mm Hg diastolically. Extremely low values in hypotensive conditions may lead to shock, which is a serious condition in which the body's organs are receiving inadequate supplies of oxygen.

Caution: In addition to those conditions listed in #3 of the previous section, do not use an arm to measure blood pressure that is the site of an intravenous device, is paralyzed, such as in a stroke, has injuries including severe contusions of the muscles, has severe skin rash, or if edema (swelling) is present.

Procedure for Measuring Blood Pressure

Before using the stethoscope:

1. Clean the earpieces with an alcohol wipe or other disinfectant, and clean the bell and the diaphragm with a different alcohol wipe or disinfectant. Allow the earpieces and diaphragm to dry before using.

2. Point the earpieces slightly forward before inserting them in your ears. Most stethoscopes allow a rotation of the earpieces in a semicircular path to provide for comfort and better acuity when listening to pulse sounds.

3. Use the diaphragm portion of the stethoscope for measuring blood pressure. The bell side of the stethoscope is used for measuring the apical pulse.

4. Be sure the bell portion is open so you will hear the beats.

5. Palpate (feel) for the pulse in the brachial artery with the fingers of your other hand.

6. Find the arrow on the cuff marked "artery." Place the cuff around the arm, except where use of the arm is contraindicated, with the arrow approximately over the brachial pulse.

7. The cuff should be no closer to the elbow than one inch, and the appropriate size should be used, as described earlier in the section related to errors of measurement. Ensure that the cuff is not excessively wrinkled or folded.

8. Place the rubber bulb pump in your dominant hand with the tubing attached to the bulb leading away from you.

9. Rapidly inflate cuff until you can no longer feel the radial pulse at thumb side of wrist. As a rule of thumb, you should add 30 more mm of mercury pressure to ensure you have exceeded pressure necessary to be above the value you will obtain for systolic pressure.

10. For most individuals, the pressure will not have to be inflated in excess of 160–180 mm of mercury.

11. Quickly and steadily deflate the cuff. Wait fifteen to thirty seconds.

12. Now that you have established the range of pressure necessary for the individual you are treating, place the stethoscope over the brachial artery.

13. Reinflate the cuff quickly and steadily to the level you estimated when you originally inflated the cuff and added additional pressure of approximately 30 mm of mercury.

14. Do not hesitate! Release the air evenly, at approximately 2 or 3 mm pressure per second. Watch the needle or the column of mercury constantly while the cuff is deflating.

15. Listen for the first pulse beat where you can hear at least two consecutive beats. Mentally note where the pressure was when you first heard the pulse. Continue releasing pressure from the cuff when you hear sound, like a regular tapping. This is the systolic value.

16. As the cuff continues to deflate at a slow but regular rate, make a mental note of the last sound of the pulse. The last sound you hear is the diastolic value. Continue to deflate the cuff; listen for 10 to 20 mm more to ensure you have the correct diastolic reading. This will avoid your determining that an auscultory gap is the diastolic value to be recorded.

17. Blood pressure values are always reported in even numbers, with the systolic (contraction of ventricles), which is the higher of the two values, on top and the diastolic (relaxation of the ventricles) on the bottom, for example, 128/82). Indicate arm used and how the patient was positioned (sitting, lying down, standing) while the measurement was being performed.

18. If you doubt the measurements you have recorded, wait two minutes and repeat the procedure. You might want to reposition the patient, or make yourself more comfortable, for the second reading.

19. Clean earpieces of the stethoscope with alcohol wipes or other disinfectant. If the tubing has contacted the patient or his linen, wipe it as well to avoid passing organisms from one patient to another. In many health care facilities, the sphygmomanometer is attached to the wall or bed; it remains with the patient and is not carried from room to room.

20. Properly document values obtained. If values exceed the normal range, report the determinations according to institutional policy. Return equipment to appropriate area.

21. Carry out any action necessary related to values determined or care of equipment.

Note: Do not leave an inflated blood pressure cuff on the patient's arm or leg for more than a moment. A patient may suffer damage if a cuff is strongly inflated and left for several minutes.

REVIEW OF BLOOD PRESSURE DETERMINATIONS

1. Blood Pressure – Force of blood against walls of arteries

    A. Systolic – pressure when ventricles contract

        a. Higher of two numbers

B. Diastolic – pressure when ventricles are relaxed

     b. Lower of two numbers

2. Pulse Pressure

    A. Difference between systolic and diastolic

       a. Should not exceed 50 mm of mercury

3. Units of measure

    A. Mm of mercury

       a. Gauges may be:

          aa. Anaeroid – needle pointing to appropriate numbers

          bb. Column of mercury with numbers printed along the column

4. Hypertension

    A. One blood pressure reading not indicative of hypertension

       a. Certain factors lead to transient hypertension

    B. Serious condition

       a. May be controlled by medication

       b. Some cases controlled by lifestyle changes

5. Measuring BP

    A. Sphygmomanometer

       a. List parts and use of

    B. Stethoscope

       b. List parts and several uses for a stethoscope

6. Factors affecting blood pressure determination

    A. List factors that may increase the blood pressure (BP). (Use your own thoughts)

    B. What are some conditions that may affect BP that you should know about?

STUDY QUESTIONS

1. T F Low blood volume will increase the blood pressure.

2. T F Strenuous exercise increases blood pressure.

3. T F To measure blood pressure accurately, you will need a watch with a second hand.

4. T F Blood pressures in the ankle will be lower than those taken over arteries closer to heart.

5. T F One blood pressure reading below 90/60 would signal hypertension.

6. T F Each small line on the blood pressure gauge is equal to two mm of mercury pressure.

7. T F Depressant drugs elevate the blood pressure.

8. T F Using a blood pressure cuff of the wrong size will give an inaccurate reading.

9. T F When measuring a blood pressure, always keep the gauge within two feet of cuff.

10. T F Stethoscope earpieces should be cleaned both before and after use.

11. T F A pulse deficit occurs with a difference between the apical and radial pulses.

12. T F The pulse is the pressure of blood against the arterial wall.

13. T F Cheyne-Stokes respirations are deep and regular.

14. T F Pulses may differ if taken at different sites, such as apical, brachial, and femoral.

15. T F The pulse rate of an infant is 80 to 100 beats per minute.

16. T F An apical phase should be counted in children.

17. T F The most often used pulse site is the carotid artery.

18. T F The respiratory system rids the body of excess carbon dioxide.

19. T F Mucus in the air passages causes wheezing.

20. T F A pulse is counted using the thumb.

B. Give the medical term for the following:

21. _____ Low blood pressure

22. _____ Lowest value in blood pressure reading

23. _____ Stretch

24. _____ Artery most commonly used for blood pressure determination

25. _____ Instrument for measuring blood pressure

C. Completion

Complete the statements by choosing the correct word

26. The closing of the heart valves is heard as the sounds. (diastolic) (systolic)

27. High blood pressure is known as (hypotension) (hypertension)

28. Blood pressure is lowered when weight is (gained) (lost)

29. Blood pressure is raised by (rest) (exercise)

30. The earpieces of the stethoscope should be pointed _____ as they are placed in the ears. (forward) (backward)

D. Challenge Questions

You are assigned to take Mr. Jones's blood pressure at 8 a.m. He is a very heavy man with an IV apparatus in his left arm. His blood pressure was 190/120 at 8 a.m. Respond to the following:

31. What size blood pressure cuff would you use?

32. Which arm would you use for the measurement?

33. Would it be necessary to report these results to the physician?

34. What is the pulse pressure derived from Mr. Jones's measurements?

35. How would occlusions in blood vessels affect the difference between apical pulse rates and that of the extremities (legs and arms)?

Give a brief description of the following:

36. brachial _____

37. diastolic _____

38. stethoscope _____

39. femoral _____

40. sphygmomanometer _____

41. hypotension _____

42. hypertension _____

43. elasticity _____

44. systolic _____

45. femoral _____

CARDIOPULMONARY RESUSCITATION BASIC LIFE SUPPORT

OBJECTIVES

Upon completion of this unit of instruction, the student will be able to:

  a. List components of an effective community response team

  b. Relate importance of rapid and effective provision of basic life support

  c. State the basic links in the chain of survival

  d. Describe factors contributing to development of cardiovascular disease

  e. Discuss the anatomy of the cardiopulmonary system and the relationship of the respiratory system to the cardiovascular component

  f. Give the signs and symptoms of an impending coronary attack

  g. Differentiate between cardiac arrest, respiratory arrest and major causes for the cessation of these functions

  h. Describe the initial assessment of a possible victim

  i. List the steps for providing cardiopulmonary resuscitation

  j. Describe follow-up treatment of a resuscitated victim, and the need for monitoring

SECTION OUTLINE

Cardiopulmonary Resuscitation – Introduction to emergency care as a community responsibility

Emergency Cardiac Care

Lifestyle and Risk Factors

Conditions that contribute to coronary heart disease

Anatomy of the cardiovascular system

Acute myocardial infarction or heart attack

Anatomy and physiology of the respiratory system

Initiation of Basic Life Support

General facts to remember

INTRODUCTION TO CARDIOPULMONARY RESUSCITATION (CPR)

Hillary Rodham Clinton's book *It Takes a Village* (Clinton, Hillary Rodham. *It Takes a Village: And Other Lessons Children Teach Us.* New York: Simon & Schuster, 1996.) would be an excellent theme for the organizing of life support systems about our country. It does take a dedicated community to provide training for laypeople that are able to provide CPR and other lifesaving maneuvers, as well as education for the public in matters of a healthy lifestyle. This section is not intended to replace the certification processes for the American Heart Association or the American Red Cross. These organizations have been in place for many years and provide research to improve techniques of lifesaving efforts. They provide educational materials for the public, instruction to the public, and guidelines for becoming certified in CPR, Advanced Cardiac Life Support (ACLS), and other areas of interest related to health.

This section is an effort to acquaint the beginning health care worker with the intricacies of providing emergency care in the community and the responsibility of the individual communities to provide a well-coordinated and effective system. There must be clear tiers of treatment through which the victim is advanced to save as many lives most effectively as possible. These tiers of care, from the basic layperson performing effective CPR to the advanced care provided at trauma centers, are discussed here. In order to become certified in life support, the student must be trained under the auspices of one of the organizations dedicated to this training. Basic facts related to basic life support (BLS) are presented to give the learner a cohesive approach to training. As a medical worker, you will be required to gain certification in CPR with the American Heart Association; this training designates you as a health care provider. Other lower levels of training are available, such as a program called "Heart Saver." Many jobs, such as child care, may require that the workers gain some sort of training for intervention in emergency situations.

While some actual procedures are listed here, this is an attempt to provide an introduction to what will be expected of you as a health care worker. No attempts will be made in this section to teach you the actual procedures involved in resuscitation of a victim. This will be left to the organizations that are so vital to our communities in providing this much-needed training and education. The requirements for becoming certified vary by facility, and some employers recognize only certain certifying bodies and will not accept the certification provided by others. Students who will perform clinical training should insure that they have the required level of training.

Emergency Care is a Community-Wide Responsibility

Education for everyone from early childhood to senescence is necessary to reduce risk factors that contribute to disease, particularly coronary disease. Effective training for everyone is necessary to enable each person to respond to an emergency situation in the correct way. Even small children should be taught to call emergency numbers and to recognize certain problems. The majority of sudden deaths caused by cardiac arrest occur before hospitalization, so the community must be viewed as part of the "coronary care unit." A well-trained group of laypeople will contribute vitally to the community by saving lives and through education in reasonable lifestyles that could ensure the survival of some of those suffering cardiac and respiratory arrest.

When the focus is on lifesaving techniques as well as prevention of disease through the reduction of risk factors, a great decrease in unnecessary deaths relating to an unhealthy lifestyle may occur. Community training programs should include a holistic approach to disease prevention, including recognizing ominous signals of cardiovascular disease. Patients known to have coronary heart disease should engage in group meetings that focus on awareness of warning signs and how to live a healthier lifestyle. It is clear that coronary heart disease and other forms of atherosclerotic vascular disease need to be supported by community nutritional patterns, as well as by offering smoking cessation seminars for children and young adults from all economic and social groups.

Training lay personnel in BLS saves lives that would be lost due to cardiac arrest. Communities with large numbers of laypeople well trained in CPR, along with a rapid response system of well-trained paramedical personnel providing ACLS, resuscitate up to 50 percent of patients who go into fibrillation. This is an ineffective quivering of the heart in which no blood is being pumped. This condition often results after a coronary attack and the heart has increased its beats–per minute (tachycardia) following the attack. While many consider the terms BLS and CPR as being synonymous, CPR is also used in ACLS, which is an advanced program used chiefly in medical facilities for treating coronary patients. This level of training is usually reserved for critical care nurses, paramedics, and physicians who perform advanced trauma life support in high level emergency units.

Basic Life Support

While often called CPR, for cardiopulmonary resuscitation, the better term to describe this range of treatments is basic life support. No bodily functions will occur if there is insufficient oxygen and nutrients reaching the cells of the body. Therefore, support of the respiratory and circulatory systems is paramount if the goal is to save the life of a person suffering from cardiac arrest due to any number of medical emergencies. Prevention of cardiovascular disease is necessary in order to prevent "sudden death" from the cessation of the basic functions of life, that of breathing and circulating one's blood. If this flow is interrupted for any significant length of time, generally considered to be six minutes, permanent brain damage occurs, and there is little possibility or even any point in resuscitating a victim. However, there is an exception to this rule. Those who are submerged in icy water may survive after thirty or even forty-five minutes or more due to a complex reaction by the body called the dive reaction. This phenomenon slows all of the functions of the body in an attempt to keep the brain alive.

Community Efforts

The community efforts are on both education and treatment following medical intervention. Prevention should be the focus of community education and should start early in life. These efforts will include the need for exercise, healthy diets, and better and less-stressful lifestyles. Studies show that those who lead sedentary lives run a higher risk of heart attack than those who have a regular program of exercise. A reasonable exercise program is instrumental in reducing the risks for diseases of all types. Regular exercise can increase the cardiovascular efficiency and may lower the demand for oxygen for any physical exercise. However, medical evaluation is needed prior to a person embarking on a vigorous physical program.

Exercise tones the muscles including the heart, stimulates the circulation, lowers the incidence of obesity, and promotes a healthy feeling among those who exercise regularly. This serves to lower the stress level associated with our fast-paced lives. Exercise may help to lower blood lipid abnormalities and a certain type of diabetes. Heart attack victims who engaged in regular exercise prior to having an attack have significantly increasedsurvival rates than those who did not exercise.

Efforts to prevent cardiovascular and cardiopulmonary disease are as important as those to provide emergency treatment for the cardiac arrest victim. Lowering risk factors has statistically been shown to save lives. The education of the community is vital in the effort to decrease mortality from Coronary Heart Disease (CHD). Education designed to recognize and modify risk factors depends on both education and understanding before a healthier lifestyle will be adopted by most of the people within the community. Efforts to educate the public must also be directed toward overcoming the denial of early signs and symptoms of cardiac disease and to encourage a quick response from the public in activating the EMS system.

What is the Role of the Health Care Provider?

We have a moral duty to help our fellow beings. Many lives could be saved annually if adequate resuscitation efforts are started soon after the arrest of either or both the respiratory and circulatory systems. Properly performed CPR along with rapid arrival of an automated defibrillator through response by an EMS team can reduce the death rate from cardiac arrest by more than half, it is estimated. The rate of cardiac arrest is falling nationwide, but ironically the death rate from cardiac arrest for younger people is increasing. It is thought that the reasons for this are a rise in obesity and an increased use of illicit drugs, particularly cocaine.

Community Role in a "Chain of Survival"

Time is of the essence! A community with a large number of well-trained laypeople who are strategically located in all areas of the community is essential in providing early and effective first aid treatment. It is vital that each community has a well-trained team that can carry out rescue efforts and provide primary care. Laypeople are often the first on the scene, and CPR provided correctly and in a timely manner, with an EMS system to respond in a reasonable period of time, should be a goal of each community. Transport to a medical facility after primary care should be provided, and the medical treatment facility, usually a hospital, should also have adequate training to provide ACLS after the layperson and the EMS have performed their duties. Each hospital should be equipped and have trained personnel to provide emergency cardiac care and trauma care in the most effective manner possible. CPR treatment by the layperson, who is then relieved by the community EMS with resources including an automated electronic defibrillator (AED), followed by transport to a nearby medical facility gives the optimal chance for survival.

Providing Training for CPR/BLS

The intent of this section is not to certify personnel in the provision of BLS/CPR. It is to be used as an adjunct for educating the health care provider in a holistic effort to understand the scope of care needed for prevention, treatment, and resuscitation of trauma victims and patients with acute and chronic heart disease. Both the American Red Cross and the American Heart Association provide training for the public and health care workers in BLS and First Aid. They provide the resources, research, and documentation literature for certification of specialists in BLS, ACLS, and First Aid as well as to meet other community training needs. Education and training in the following areas are provided:

1. Written information and procedures necessary for providing cardiopulmonary resuscitation for both adult and pediatric patients

2. Procedures and resources needed during special rescue situations

3. Structure and function of the respiratory and circulatory systems needed to understand all aspects of resuscitation efforts

4. Risk factors for diseases, particularly risks for vascular disease, heart attack, and stroke related to heredity and lifestyle

5. Signs and symptoms that warn of impending illness; actions and changes in lifestyle needed to minimize risk of disability and sudden death from cardiac arrest or stroke

6. Injury prevention for various stages of life, from birth to the elderly

7. Knowledge needed to safely carry out rescue activities

8. Ethical and legal requirements that provide protection for the rescuer/first aid provider

9. Quality of life for all citizens of a community often rests with volunteer agencies that teach lifestyle improvement, such as smoking cessation, preparing healthy diets, as well as keeping the citizens of a community healthier and safer as a result of education

Community Response in Medical Intervention for Cardiovascular Disease

Statistics indicate that the overall number of deaths from cardiovascular disease has decreased during the past three decades. But there is still much to do to educate the public in lifestyle matters, as well as research to provide the latest methodology found to be effective in aiding the victim of disease or injury. Healthier lifestyles, including diet and exercise, could do more to reduce these statistics.

Cardiovascular disease accounts for possibly 1 million deaths each year in the United States. Half of these deaths are said to occur suddenly and are due to coronary heart disease. Several million Americans have some sort of coronary heart disease and therefore are at risk for a heart attack or stroke. Rapid treatment extending throughout the "Chain of Survival" network would be quite effective in reducing these death rates, along with advances in medical treatment. Prompt BLS and ACLS, with rapid availability of an EMS system, layperson CPR, and early defibrillation are paramount in our efforts to control these numbers of preventable deaths.

Intervention by a well-trained layperson or professional is not intended for adults with coronary heart disease alone. Other community health risks that are left untreated or the sufferers uneducated about their respective conditions exact a toll in long-term suffering and economic hardship, often causing public outlay of funds to care for the victims and their families. People who are victims of trauma or illicit drug use also have a need for quick response by trained personnel. Results of drug use and other elements of a dangerous lifestyle may be respiratory failure or congenital birth defects in children of parents who use drugs, to list only a couple. Many community statistics for various disabling conditions are related to age, such as trauma, which is prevalent in children and young adults. These statistics are greatly improved with better education for prevention and treatment of existing conditions. Often, a mere change in lifestyle will head off a serious cardiac emergency, improving the lives of a community's citizens and lowering the financial burden of providing high-level care for a seriously ill person.

EMERGENCY CARDIAC CARE

While the community is concerned about emergency care for all types of emergencies, Emergency Cardiac Care (ECC) is a vital component of the emergency response system. The majority of cases treated in our country are related to life-threatening conditions of the cardiovascular and pulmonary systems. ECC includes all the resources of a community, from the layperson performing CPR as a first-responder to the advanced medical facilities. Emergency transportation alone, without life support, does not constitute ECC. Although transportation is an important aspect of

ECC, it is just a link in the chain of efforts to treat and save lives effectively. Treatment performed properly as first aid on the scene of the accident or illness is as or more important than transportation. Lengthy delays at the scene must be avoided, with stabilization achieved and defibrillation provided as necessary before and even during movement of the victim to a well-prepared medical site.

The two components of ECC are BLS and ACLS. CPR is an integral part of the lifesaving process in both. The ECC includes the following:

1. Warning signs of heart attack

2. Activating the EMS system

3. Preventing complications and further injury

4. Emotional support for the patient

5. Prompt availability of monitoring equipment

6. Providing immediate BLS at the scene, when needed

7. Providing ACLS at the scene with defibrillation, if needed

8. Stabilizing the victim before transportation

9. Safely transferring the patient to advanced medical care facility

Varieties of Conditions Other than Cardiovascular Requiring Treatment

Resuscitation is required in various injuries and diseases not caused by cardiovascular disease. Other life-threatening conditions that don't involve the heart in the initial stages of the condition may eventually require CPR. Some of these injuries or diseases are:

1. Asthmatic attack

2. Mechanically obstructed airway

3. Cardiovascular accident (stroke)

4. Near-drowning

5. Heat injuries (hyperthermia)

6. Electric shock

7. Trauma

8. Cold injuries (hypothermia)

9. Infant and child resuscitation

CPR includes **rapid** assessments and **aggressive** treatment to aid the cardiopulmonary systems in order to stabilize the victim. The application of CPR may avoid cardiac arrest or respiratory arrest. Proper CPR may be performed anywhere and with little or no equipment and can be learned by anyone. CPR skills should be taught to everyone capable of reacting in an emergency situation.

Layperson CPR is critical in resuscitation and can in many cases return cardiac and respiratory functions to a victim. When symptoms indicate circulatory failure, the bystander should be able to recognize these symptoms and react properly until advanced help is received. The victim should be immediately brought to the nearest emergency department or other facility with properly trained life support personnel. Each community should strive to have such a facility within a reasonable distance of all citizens. Early treatment coupled with quick arrival of advanced help to stabilize the victim and transport them to a medical facility provides an excellent chance of survival for many victims.

First Step in Resuscitative Efforts is Assessment

Any person present when cardiac or respiratory arrest occurs should initiate BLS. To be successful, Emergency Cardiac Care depends on the layperson's understanding of the importance of early activation of the EMS system and willingness and ability to initiate prompt and effective CPR. Accordingly, providing lifesaving BLS at this level can be considered primarily a public, community responsibility. The health care community, however, has the responsibility to provide leadership in educating the public and to support community education and training by volunteering time and equipment.

Survival of cardiac arrest depends on a series of critical interventions. If any of these critical actions is neglected or delayed, survival rates are greatly diminished. The American Heart Association (AHA) has educated the communities in the ECC systems concept for a number of years. The AHA and the American Red Cross have been invaluable in providing training and conducting research to provide the latest and best technology and procedures possible in the fight for disease prevention and survival of victims of disease. While BLS is vital in the immediate efforts to sustain life and stabilize victims, ACLS must be within reach in order to take over from the bystander, providing more advanced and sustained efforts while transporting the victim to medical treatment facilities.

ACLS includes BLS along with equipment for providing better ventilation, intravenous (IV) lines for administration of drugs, monitoring of the heart, defibrillation for arrhythmias, and continued care and monitoring following successful resuscitation. It also includes the establishment of communication necessary to ensure continued care. A physician supervises and directs ACLS personnel, often using radio communication to provide a set of "standard orders."

Full Scope of ECC Operations

As a health care worker and by virtue of receiving training for intervention in an emergency, you will become part of the community ECC. You may be called upon at any time to render aid to neighbors, relatives, or strangers who are injured or have fallen ill. You will be looked upon as a medical expert. Each community ECC will be based on needs for patient care and available resources. State, regional, and federal requirements are defined in many areas of our country. Often, resources are shared across political boundaries, such as county lines and states. Success of the system requires planning between participants to ensure a smoothly working system. The community must be willing to fund the program it develops and review its operations. Planning and monitoring of the system should be through an advisory board on emergency services and should assess community needs. It should have multidisciplinary participation in order to provide for smooth operations among different entities within the system. Continuing education programs must be provided for all components of the ECC to provide for a sustained skill level of the responders. Recertification on a periodic basis is necessary due to changes mandated by research, and the fact that a person's skills become rusty when not practiced for a period of time.

The Chain of Survival

In order to afford patients the best chance for survival, weaknesses in the community ECC system must be identified and remedied. Any breaks in the links of the chain of survival will serve to lower the survival rate and may be fatal to individual victims. Based on the population and available resources, unfortunately the survival rate in one community might be totally unacceptable in another. Community ECCs must assess whether their ECC systems actually do optimize a patient's chance for survival. Achieving the optimal survival rates for cardiac and/or respiratory arrest is the challenge in every community. Basically, the links in this chain of survival, whether in a hospital or in the community at large, are basically the same for an effective response and rescue system.

Basic Links in Chain of Survival

1. Quick access to the EMS system by effective community organization

2. Early CPR through a large number of well-trained laypeople

3. Early defibrillation by having strategically located portable defibrillators about the community

4. Early advanced cardiac care in well-staffed and trained hospitals and personnel, with rapid transportation

1. Quick Access

Immediate access following the patient's collapse until EMS personnel arrive, prepared to provide care, will enhance survival. Recognition of early warning signs, such as angina pectoris (chest pain) and shortness of breath before collapse, are key components about which the people of the community need to be educated. Significant symptoms and signs should precipitate the following:

A. Early identification of patient who has collapsed or is likely to collapse by someone who can activate the EMS system is important. 911 is the number for most community EMS dispatchers and other emergency personnel. If inside some building, establish an outside line before dialing 911.

B. Following collapse, establishment of unresponsiveness

C. Rapid notification to the EMS dispatchers

D. Rapid recognition by the dispatchers of an actual or pending cardiac arrest

2. Early CPR

A. Proper and quick dispatch instructions to available responders (local CPR trained lay people and nearest EMS station) to guide them to the patient

B. Quick initiation of CPR

    a. Adult victim – activate EMS system **prior to beginning CPR**

    b. Child and infant – activate EMS **after one minute of rescue effort**

3. Early Defibrillation

A. Rapid arrival of EMS personnel with necessary equipment and supplies including a defibrillator, to be used if necessary

B. Identification of the arrest

4. Early Advanced Cardiac Care

A. Transport to a medical facility while providing support during transport

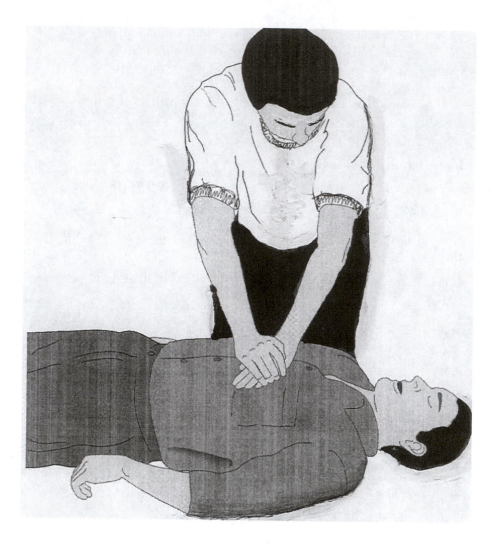

Special Instructions to Layperson Providing Life Support Activities

Some EMS dispatchers are able to provide information regarding the performing of CPR by the layperson on the scene. Dispatchers offer instructions to the caller on how to perform CPR until the EMS responders arrive. This approach has been met with some success in a number of communities, but the optimum situation would be that in which most laypeople of are already adequately prepared to perform CPR.

LIFESTYLE AND RISK FACTORS – AFFECT ON CARDIOVASCULAR AND RESPIRATORY HEALTH

It has been well established for many years that certain lifestyles put people at risk for many diseases, particularly coronary disease and diseases of the respiratory system. Some aspects of health cannot be controlled and some people have a predisposition to contracting certain diseases. However, many diseases are in part caused or aggravated by our lifestyles. Multiple risk factors increase the chance for developing coronary and respiratory diseases. Even those with an inherent predisposition for certain diseases may improve their long-term chance for survival for many years by adopting a healthy lifestyle. There are three categories of risks that are involved in the development of heart disease.

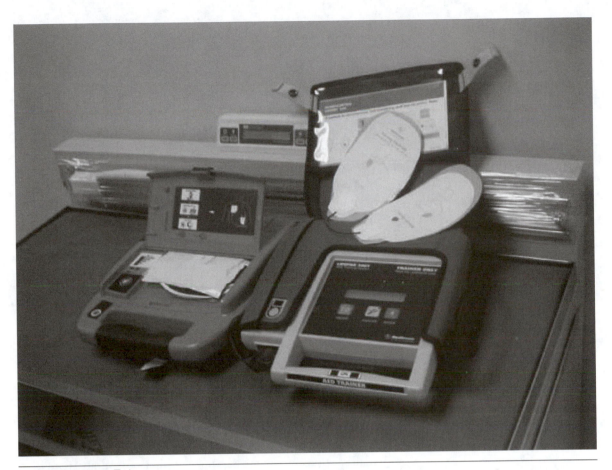

Portable Defibrillator Trainers

1. **Risk Factors that Cannot Be Changed**

   A. **Gender (Sex)**
   Of course, none of us is able to change our sex. Even those who undergo sex change operations have not changed genetic components of their sexual identity.

   B. **Heredity (Who your immediate relatives are)**
   We all know families that seem to have a greater than normal number of people dying at an early age with heart disease. Many inherited diseases of the heart are carried on for generations.

   C. **Age (Number of decades lived increases risk)**
   Age is a naturally occurring phenomenon about which we can do nothing. For every year we live, certain risks increase. Approximately one-fourth of the deaths from heart disease occur before the age of 65.

2. **Risk Factors that Can Be Changed**

   A. **Cigarette Smoking**
   The death rate from coronary disease among smokers is significantly higher than that for nonsmokers. The younger the smoker was when they began smoking correlates with the rate of deaths where cigarettes are an implicating factor.

B. Hypertension

Untreated high blood pressure, or hypertension, has been implicated in heart disease. Hypertension over the course of a number of years does damage to the heart as well as other vital organs. There are two types of hypertension:

a.   Primary   Cause or origin is unknown

b.   Secondary   Caused by chronic disease conditions

C. High Cholesterol

Cholesterol sometimes has a hereditary or familial component. Increased cholesterol has been associated with the development of coronary heart disease. There are a number of types of cholesterol, broken down basically into LDL (low-density lipoproteins), HDL (high-density lipoproteins), and VLDL (very low-density lipoproteins). The low-density molecules have been implicated most often in the development of atherosclerosis.

Cholesterol is a substance that is manufactured by the body but is also present in the animal products we eat. It is found in especially large amounts in egg yolk and organ meats. Excess cholesterol is deposited in the arteries and may lead to atherosclerosis. Diets high in saturated fats normally increase blood cholesterol. Saturated fats are found in meat, animal fats, and even some plant oils. Palm oil, coconut oil, cocoa butter, and hydrogenated margarine and shortening, whole milk, cream, butter, ice cream, cheese, and bakery goods with shortening added are loaded with saturated fats. Polyunsaturated fats and monounsaturated fats actually lower the cholesterol. Using polyunsaturated and monounsaturated fats instead of saturated fats from the previously listed sources and by increasing complex carbohydrates intake, a person may reduce their risk for atherosclerosis. More fresh fruits and vegetables in the diet go a long way toward lowering the cholesterol in most people. Eat fish or poultry instead of red meats, such as beef, pork, and lamb, trim off excess fat, and remove the skin. Serve small portions of any meat. Cook with limited amounts of liquid vegetable oils and polyunsaturated oils such as canola, corn, cottonseed, soybean, and safflower products. Olive oil is an excellent source for monounsaturated fat.

D. Sedentary (Low Activity) Lifestyle

Almost everyone can do more to avoid a sedentary lifestyle. Activities as simple as walking up stairs instead of taking the elevator and walking to nearby destinations instead of taking a car are easy lifestyle modifications. Strenuous and unaccustomed activity occasionally brings on a heart attack in an apparently healthy person who has undiagnosed heart disease. Before someone over 40 years of age or with a known risk of cardiovascular disease undertakes an exercise program or engages in heavy physical labor, a physician should be consulted. A stress test may be performed. Physical activity should be increased gradually in any exercise program. Sports that the patient enjoys are excellent means for achieving a higher level of activity, both as a preventive measure as well as for rehabilitation following a heart attack.

3. Factors that May Contribute to Coronary Disease

A. Obesity (Extremely overweight is morbid obesity)

Sudden death related to obesity, particularly those who add weight to their frames after completing their growth at about age 25, increases the risk of having coronary heart disease dramatically. Life expectancy for people who are considerably overweight is shortened, and significantly overweight middle-aged men are three times more likely to have a fatal heart attack. As people age and become less physically active, fewer calories are needed to maintain an ideal weight. Obesity has been traced to an increased occurrence of CHD and sudden death largely as a consequence of its influence on other risk factors. The rates for hypertension, hyperlipidemia (high level of fatty substances in the blood), and diabetes are greater among the obese. Obesity may directly contribute to CHD, as few people become obese without developing a high coronary risk status through an unhealthy lifestyle. There is no quick, easy diet to magically provide for drastic losses of weight. Losing weight should be accomplished in a slow, measured fashion, through a combination of sensible diet and regular exercise.

B. Stress

Stress-reducing activities, such as exercise, meditation, and rest, are necessary to lower many of the body's defense reactions against stressors. While the exact damage that stress does to the body's organs is not entirely clear, it certainly has an effect on the blood pressure and muscle tone. Emotional stress and situations or occurrences with a personal impact, such as the death of a close relative or friend, divorce, or loss of a job, are common before myocardial infarction. It is not possible to measure a person's emotional stress. Everyone feels stress, but some feel it more acutely than others and manifest it differently. Excessive stress over a long period may create health problems in some people. Many health care practitioners believe that reduced emotional stress would benefit the population of the world.

C. Diabetes

The risk of coronary heart disease among people with diabetes is two to three times greater than among those without diabetes for men and women, respectively. Risk factors such as high cholesterol, hypertension, and obesity seem to be exacerbated by diabetes. Also, peripheral vascular problems develop after years of suffering with diabetes.

CONDITIONS THAT CONTRIBUTE TO CORONARY HEART DISEASE

As people grow older, atherosclerosis causes the blood vessels to become hardened and less elastic. This change takes place gradually and occurs in those without hypertension, but the condition does hasten the process of hardening of the vessels. The incidence of stroke increases with high blood pressure and age. Uncontrolled high blood pressure may cause kidney damage and heart damage. The heart may become enlarged and less efficient, but damage may be limited if proper treatment is initiated early in the disease process. Minor cases of hypertension may be controlled by diet and weight control. Increased sodium may be related to hypertension but has not been directly implicated.

Cardiopulmonary Anatomy

The anatomy or structure and the physiology or function of the cardiovascular and respiratory systems are important components and understanding them is necessary to gain an understanding of the clinical implications of heart diseases. The physical aspects of how CPR procedures work to improve the chance for survival following an arrest require a basic knowledge of both the coronary and the respiratory systems. These two systems work hand-in-hand; it is difficult to separate the two as they are intrinsically interconnected to provide oxygenated blood and nutrients to the entire body. A cessation of this supply of oxygenated blood to the vital organs spells death within minutes if artificial means are not employed to restore the circulation.

ANATOMY OF THE CARDIOVASCULAR SYSTEM

The cardiovascular system is composed of the heart, arteries, capillaries, and veins. The normal adult heart is the approximate size of a large fist. It lies to the left of the center of the chest, behind the sternum (breastbone). The heart is above the diaphragm and shares the thoracic cavity with the heart. The heart is also somewhat surrounded by the lungs and other visceral organs.

The heart may be simply described as a hollow, four-chambered organ with tough, muscular walls of muscle called myocardium; a sac called the pericardium surrounds it. A wall, called the septum, separates the heart cavity into right and left sides, and each side is divided into an upper chamber (atrium) and a lower chamber (ventricle). Valves regulate the flow of blood through the heart chambers and out to the lungs to pick up oxygen and then back to the lungs to be pumped out to the cells of the body. The heart simply pumps blood from the right ventricle (lower chamber) to the lungs through the pulmonary artery where oxygen is bound to the red blood cells. The blood then returns to the heart through the pulmonary vein to the left upper chamber (atrium). The blood then goes through the mitral valve to the left ventricle (lower chamber), where it is pumped through the aortic valve into the aorta. There, it is divided into arterial branches going toward the head and the main aorta, which descends to provide oxygen for the lower body and its organs. Arteries carry oxygenated blood to the body's cells and pick up carbon dioxide.

This gas exchange of oxygen and carbon dioxide takes place in the capillaries, the smallest vessels in the body. The cells of the body will quickly die if the flow of oxygen to them is interrupted, so immediate reaction by the rescuer is necessary to save a life. The red cells then bind with carbon dioxide and return to the heart through the veins. The venous blood returns to the left atrium (upper chamber), where it is pushed into the left ventricle and goes through the cycle of being oxygenated and losing its load of carbon dioxide. The blood then returns to the left atrium and then to the left ventricle where it begins its journey all over again to nourish the tissues and organs of the body.

The body essentially pumps hundreds of gallons of blood per day, and it is vital that the heart be well nourished by diet as well as exercise in order to continue effectively pumping the blood 24 hours per day for our entire lives. The bodily functions of providing oxygenated blood to the body are accomplished by performing CPR when the body has lost its capability to accomplish this important task on its own. The rescuer or rescuers supply air to the lungs by breathing into the victim's mouth and then compress the sternum over the heart to force blood from the heart and into the arterial system. The more competent and proficient a person is in delivering cardiopulmonary resuscitation, the better the chance a victim has for survival. The trained rescuer who is first on the scene has no equipment other than their hands and their own lungs and mouth to use in delivering the care the victim needs. Undoubtedly, they will soon become exhausted, so it is necessary that the EMS system be activated as soon as possible after assessing a victim and finding them unresponsive and without heartbeats or respirations. Remember, start CPR on a child or infant and perform the procedures for one minute PRIOR to calling for help. For an adult, activate the EMS and then begin giving CPR. Often, children may be resuscitated quickly with only a small amount of CPR, and this is the reason for beginning the treatment before taking time to activate the EMS. The entire vascular system of an adult contains five to seven liters of blood, and each heartbeat ejects about 70 mL (or cc's) of blood. Therefore, the heart may pump up to 35 liters of blood per minute during strenuous exercise.

Cardiac muscle contractions or heartbeats are started by electrical impulses from a natural pacemaker in the heart, the SA node, and are transmitted through the heart muscle by a system of conduction over nerves. Heartbeats are coordinated to allow blood to enter the atrium, be pumped into the ventricles, and out to the lungs or the body, depending on the side of the heart being examined. Heart muscle contracts after stimulation by this electrical impulse. In some heart disease, this stimulation is not coordinated and the heartbeats ineffectively. This is called an arrhythmia and medications may relieve the condition. During cardiac arrest, the heart may beat wildly and then revert to fibrillation, an ineffective quivering of the heart muscle. When this happens, defibrillation is necessary to restore the normal rhythm of the heart. That is the reason the EMS with ACLS capabilities should be enroute as soon as possible to aid the person who responded to the emergency initially.

Coronary Diseases

Two terms commonly used in disease of the cardiovascular system, which includes the heart as well as the vessels of the circulatory system, are termed Coronary Artery Disease, or CAD, and arteriosclerosis. Arteriosclerosis is often called "hardening of the arteries." The condition causes the arteries to thicken over a period of time and to lose their elasticity, or ability to stretch. This causes a rise in blood pressure. Atherosclerosis is a form of arteriosclerosis where the inner layers of the arteries become thick and are not smooth due to deposits of fatty substances, ostensibly from high levels of cholesterol over a period of time. This deposition of "plaque" in the arteries serves to narrow the arteries and restrict the flow of blood to the organs of the body. Coronary heart disease (CHD) is a disease of the coronary arteries along with a concomitant presence of symptoms, usually resulting in angina pectoris (chest pain). Ischemia is a general term that indicates a diminished flow of blood to any organ, including the heart.

Atherosclerosis is a progressive disease and appears to begin early in life as is manifested by postmortem examinations of the very young. Advanced atherosclerosis has been seen in 20-year-olds. The disease may not exhibit any symptoms until the restriction of blood flow is severe. The disease process may be halted or even reversed to an extent when risk factors, which may be changed, are removed. Eventually, the heart muscle is impaired, and a clot may occur due to sluggish blood flow. When the blood flow is completely or almost completely halted, injury to the heart muscle occurs. When the oxygen supply is insufficient to provide for the muscle of the heart, pain may occur.

Angina pectoris is a term for a common symptom of CHD and is often transient, meaning the pain comes and goes. In angina, nitroglycerin is used for relief in the form of patches, cream, or sublingual preparations designed for placement under the tongue for absorption. These forms of medication often relieve the discomfort, since the medication constricts the vessels, effectively increasing the blood flow to the heart. Stress, or more often exercise, is sometimes implicated in making the pain level increase. Pain may occur in a number of locations, including the center of the chest or across the front of the chest. It may also be focused in the neck, back, shoulder, or arm. It may be described as crushing, piercing, tightening, or heavy. The pain is often a steady discomfort, but in some it fluctuates. It is often brought on by an increase in heart rate, exercise, or exertion, and/or when anxiety is present. If the pain is persistent and does not diminish after thirty minutes of rest or medication, the person experiencing the pain may require medical attention. Coronary atherosclerosis is the most frequent cause of angina and often precedes a myocardial infarction (heart attack). In severe cases of CHD, and sometimes for a few days or weeks before an attack, angina may occur while resting. Quite often, coronary attacks occur while the victim is asleep, and frequently the person is awakened from deep sleep by angina. Angina pectoris that comes on while the person is asleep or at rest, or becomes worse over time, is known as unstable angina. Unstable angina often precedes a severe heart attack.

ACUTE MYOCARDIAL INFARCTION OR HEART ATTACK

A heart attack is a situation in which an area of heart muscle has a diminished or obstructed flow of its blood supply for a period of time. Complete blockage or narrowing that almost completely stops the flow of blood to the heart muscle results in necrosis (death) of the heart muscle tissue supplied by the obstructed artery. A heart attack often leads to arrhythmias, including ventricular fibrillation, which can be detected by an electrocardiogram. Ventricular fibrillation, if untreated, will lead to death, while atrial fibrillation, while dangerous, may not lead to death over a short period of time. Fibrillation often occurs following a heart attack, and this is the reason for having highly trained rescue providers on the way when the layperson begins BLS efforts. At any time, a person who has had a coronary attack may revert to ventricular fibrillation, a condition where the heart merely quivers uncontrollably and does not adequately provide a flow of blood to vital organs.

Signs and Symptoms of an Impending Coronary

The victim of a heart attack may not have severe symptoms and may not appear to be ill. The pain or discomfort may be mild and be confused with "indigestion." Often, the victim will complain of indigestion but will deny that they are having a coronary. The victim of a coronary may have some or all of the following symptoms:

1. Chest discomfort that lasts longer than angina and is not relieved by rest or nitroglycerin remember the term "unstable angina"

2. Sweating, nausea, or shortness of breath

3. Feelings of intense indigestion

4. General weakness or "feeling tired" for several days prior to heart attack

5. Vague feelings of unease and discomfort

Treatment to Ensure Survival

While prevention is the best way to avoid deaths from cardiopulmonary disease, we will never completely eliminate the associated conditions related to disease of these systems because of heredity and lifestyle. Many deaths that occur before the victims arrive at a medical treatment facility could be prevented with prompt and effective treatment. It has only been in the past few decades that communities realized the need for trained laypeople, portable defibrillators easily accessed around the community, and a rapid response team that can be reached at a moment's notice.

Cardiac Arrest

Sudden cardiac death or cardiac arrest occurs when heartbeat and breathing stop abruptly, and no warning signs are usually perceived. Sudden cardiac arrest often appears to occur with no warning signs or symptoms of coronary heart disease, but sometimes later a family member or the victim will remember some vague symptom that was ignored. The arrest most often occurs within an hour or two following the beginning of a coronary attack, so definitive treatment is of the essence immediately after the attack. The victim often loses consciousness within a brief moment of the arrest, and this is the condition in which the layperson usually finds the victim. Returning circulation to the brain as quickly as possible gives the best chance for a full recovery with little or no brain damage. After four to six minutes of a loss of oxygenated blood to the brain, irreversible brain damage has already occurred. Children and victims of cold exposure or barbiturate overdose may recover normal brain function after much longer periods of no circulation.

Causes for Cardiac Arrest

Cardiac arrest is most commonly attributed to CHD (coronary heart disease), caused usually by a poor diet high in saturated fats and little exercise. Any condition that can change the blood transport system to the heart could result in a cardiac arrest. This could be attributable to narrowing of the arteries, clots, brain trauma, or drug and alcohol overdoses that affect respiration and may lead to respirations coming to a halt. The heart will function even with brain injury. But if the respiratory system fails, a cardiac arrest is imminent and sure. When respirations end, the heart may beat for several minutes before stopping, which it will do when deprived of adequate oxygenated blood. Ironically, a person may have a pulse with no respirations, or respirations without any pulse. Sudden death is often preceded by ventricular fibrillation, and if a defibrillator is not available, death is certain. Fibrillation is not an effective functioning of the heart, causing a lack of oxygen to the body's tissues. Sudden death victims who showed no symptoms prior to arrest and have been resuscitated often show extreme CHD but do not show evidence of having had a heart attack. Competent early CPR coupled with availability of defibrillation and a rapid EMS response for advanced life support gives the victim of cardiac arrest an excellent chance of surviving the episode. Automated external defibrillators are now widely available in many communities and are smaller and more affordable. National efforts are ongoing to provide these devices in every city, every police department, and every large, public gathering place. A layperson may use one of the automated AEDs (automated electronic defibrillator) without causing harm to the patient, as instructions are given by synthetic voice from the instrument. The AED is programmed to assess the cardiac status of the patient and will not deliver shocks unless there is an arrhythmia indicating the need for defibrillation.

Initial Treatment

1. Help the patient rest quietly.

2. Keep activity level at a minimum.

3. Reassure the victim and monitor to determine if CPR or defibrillation is indicated.

4. Allow victim to assume position of greatest comfort, either lying down or sitting up, so as to breathe most easily.

5. If nitroglycerin is available, administer it with patient lying or sitting down, as blood pressure is lowered by the medication.

6. Monitor the pulse, as an arrhythmia may occur and defibrillation will be necessary.

7. If available, oxygen should be administered.

ANATOMY AND PHYSIOLOGY OF THE RESPIRATORY SYSTEM

The respiratory system brings oxygen from the outside air into the blood and is called external respiration. The blood also picks up and eliminates carbon dioxide from the body as it is released from the cells during their metabolism (internal respiration). The cells of the body require a continuous supply of oxygen and a mechanism by which to release carbon dioxide. The two types of respiration are inextricably interwoven and both are necessary for life. They are:

1. External respiration
   In external respiration, the lungs gain oxygen from the outside atmosphere. The oxygen binds to the red blood cells of the vascular system and is carried to all of the cells of the body.

2. Internal respiration
   Internal respiration occurs where the capillaries have contact with the individual cells and release their oxygen to the cells while picking up the carbon dioxide produced by cellular metabolism.

Organs and Systems Producing Respirations

The neuromuscular system is also extremely important in respiratory functions of the body. The respiratory center of the brain, nerves to the muscles of respiration, and muscles of respiration all play a part in effective respiratory functions. The chest cage includes ribs, spine, and sternum to protect the lungs and aid in breathing. The major muscle of respiration is the diaphragm, a sheet-like muscle attached to the margin of the lower ribs and extending from front to back of the thoracic cavity, separating the chest cavity from the abdominal cavity. A number of smaller muscles of the neck and shoulder girdle are involved in effective breathing.

The lungs can be pictured as a tree. The bronchi and bronchioles lead from the mouth and nose to the lungs. They are cartilaginous tubes that are rigid so they don't easily collapse. The bronchi resemble the trunk of the symbolic respiratory tree, and the bronchioles are the limbs. The alveoli, or the leaves of the respiratory tree, are composed of millions of tiny air sacs that hold carbon dioxide and oxygen and are lined by a moist membrane. On the inner side of the membrane is a fine system of capillaries, and this is where the blood is in contact with the oxygen from the outside air. These leaves or alveoli, along with their contiguous capillaries, are the basic lung units. Remember, the heart has two sides; the pulmonary arteries carry blood their oxygen is released to the cells, from the right heart. The capillaries surround the alveoli. The pulmonary veins carry the oxygenated blood back to the left heart. Carbon dioxide in the blood remains fairly constant, but when the level rises substantially, the body is adversely affected.

The stimulus to breathe comes from the respiratory center in the brain, but the level of carbon dioxide in the arteries regulates the body's need for oxygen. As the CO_2 level rises, the respiratory center in the brain sends signals to the muscles of the chest wall to stimulate faster breathing. The breathing rate and depth are increased until the level of carbon dioxide falls, and this is often called "blowing off" CO_2. The body constantly monitors the CO_2 level and the number and depth of breaths. This serves to maintain the level of CO_2 in the blood.

Atmospheric air contains about 20 percent oxygen and a small amount of CO_2. Only a fraction of the oxygen in the inhaled air is taken up by the blood during respiration; exhaled air still contains about 16 percent of the atmospheric level of oxygen. This is enough oxygen to enable the exhaled air from the rescuer to provide sufficient oxygen for resuscitation. ACLS personnel use a bag-valve mask with adjunctive oxygen. This gives a higher level of oxygen to the victim.

Respiratory Arrest and Inadequate Respiration

Respiratory arrest refers to the absence of respiratory functions. Inadequate respiration indicates that some breathing may occur, but it is insufficient to provide enough oxygen to rid the body of excess carbon dioxide in the blood. The brain stimulates respiratory functions. Interrupted blood flow to the brain is a stroke or cerebrovascular accident (CVA). A blood clot blocking flow to portions of the brain, a bleeding condition within the brain, or cardiac arrest will cause breathing to cease. If oxygenation of the brain is stopped, respiratory arrest will occur quickly. Drug overdoses and certain medications, which reach a high level in the body, or head injury could all affect the thoracic muscles of the chest and affect respirations.

An obstructed airway is another common cause of respiratory functions, particularly in infants and young children. Prompt and proper treatment for an obstructed airway is necessary to save the victim. Proper emergency training, including opening of the airway in emergency situations, is vital for safety in the home, eating establishments, and any place where crowds gather, such as sporting events. We must also remember that a heart without oxygen soon stops beating, so the *airway must be addressed first*.

Signs and Symptoms of Respiratory Insufficiency

Respiratory failure may occur from disease as well as trauma. Such well-known conditions as emphysema and asthma may affect the respirations to an extent that the body is unable to function normally. Often heart damage and respiratory failure are found in tandem in a debilitated patient. Damage to one of these systems often leads to secondary damage in the other.

Basic Life Support

There are subtle differences in the treatment and intervention process between adults, children, and infants. However, the goal is the same. To restore respirations first of all is paramount. As was presented earlier, the lack of respiratory functions will cause the heart to stop beating, and cardiac death will soon occur. In some cases, the heart may beat for a few minutes following respiratory arrest until it has insufficient oxygen to operate on its own.

The first phase of BLS in the ECC is designed to prevent respiratory or cardiac arrest by supporting the circulation and respirations for a victim of cardiac or respiratory arrest. The goal of CPR is to provide oxygen to the brain and heart until advanced medical treatment can restore normal cardiopulmonary functions. Promptly starting CPR and having advanced medical care on the way is vital. In respiratory arrest, success is often achieved with restoration of breathing, and rescue breathing is started within a matter of minutes. If CPR is started in cases of cardiac arrest within three or four minutes, and ACLS is started within a few minutes after initiation of CPR, the success rate is good. Improvement of lifestyles including diet and exercise coupled with timely CPR and ACLS spells a high degree of success in resuscitation of victims of both cardiac and respiratory arrest. The American Heart Association studies suggest that victims may be saved up to 61 percent of the time with timely and effective action by the layperson initiating CPR and the quick arrival of advanced care personnel.

Response by Laypeople to Cardiac and Respiratory Emergencies

Previous guidelines have called for a single rescuer who is alone to perform CPR for one minute and then activate the EMS system. This has now changed to indicate the need for the single rescuer to activate the EMS prior to beginning CPR. Studies have shown that AED availability soon after the start of CPR maximizes the potential for saving many lives. The time from collapse to defibrillation is most important. Education in BLS training under the auspices of the American Heart Association includes training in the use of the AED. The witness to a collapse must not waste time calling neighbors and relatives but should immediately activate the EMS.

Untrained laypeople may be used to help perform CPR when the primary rescuer becomes exhausted. Specific instructions and monitoring of the untrained person may be necessary to continue the efforts to resuscitate a person. Instructions can be relayed by telephone to the untrained person by trained medical personnel, such as paramedics and emergency medical technicians, when immediate resuscitation is necessary and a trained person is not available.

INITIATION OF BASIC LIFE SUPPORT

First to be established is, "Does the victim need resuscitation?" No victim should be "resuscitated" until the need has been clearly determined. It is dangerous to do chest compressions on a person who has an effective pulse rate. Assessment of the victim includes determining if the victim is unconscious or is merely sleeping. Assessment continues throughout the process of resuscitating the cardiac or respiratory arrest victim. Also remember that after determining unresponsiveness in an ADULT, the EMS must be activated immediately prior to performing CPR if possible.

Initial Sequence of Basic Life Support

1. Assessment   Does the patient need BLS? Assess for injuries; if spinal injury is suspected, a modified manner of opening the airway is used.
   If the patient is unresponsive to the spoken or shouted word and to a physical touch, the EMS must be activated.

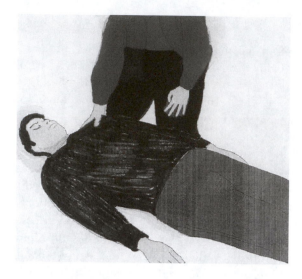

2. EMS
   Activation

If someone is available, send the person to contact EMS by the most convenient means. In most communities, 911 is the number of choice. If the rescuer is alone in an isolated area and no one is near to hear a cry for help, CPR must be initiated.

   A. Good communication is necessary, so speak calmly.

   a. Give location with landmarks if appropriate

   b. Provide telephone number and stay on line until EMS personnel conclude the call

   c. Types and numbers of injuries if known

   d. What is the status (condition) of the victims?

   e. Who is providing aid, and what kind of aid is being provided? Some EMS personnel are trained to instruct rescue efforts by telephone

   f. Hold the phone until EMS personnel have completed their information gathering. Sometimes, the EMS responder is consulting with other EMTs or with a nearby health care facility for advice.

Basic Steps in Resuscitation

Remember, if there is no air going into the body, providing circulation artificially will do no good, even if chest compressions are performed flawlessly. The following section is merely to show the sequence of steps necessary to resuscitate a victim. It is not specific as to the tasks necessary to resuscitate various categories of patients relative to age.

Step One   Determine Responsiveness Call to the victim and shake the victim gently to determine if he or she is unconscious.

Step Two   Position the victim
When the victim is unresponsive, the rescuer must determine if the victim is breathing. This assessment requires that the victim be positioned properly with the airway opened. For effective CPR, the victim must be flat on the back (supine) and on a firm surface. This facilitates both the chest compressions and the blood flow to the brain. Airway management and rescue breathing are also more easily achieved with the patient supine. An unconscious victim must be

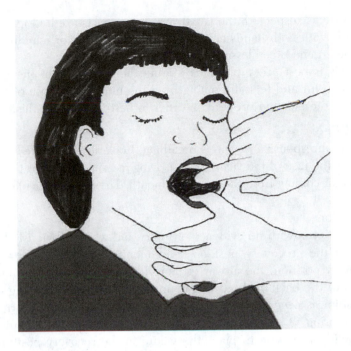

positioned quickly for CPR. A victim lying face down must be rolled onto their back for CPR. If a spinal injury is suspected, the head must be supported without twisting the spine as the body is rolled over. In order to easily roll the victim; raise the arm on the side to be rolled on straight above the victim's head. Then grasp the shoulder and hip on the side opposite the raised arm and roll the victim toward the rescuer.

Step Three   Open the Airway

In an unconscious victim, the tongue may be occluding the airway. If the lower jar where the tongue is attached is moved forward, the tongue is lifted away from the back of the throat. Any foreign material including vomitus must be removed from the mouth and throat. The head tilt-chin lift maneuver is performed by placing one hand on the victim's forehead and the fingers of the other hand under the bottom of the chin. Lift the chin and jaw while tilting the head back. If a spinal

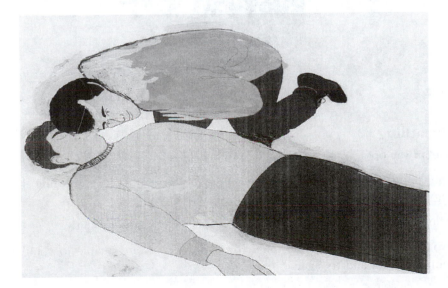

injury is suspected, the jaw-thrust maneuver is used. Grip the lower jaw on each side with both hands and displace the lower jaw or mandible forward.

Step Four   Determine Breathlessness
This is best accomplished by using the sensitivity of the ear and the cheek to listen for and feel air coming from the mouth and nose of the victim. One must get into position properly in order to best accomplish this determination.

Look, Listen, and Feel

Determine if the unresponsive person is breathing. Look, listen, and feel. You should place the side of your face over the face of the victim, who is lying face-up. **Look** for the chest to rise. **Listen** for breaths. **Feel** for air coming from the nose and mouth. The ear is particularly sensitive to airflow.

Note: Recovery Position

An unresponsive victim with no evidence of injury and who is obviously breathing adequately should be placed in the "recovery position" and monitored regularly for possible respiratory arrest. In the recovery position, the airway is more likely to remain open, and obstruction from the tongue falling into the back of the throat is unlikely. Careful monitoring of the victim placed in the recovery position is necessary until the victim responds or is transported to a medical care facility. When monitoring of successfully resuscitated victims has to be interrupted to provide care for another victim, it is wise to place the victim in the recovery position.

Step Five   Perform Rescue Breathing
Mouth-to-mouth rescue breathing is a quick and effective way to provide oxygen for the victim. Exhaled air contains enough oxygen to fulfill the victim's needs. The rescuer must inflate the victim's lungs fully with each breath. Time between breaths must be sufficient to allow the victim's lungs to deflate after air is breathed into them. Failure to do so will cause the air to be eventually forced into the victim's stomach, which is no help at all.

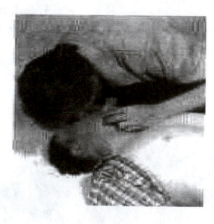

Rescue Breathing

1. Keep the airway open by the head tilt-chin lift maneuver.

2. Close the victim's nose by placing a hand on the forehead of the victim, while at the same time pinching closed the nose between index finger and thumb.

3. Take a deep breath and seal your lips around the victim's mouth tightly.

4. Give two slow breaths. Allow the lungs to deflate. If you are unable to ventilate the victim, reposition the head and try again.

5. Each ventilation should include enough air and force to make the chest rise visibly. The rescuer should watch from the corner of their eye for the chest to rise. The lungs of most adults will hold as much as one liter of air (a little more than a quart). The oxygen that the rescuer has breathed in and is forcing into the victim's lungs is not oxygenated at the percentage that the rescuer is enjoying, but there is enough residual oxygen left in the lungs of the rescuer to resuscitate the victim effectively.

6. Rescue breathing for adults is about 12 breaths per minute, while for children and infants it is higher as the younger victims have a higher rate of both respirations and heartbeats.

7. Allow for the chest to fall before giving the second breath. If you are unable to ventilate the victim the first time, ALWAYS reposition the head to open the airway and try again.

8. If the stomach begins to become full and distended, the rescuer is probably giving the rescue breaths too quickly and with too much force. Air in the stomach will do nothing to help oxygenate the victim.

Special Situations

1. Mouth to Nose
   Sometimes it is impossible to breathe through the victim's mouth due to injury of disease. In this situation, a mouth to nose technique is used.

2. Stoma (surgical opening such as a person with a tracheostomy)
   The mouth and nose must be sealed or a tightly fitting face mask used to prevent air leakage. If you are not able to provide rescue breathing through the tracheostomy tube, the tube is extracted and ventilation is provided directly through the stoma (opening in the throat).

3. Barrier Device
   If possible, a mask or other barrier device should be used when ventilating a patient. Medical care provider students will be trained in the use of a barrier device during CPR training. There are two basic designs, the mask and the shield. There are a large number of various types and designs, ranging from a simple disposable plastic sheet with openings for the mouth of the victim, to the ones pictured here. Bag-valve masks are also effective in delivery of air to the victim and are available in sizes from infant to adult.

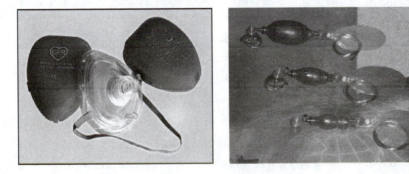

(a) Bag-Valve Masks With Covers
(b) Bag-Valve Masks – Use With O_2
Examples of a barrier device to prevent transmission of infectious diseases

GENERAL FACTS TO REMEMBER

A child is from 1 year of age through 8 years of age. An infant is less than 1 year old. Children over the age of 8 years of age are treated as adults.

1. Never attempt to perform chest compressions on a person who has a pulse.
   In your assessment, always assess for a pulseless state.

Check the pulse at the carotid artery for an adult. Use the brachial (arm) for infants and small children. The carotid artery is in front of the large muscles going down the side of the neck. It is under the jawbone and toward the back of the neck from the trachea (Adam's Apple).

2. Remember the ABCs of CPR.

    A. Airway first

    B. Breathing second

    C. Circulation is important but comes after a patent (open) airway is established.

3. Always start with two slow breaths. Remember the ABC's of resuscitation. First the airway must be opened. It will do no good to perform chest compressions and circulate blood that contains little or no oxygen.

4. Rates of respirations and pulse
These vary for age groups. A higher rate is necessary for infants and children than for adults. Through determinations reached by research, certifying bodies will alter the rates. The current requirements will be listed in the manuals provided by the certifying bodies and will change periodically.

5. Depth of chest compressions
The depth for compressions varies by age and are as follows:

    A. Adult   1 ½ to 2 inches   Performed with heels of both hands

    B. Child   1 to 1 ½ inches   Performed with heel of one hand

    C. Infant   ½ to 1 inch   Performed with two fingers

6. **If pulse is present** but there is no spontaneous breathing
Rescue breathing at approximately twelve times per minute or once every five to six seconds for adults
If there is no pulse:
A. For adults, EMS system should be activated and them CPR initiated.

    B. For children and infants, perform one minute of CPR PRIOR to activating EMS. Children and infants may respond almost immediately to resuscitation.

7. Patient must be on a firm surface and supine (on the spine) before performing chest compressions. Chest compressions must be regular and rhythmic. Avoid jerky motions and keep the arms straight while leaning on the sternum to avoid excessive fatigue.

8. One must learn both one-person and two-person CPR. It is necessary to practice both techniques, as we cannot always choose the situation we may find ourselves in when we are called upon to perform CPR.

9. Often, the cause for cardiac arrest or respiratory arrest is obvious. For example, a child often has an obstructed airway, leading to respiratory arrest and possible cardiac arrest following. The Heimlich maneuver in most cases will clear an obstructed airway for infants, children, and adults. Differences exist in the methodology employed for various age levels. In this procedure, residual air in the lungs is used to force the obstructing material from the respiratory system. The Heimlich maneuver may be performed on either a standing victim (conscious) or a patient who has collapsed and is on the floor. Occasionally, a person with an obstruction will collapse, and in doing so, hit the floor with enough force to dislodge the obstruction.

Monitoring the Victim

1. The victim's condition must be monitored to assess the effectiveness of resuscitation efforts. In two-person CPR, the person at the head of the victim may assess the effectiveness of chest compression by checking for carotid or brachial pulse while compressions are being performed.

2. If the victim resumes spontaneous circulation and breathing, efforts by the rescuer(s) will be stopped, but the victim must be monitored to determine if arrest reoccurs.

3. Place successfully resuscitated victim in a rescue position and monitor vital signs regularly.

4. **DO NOT abandon the patient. You are the patient's last and only hope, as time is of the essence!**

GLOSSARY

Terms Related to Infectious Diseases and Allied Health Professions

absorption Act of soaking into an item, such as an absorbent pad; the taking up of liquids or gels

active immunity Produced by either immunizing an individual or by the person having been infected and having recovered from the infection.

acute Lasting for a short period of time and in a severe condition; acute condition usually occurs early in a disease process when the body's immune responses first react to a condition such as an infection

advanced directive Legal document detailing the wishes of a person who may become ill and be unable to make decisions due to a diminished mental state

aerobic Condition requiring oxygen; includes certain growth requirements for various species of bacteria

afebrile Patient is not reacting to a disease process by a rise in body temperature

agent Infectious organism; may be viral, bacterial, protozoal, fungal

AIDS Acquired Immunodeficiency Syndrome is a disease that results from HIV infection

anaerobic Condition of not having or requiring oxygen in order to metabolize, as in bacteria that can survive conditions of no oxygen

anemia Insufficient blood supply, absence of blood supply, or a physical condition affecting the red blood cells

anorexia Loss of desire for food intake or appetite

anoxia Condition of being without oxygen

antecubital Space located on inner part of elbow where arterial pulse may be palpated or felt

antibody Protein developed by certain white blood cells of the body against a foreign body or substance

antibody screen/titer Test to check for presence or level of antibodies; occurs following exposure to infectious agent

anticoagulant Medication or substance that delays or prevents clotting of blood

antigen A substance that is foreign to the body and causes antibody formation

antisepsis Measures taken to retard, prevent, or inhibit growth of pathogenic organisms

apical pulse Pulse taken by stethoscope (auscultation) near the apex of the heart

apnea Cessation of breathing – may be temporary or permanent

arterial Adjective; pertaining to an artery

arteriosclerosis Hardening, thickening, and/or narrowing of the arteries

asepsis State of being free from infection

assault Includes both physical and verbal attack on another; also providing of care without consent unless covered by applicable laws

(see informed consent, treatment of minors and incapacitated people)

atherosclerosis Cholesterol-lipid-calcium deposits on lining of arteries

atrium Upper chamber of heart (left and right); auricle

atrophy Wasting away or diminishing of size

auscultation Listening for sounds in the body; usually refers to use of stethoscope

autoclave Uses either heat or steam to sterilize reusable equipment

axilla Under the armpit

benign Not malignant or cancerous

biohazardous Contaminated by any sort of waste capable of causing infection

blood The OSHA standard refers to human blood, human blood components, and products made with human blood

bloodborne pathogen A pathogenic microorganism that is present in human blood and can cause disease in humans

brachial Brachial artery is the main artery in the arm

bradycardia Slow pulse rate that is generally interpreted as below 60 beats per minute

bulimia Condition in which person may eat excessively and then may refuse to eat; often accompanied by purging

capillary Smallest blood vessels that transition between arteries and veins; oxygen exchange and nutrients occur here between blood vessels and cells

cardiac Pertains to the heart

cardiopulmonary Refers to system containing both heart and lungs; includes provision of providing oxygen and chest compressions to victim without pulse and/or respirations

chain of infection Steps involved in transmitting or spreading disease from a source to an individual or group

chronic Opposite of acute; period of lasting a long time, or is recurrent

communicable disease Disease that may be communicated or transmitted to another through contact with the source individual or equipment or supplies contaminated by an infected person

confidential Medical or personal information that is not to be shared with others not involved with the care of the individual or that has no need to know the information; divulging of confidential information may have legal ramifications

contaminated The presence or the reasonably anticipated presence of blood or other potentially infectious materials on an item or surface

contaminated laundry Laundry that has been soiled with blood or other potentially infectious materials or may contain sharps

contaminated sharps Any contaminated object that can penetrate the skin including, but not limited to, needles, scalpels, broken capillary tubes, and exposed ends of dental wires

culture specimen Sample of organisms (viral, bacterial, fungal, protozoal, or other) that may be used to identify causative organism

cyanosis Blue color of skin, nail beds, and/or lips resulting from insufficient oxygen in blood

decontamination The use of physical or chemical means to remove, inactivate, or destroy bloodborne pathogens on a surface or item, to the extent that they are no longer capable and the surface or item is rendered safe for handling, use, or disposal

decubitus ulcer Pressure bedsore that sometimes results from neglect of bedridden and chronically ill patients

dehydration Insufficient water or liquids in tissues of body

dermis General term related to the skin

dialysis Removal of waste products from the blood by use of machine utilizing filter membranes

diaphoresis Excessive perspiration, usually from disease process

diastole Period of the heart's contraction where muscles are relaxed

diastolic pressure Blood pressure measurement when heart is at rest

digital Pertains to toes and fingers and is manner in which counting may be performed

dilate Make larger or expand

disease Any condition in which the body is not functioning normally

distal Position most distant from the center of the body, or the trunk

disinfection Application of a substance designed to destroy organisms. Some disinfecting agents will kill only limited types of organisms. Disinfecting does not ordinarily kill all organisms on an item

diuretics Medications that increase urinary output to avoid retention of fluids

dyspnea Labored or difficulty in performing respirations

edema Swelling from accumulation of fluids in tissues of the body

EKG/ECG Mechanical tracing of electrical activity of the heart

embolus Blood clot capable of circulating about the body; may cause cessation of blood flow to vital organs

emesis Vomiting (regurgitation) to rid the body of contents of stomach

engineering controls Physical equipment, such as sharps disposal containers, self-sheathing needles, and eyewash stations, that isolate or remove the potential hazard from the work area

epigastric Area of the abdomen just above the stomach

epidermis Outer layer of skin

epilepsy Chronic disease of nervous system, often accompanied by convulsions and unconsciousness

epistaxis Nosebleed

erythema Skin redness

erythrocyte Red blood cell

esophagus Tube extending from mouth to stomach

etiology Study of cause of a disease process

exposure incident Exposure of an eye, mouth, other mucous membrane, non-intact skin, or parenteral contact with blood or other potentially infectious materials that occurs in the workplace

fainting Complete or partial loss of consciousness due to temporary loss of circulation of blood to brain

false imprisonment Restricting freedom of movement of an individual; includes medical patients

febrile Elevated body temperature

first aid Immediate care given to an injured person or one who has become unexpectedly ill

fungi Simple, plant-like organisms that grow on organic material

gastric Pertaining to the stomach region

geriatrics/gerontology Pertains to care and treatment of disease chiefly confined to the elderly

glucometer Instrument to measure glucose content of the blood

hand washing facility A facility designed to provide running and clean water, soap, and disposable, *single use towels* or warm air-drying machines

HBV Hepatitis B virus. One of the viruses that causes inflammatory diseases affecting the liver. It is a bloodborne pathogen

heat exhaustion Illness resulting from excessive heat and loss of bodily fluids

heat stroke Emergency condition in which the body has lost its capacity to lose heat through sweating and other normal mechanisms

hematuria Passage of blood in the urine

hemoptysis Expectoration (spitting) of blood

hemorrhage Bleeding excessively

hepatitis A type of disease that causes swelling, soreness, and loss of normal function of the liver. Symptoms may include jaundice, weakness, fatigue, anorexia, nausea, abdominal pain, fever, and headache. (Jaundice is a sign that may develop later, usually in adults).

HIV Human immunodeficiency virus is a virus that infects immune system white blood cells (type of lymphocyte). Loss of this immune response leads to infection with opportunistic organisms

hygiene Practice of cleanliness to prevent or avoid infection

hypertension Blood pressure exceeding the normal levels

hypotension Low blood pressure

hyperthermia Extreme heat in the body

hypothermia Lower than normal body temperature

immune Resistant to infectious disease and may result from acquired immunity, body structures, such as intact skin, or immunization

immunization A procedure by which resistance to organisms is produced by the body.

inflammation Tissue reaction to infection; heat, redness, swelling, and pain

inspiration Inhaling, or taking in of air into the lungs

intact skin Skin, with no breaks or rash.

integument Skin, or outer covering of body

intercostals Between the ribs

ischemia Poor, diminished blood flow to body tissues due to obstruction

isolation Removing of patient from normal contact with staff and visitors due to communicable disease

jaundice Yellowing of the skin and sclera of the eyes related to destruction of red blood cells. This is usually associated with conditions of the liver

laceration Wound with jagged and irregular edges

lacrimal Related to tears and the glands that secrete them

larynx "Adam's Apple," located between pharynx and trachea

leukocyte White blood cell

living will Legal document stating measures to be taken in a medical emergency

lymph node Nodular or round portion of lymph vessels

mucous membrane Lining of skin in the mouth, nose, eyes, genitals, anus, and to a lesser extent, ears of a human body

malpractice Improper or unprofessional treatment of a patient that results in harm to the person

mandible Lower jaw; only movable bone of the skull

manubrium Upper segment of the sternum, articulating with the clavicles

metabolism Use of food for energy to provide for bodily functions

mucus Clear secretions from mucous membranes of the body. This substance acts to promote immunity by trapping organisms

muscle tone Partial contraction of muscles as in a state of alert

myocardial infarction Heart attack or "coronary"

natural immunity Naturally occurring immunity is genetic immunity. Certain species of animal including humans are immune to certain diseases

nausea "Sick" feeling in which a person feels that they will regurgitate

necrosis Death of tissue

negligence Withholding of usual and customary care that results in injury

non-intact skin Skin that has a break or rash on surface

nosocomial Disease that originates in a hospital or other health care facility

occupational Related to duties normally performed in a particular job

occupational exposure Potentially infectious materials found in the workplace, and to which certain employees would ordinarily be exposed in their normal course of duties

paralysis Loss of use of a part of the body

parenteral Other than by mouth, process by which a sharp object pierces the skin, opening the barrier to invasion by organisms

pathogen Includes viruses, bacteria, protozoa, and all one-celled organisms which may cause illness if infected

patients' rights Normal care that all patients should expect to receive

percutaneous Procedure requiring a puncture or incision through the skin.

PPE – personal Clothing or equipment designed to provide protection

protective equipment used for handling of hazardous materials or organisms

prophylactic Preventative measures that prevent disease

pulmonary Pertaining to the lungs

pulse Pressure of arterial walls as heart contracts

pulse deficit Difference between rate of apical pulse and one taken radially

pyrexia Fever

rale Bubbly or noisy sound caused by fluids in the air passages

rate Number of beats or respirations per minute by the heart and the lungs

respiration Taking in of oxygenated air by the lungs; includes both inhalation and expiration as one respiration

restraints Protective devices that restrict movement by an individual

reverse isolation This process is to protect an immunocompromised patient against exposure to organisms that may be transmitted by hospital staff and visitors

sclera Whites of the eyes; may become yellow with jaundiced condition

senility Loss of mental faculties and physical abilities due to aging

smear Biological material spread on glass slide to be examined for presence of organisms and/or cells from the body

source individual An individual harboring an organism that may prove potentially harmful to an employee or another patient. The source individual may be either living or dead

sphygmomanometer Instrument for listening to arterial blood pressure indirectly

spleen Gland below diaphragm and normally in upper-left quadrant of abdomen – may be multiple spleens (3–5), serving to store and filtrate blood

sputum Substance secreted in bronchi and composed of saliva and mucus

sterilize Process by which ALL microorganisms are killed

sternum Breastbone

stethoscope Instrument for listening for internal body sounds

stroke Cerebral vascular accident; bleeding or clotting in the brain

tachycardia Rapid heart rate, usually determined to exceed 100 beats per minute

T4 cells Type of white blood cell (lymphocyte) that acts to recognize harmful organisms

thrombus Stationary blood clot

tourniquet Elastic band used to compress blood vessels

trachea Windpipe, from larynx to bronchi

Universal Precautions An overall approach to infection control in which most body fluids are treated as though they were known to contain infectious organisms

vaccine Suspension of inactivated or dead organisms (antigens) that is administered by mouth or parenterally into a human or other animal to cause production of antibodies against the specific organism. This is known as active immunity to an organism

varicose veins Distended, swollen veins near the surface of the skin

vertigo Dizziness

virus Very small organisms that cause disease by entering the cells of the body

vital signs Information related to body conditions, including temperature, pulse, respiratory rate, and blood pressure

xiphoid process Small, bony projection at the end of the sternum and superior to the upper abdomen

Subject Index